FOR ORGANS, PIANOS & ELECTRONIC KEYBOARDS

E-Z PLAY® TODAY

125

THE GREAT BIG BOOK
OF CHILDREN'S SONGS

C000156865

ISBN 978-0-634-00045-4

HAL•LEONARD®
CORPORATION

7777 W. BLUEMOUND RD. P.O. BOX 13819 MILWAUKEE, WI 53213

CONTENTS

ABC-DEF-GHI

Registration 4
Rhythm: Waltz or 6/8 March

Words by Joe Raposo and Jon Stone
Music by Joe Raposo

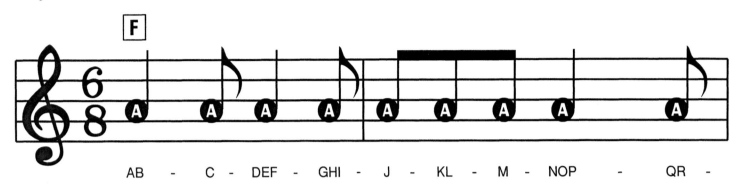

AB - C - DEF - GHI - J - KL - M - NOP - QR -

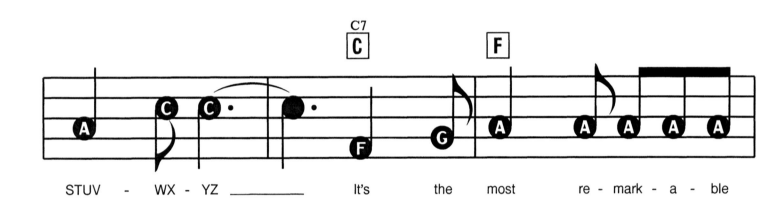

STUV - WX - YZ _____ It's the most re - mark - a - ble

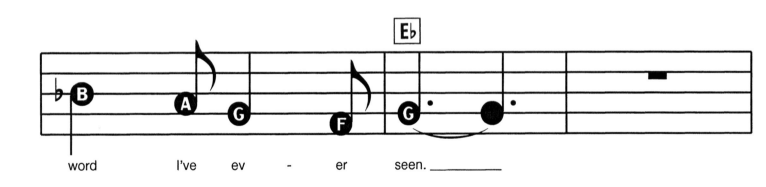

word I've ev - er seen. _____

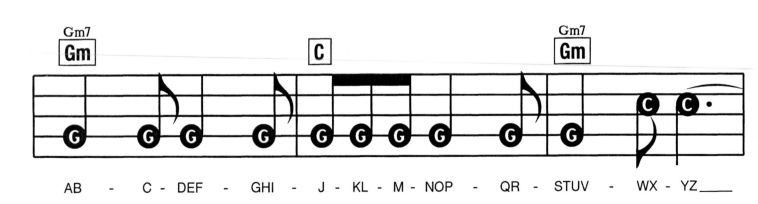

AB - C - DEF - GHI - J - KL - M - NOP - QR - STUV - WX - YZ____

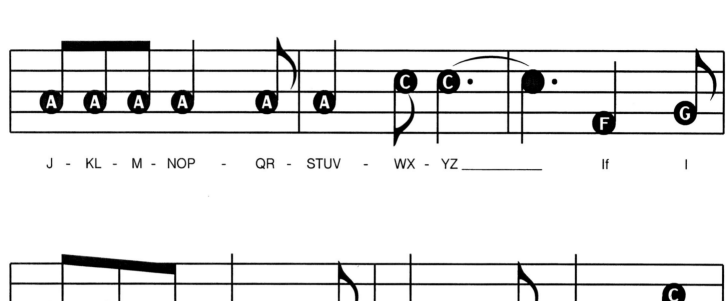

J - KL - M - NOP - QR - STUV - WX - YZ _____ If I

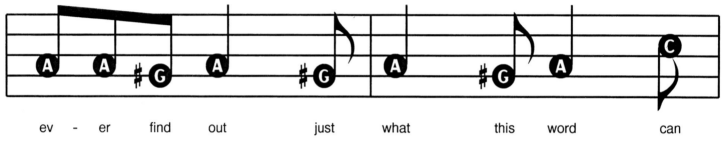

ev - er find out just what this word can

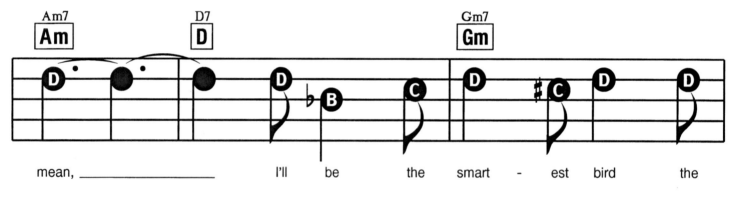

mean, _____ I'll be the smart - est bird the

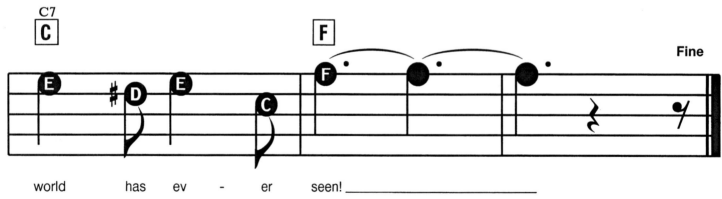

world has ev - er seen! _____

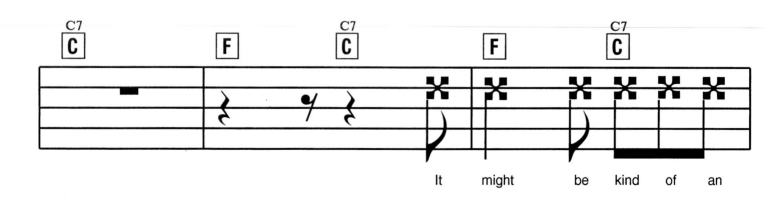

It might be kind of an

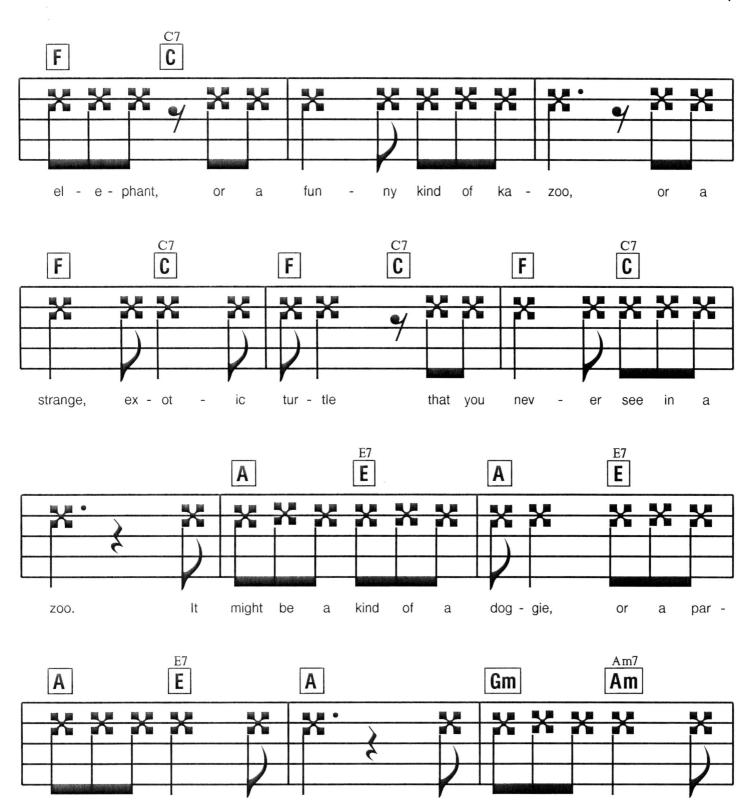

el - e - phant, or a fun - ny kind of ka - zoo, or a

strange, ex - ot - ic tur - tle that you nev - er see in a

zoo. It might be a kind of a dog - gie, or a par -

tic - u - lar shade of blue, or may - be a pret - ty

D.C. al Fine
(Return to beginning
and Play to Fine)

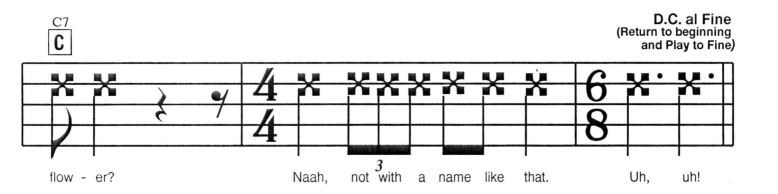

flow - er? Naah, not with a name like that. Uh, uh!

Are You Sleeping

Registration 4
Rhythm: Fox Trot or Swing

Traditional

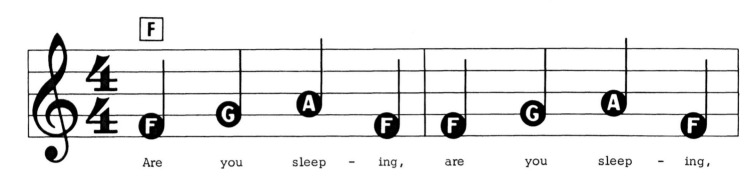

Are you sleep - ing, are you sleep - ing,

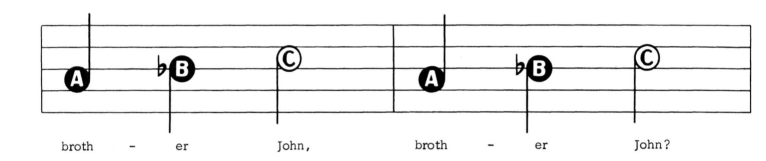

broth - er John, broth - er John?

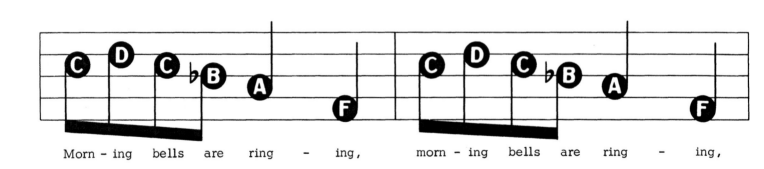

Morn - ing bells are ring - ing, morn - ing bells are ring - ing,

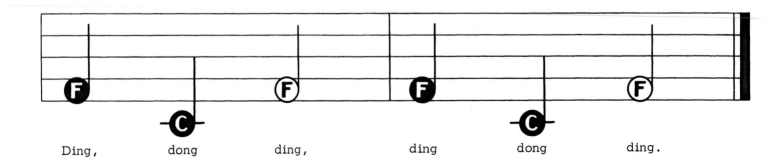

Ding, dong ding, ding dong ding.

Be Kind To Your Parents

from FANNY

Registration 5
Rhythm: Polka or March

Words and Music by
Harold Rome

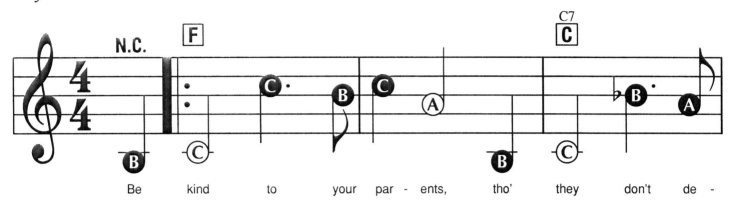

Be kind to your par - ents, tho' they don't de -

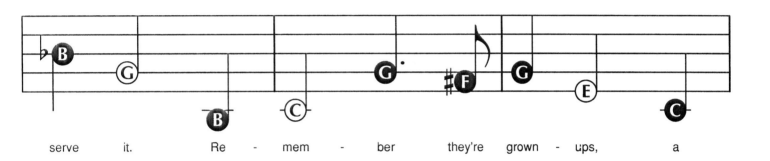

serve it. Re - mem - ber they're grown - ups, a

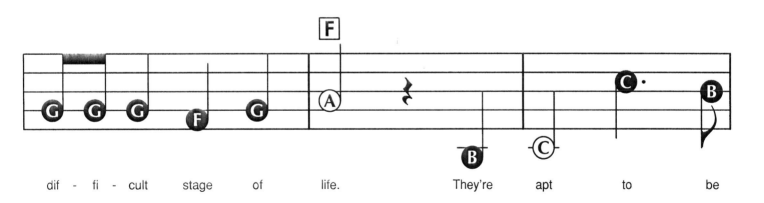

dif - fi - cult stage of life. They're apt to be

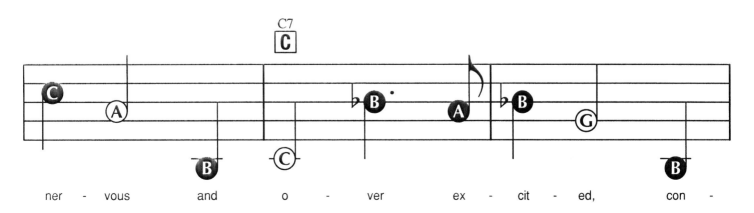

ner - vous and o - ver ex - cit - ed, con -

10

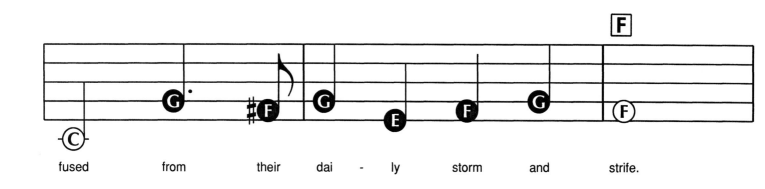

fused   from   their   dai - ly   storm   and   strife.

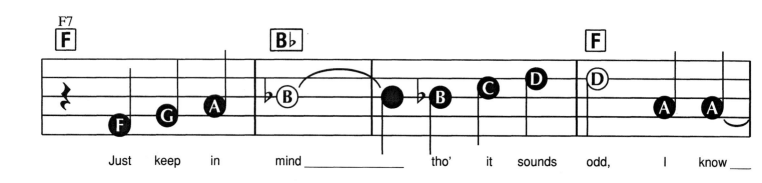

Just   keep   in   mind _____   tho'   it   sounds   odd,   I   know ___

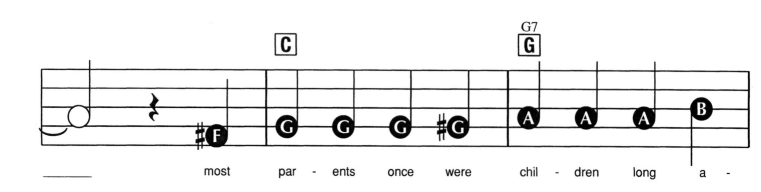

_____   most   par - ents   once   were   chil - dren   long   a -

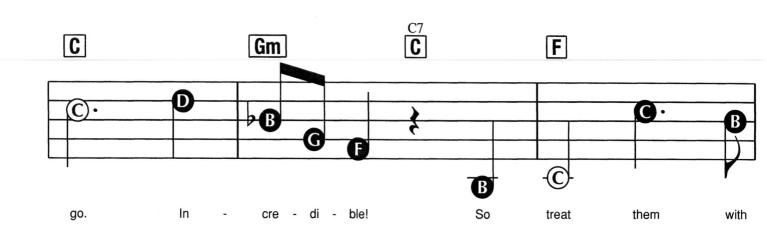

go.   In - cre - di - ble!   So   treat   them   with

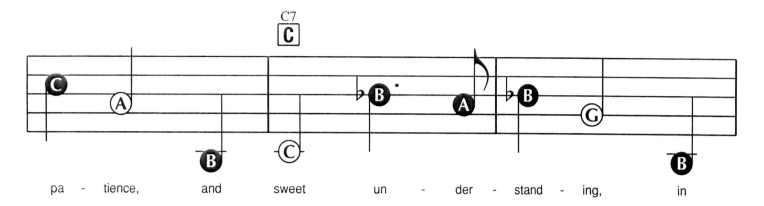

pa - tience,   and   sweet   un   -   der   -   stand   -   ing,   in

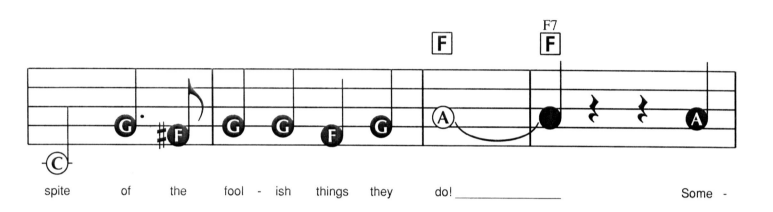

spite   of   the   fool - ish   things   they   do! _____   Some -

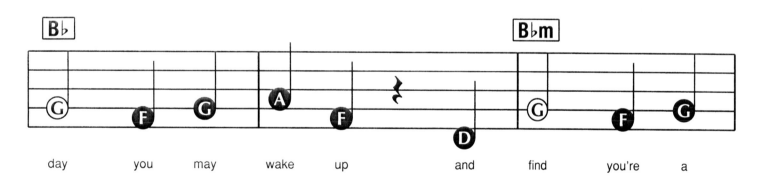

day   you   may   wake   up   and   find   you're   a

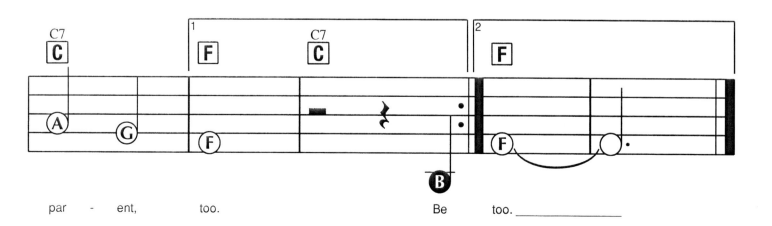

par - ent,   too.   Be   too. _____

The Ballad of Davy Crockett

from Walt Disney's Television Series DAVY CROCKETT

Registration 2
Rhythm: Fox Trot or Swing

Words by Tom Blackburn
Music by George Bruns

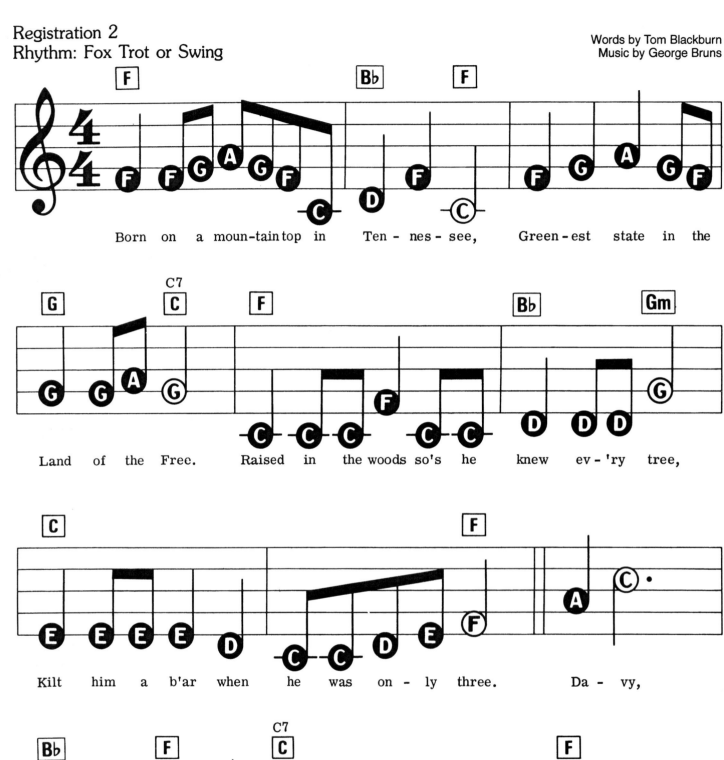

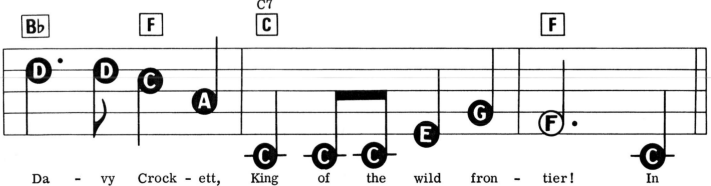

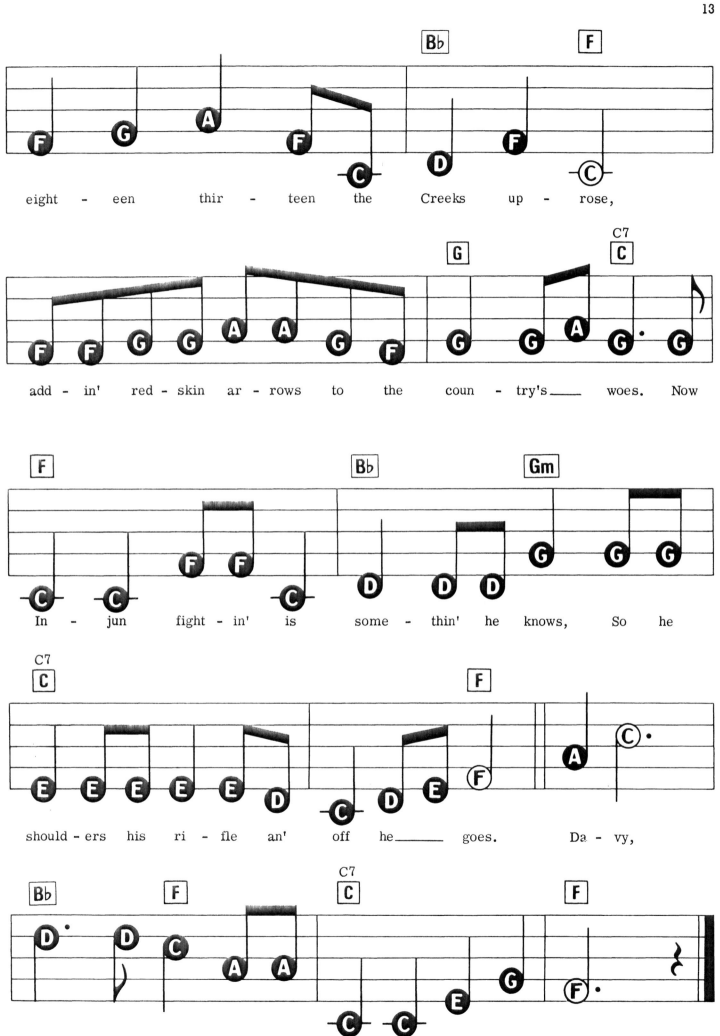

The Bare Necessities

from Walt Disney's THE JUNGLE BOOK

Registration 4
Rhythm: Fox Trot or Swing

Words and Music by
Terry Gilkyson

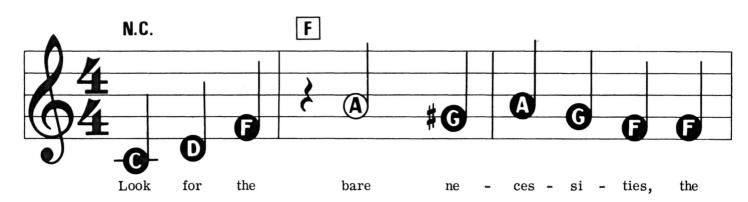

Look for the bare ne - ces - si - ties, the

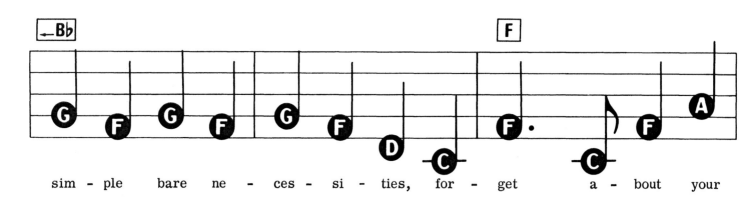

sim - ple bare ne - ces - si - ties, for - get a - bout your

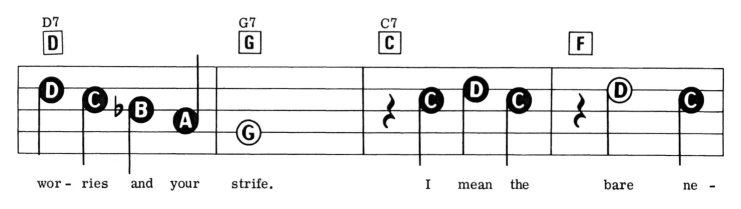

wor - ries and your strife. I mean the bare ne -

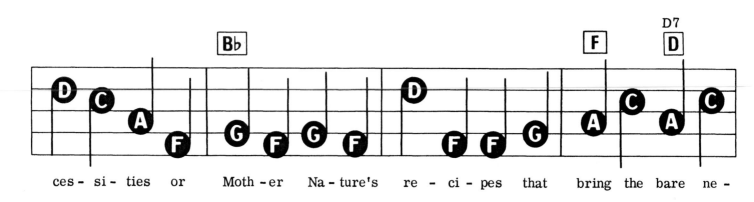

ces - si - ties or Moth - er Na - ture's re - ci - pes that bring the bare ne -

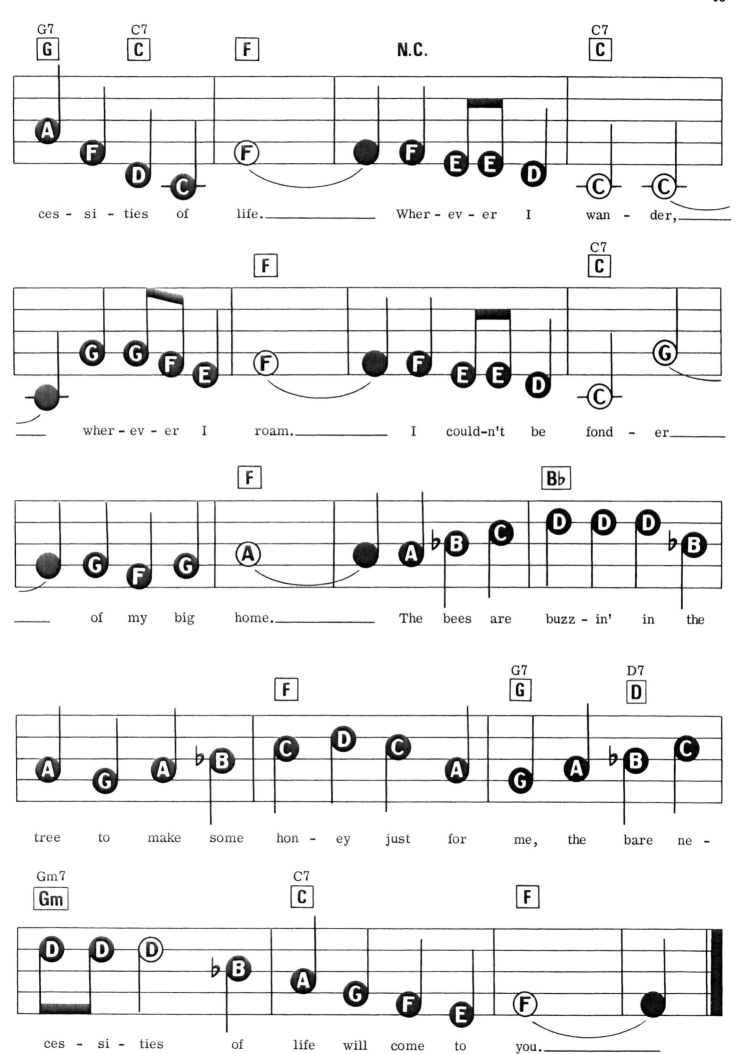

Beauty And The Beast

from Walt Disney's BEAUTY AND THE BEAST

Registration 1
Rhythm: Pops or 8 Beat

Lyrics by Howard Ashman
Music by Alan Menken

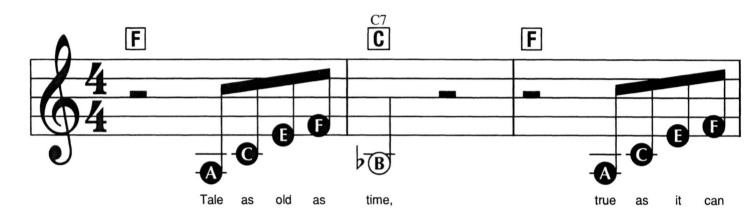

Tale as old as time,   true as it can

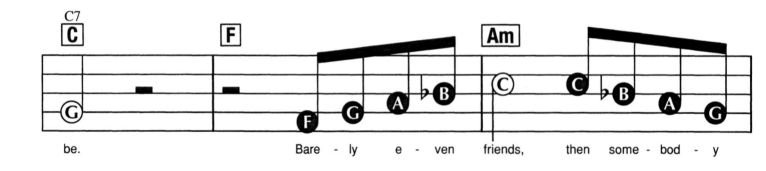

be.   Bare - ly e - ven friends, then some - bod - y

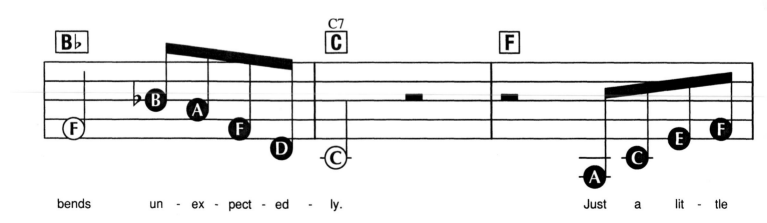

bends un - ex - pect - ed - ly.   Just a lit - tle

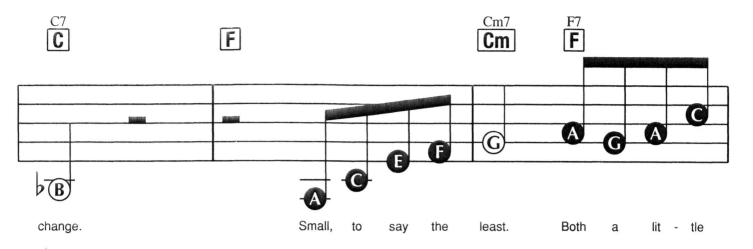

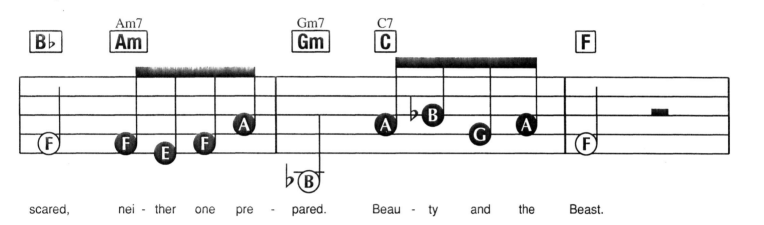

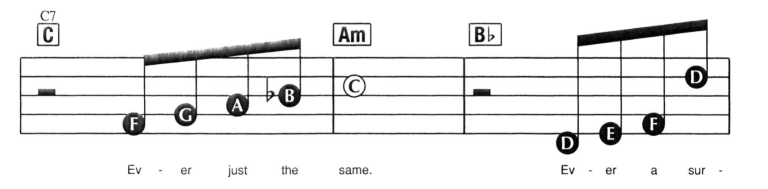

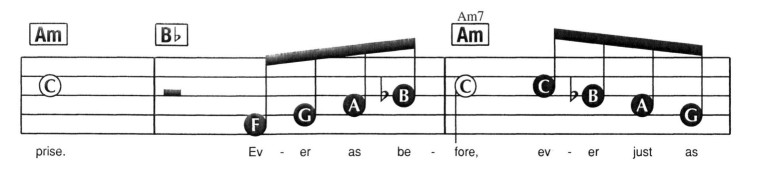

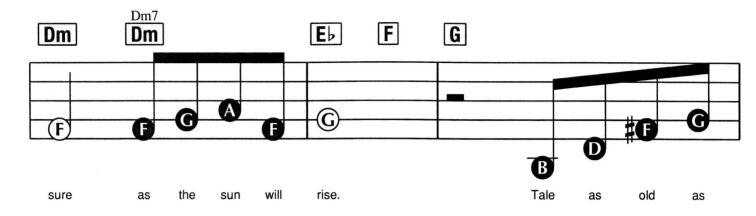

sure   as   the   sun   will   rise.   Tale   as   old   as

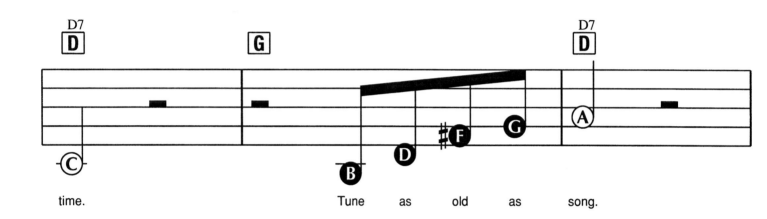

time.   Tune   as   old   as   song.

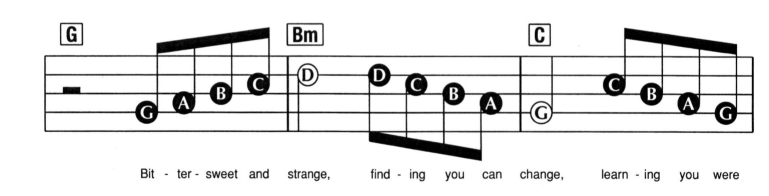

Bit - ter - sweet and strange,   find - ing you can change,   learn - ing you were

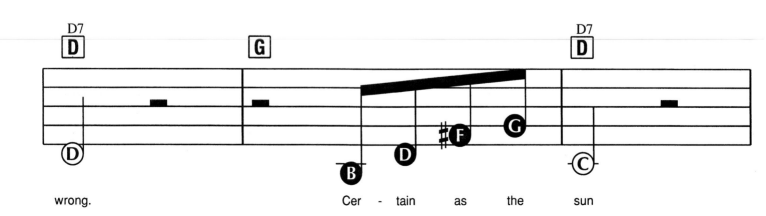

wrong.   Cer - tain   as   the   sun

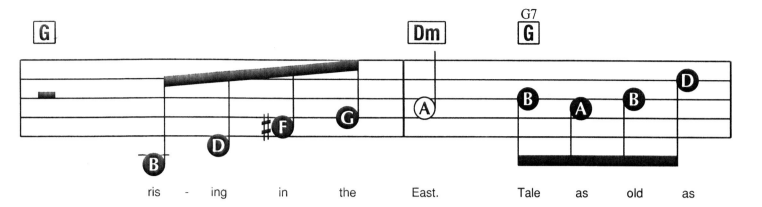

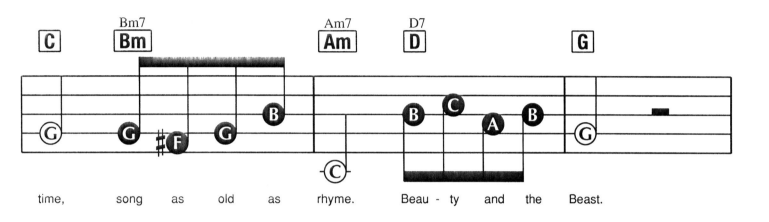

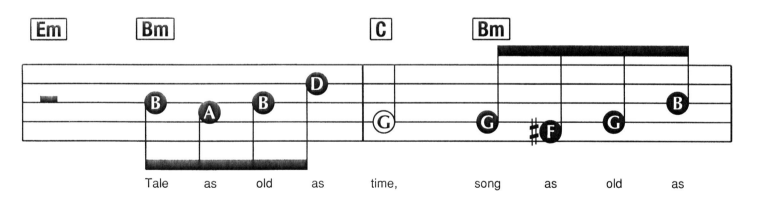

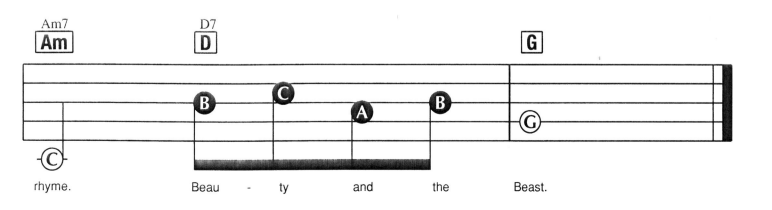

Bein' Green

Registration 3
Rhythm: Pops or Rock

Words and Music by
Joe Raposo

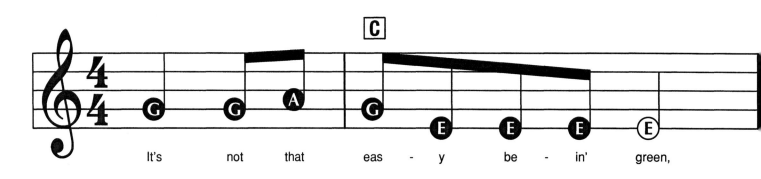

It's not that eas - y be - in' green,

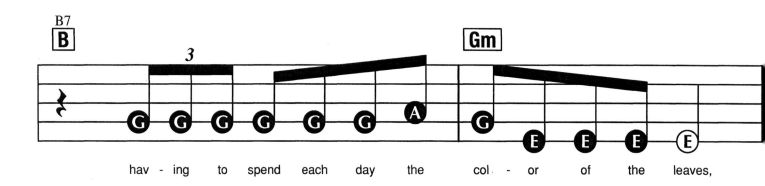

hav - ing to spend each day the col - or of the leaves,

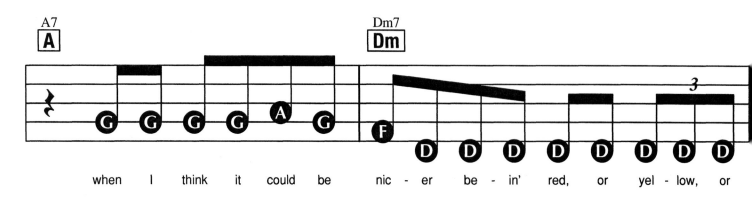

when I think it could be nic - er be - in' red, or yel - low, or

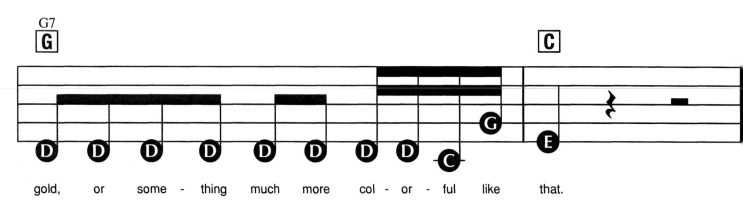

gold, or some - thing much more col - or - ful like that.

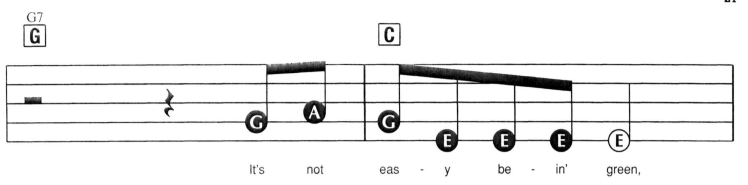

It's not eas - y be - in' green,

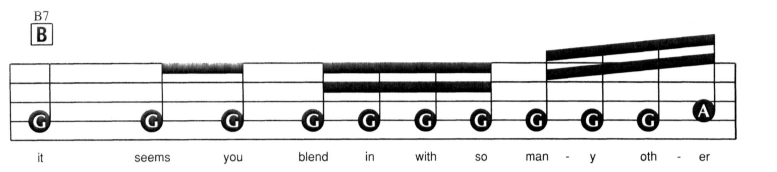

it seems you blend in with so man - y oth - er

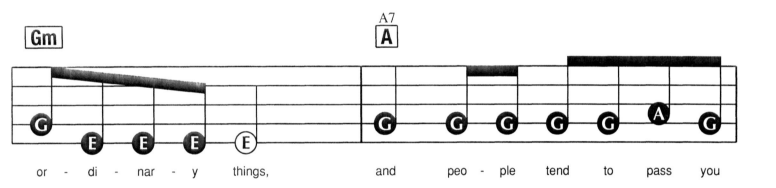

or - di - nar - y things, and peo - ple tend to pass you

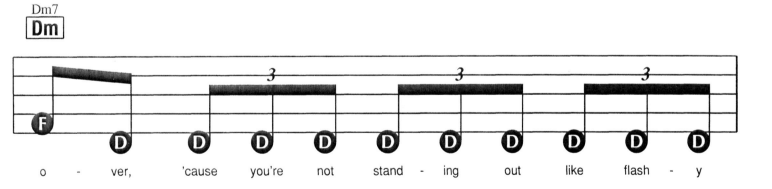

o - ver, 'cause you're not stand - ing out like flash - y

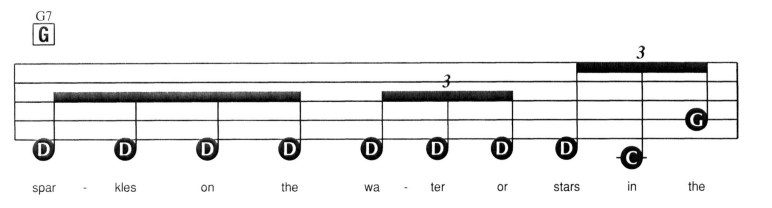

spar - kles on the wa - ter or stars in the

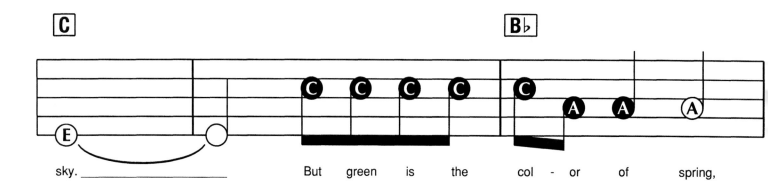

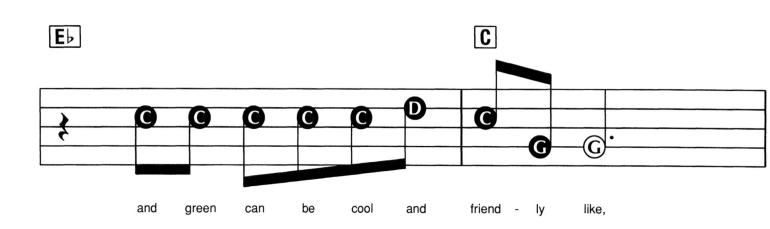

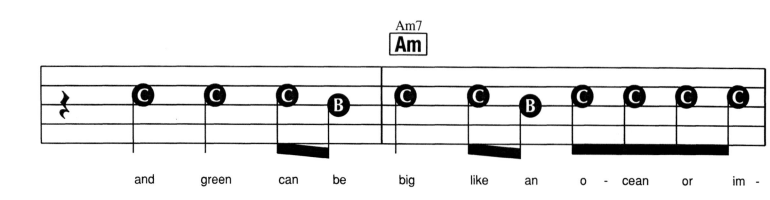

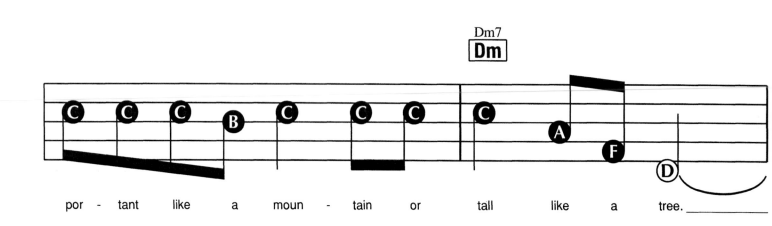

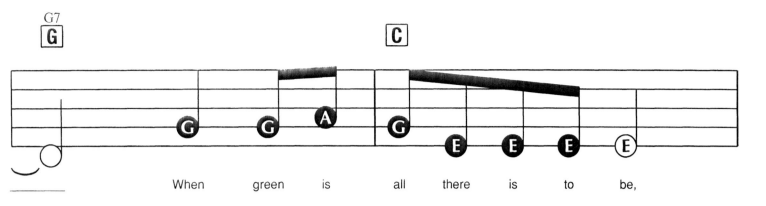

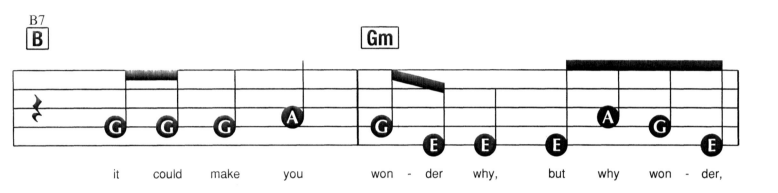

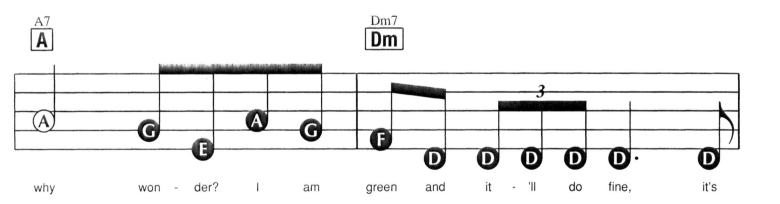

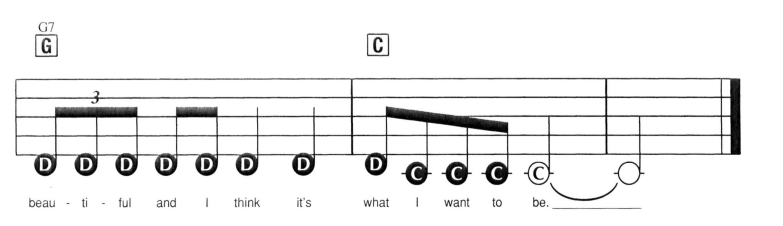

Bibbidi-Bobbidi-Boo
(The Magic Song)
from Walt Disney's CINDERELLA

Registration 8
Rhythm: Swing

Words by Jerry Livingston
Music by Mack David and Al Hoffman

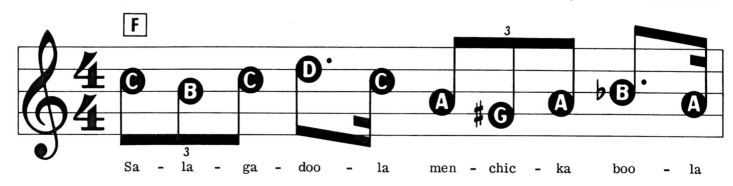

Sa - la - ga - doo - la men - chic - ka boo - la

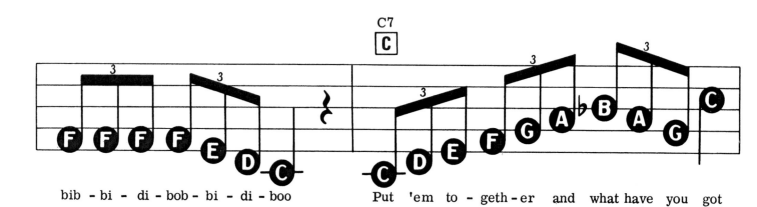

bib - bi - di - bob - bi - di - boo   Put 'em to - geth - er and what have you got

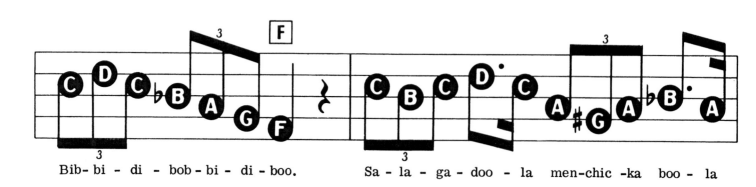

Bib - bi - di - bob - bi - di - boo.   Sa - la - ga - doo - la men - chic - ka boo - la

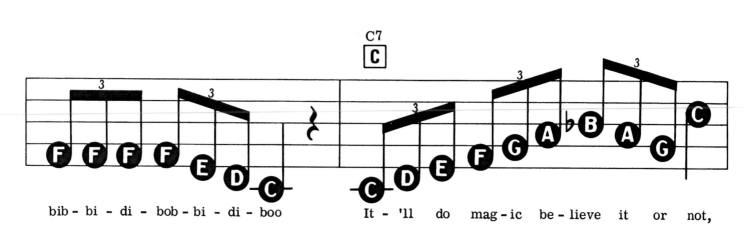

bib - bi - di - bob - bi - di - boo   It - 'll do mag - ic be - lieve it or not,

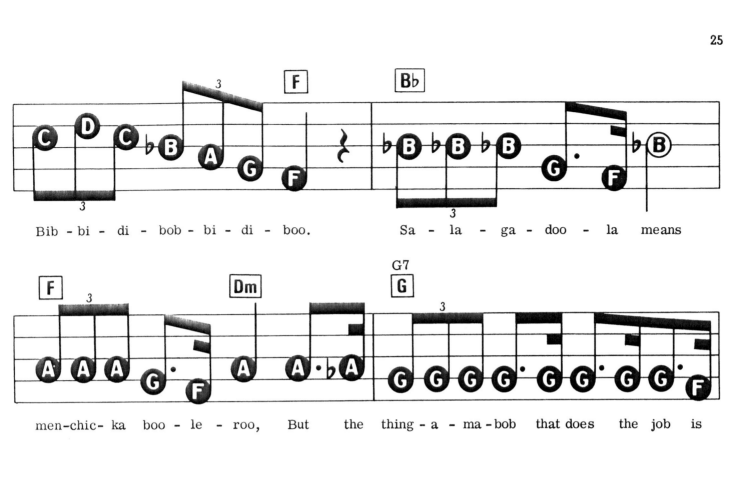

Bib - bi - di - bob - bi - di - boo.   Sa - la - ga - doo - la means

men-chic- ka boo - le - roo,   But   the   thing - a - ma - bob   that does   the   job   is

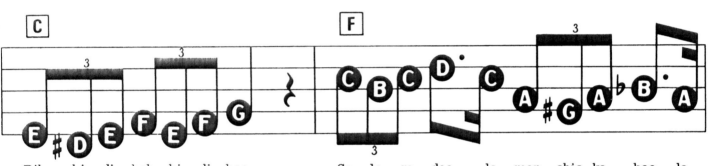

Bib - bi - di - bob - bi - di - boo.   Sa - la - ga - doo - la men - chic - ka   boo - la

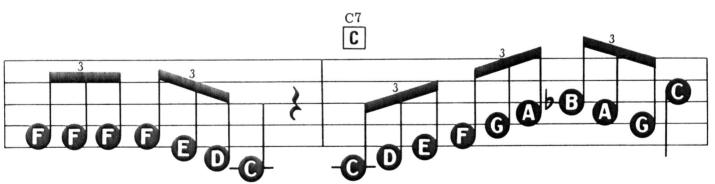

Bib - bi - di - bob - bi - di - boo   Put 'em   to - geth - er   and   what have you   got

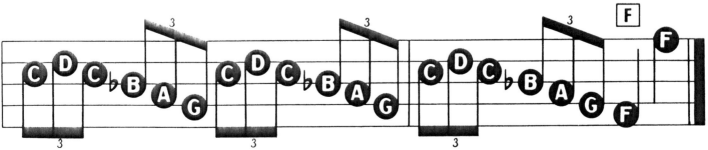

Bib - bi - di - bob - bi - di - bib - bi - di - bob - bi - di   Bib - bi - di - bob - bi - di - boo.

The Bible Tells Me So

Registration 7
Rhythm: Swing

Words and Music by
Dale Evans

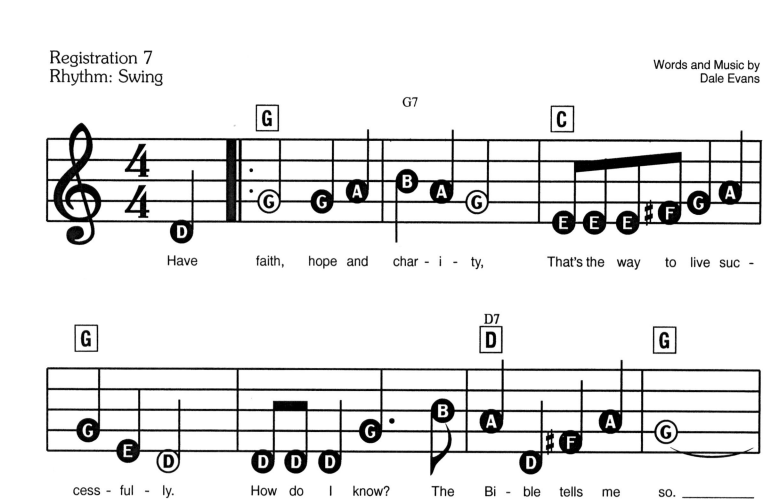

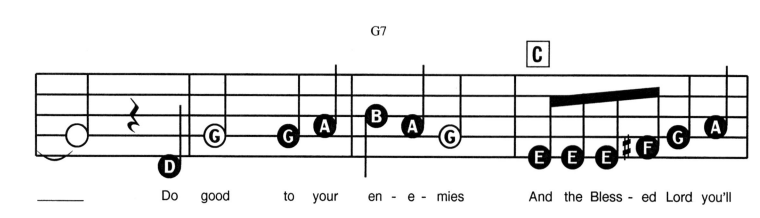

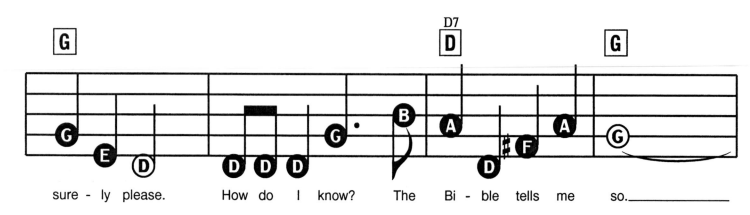

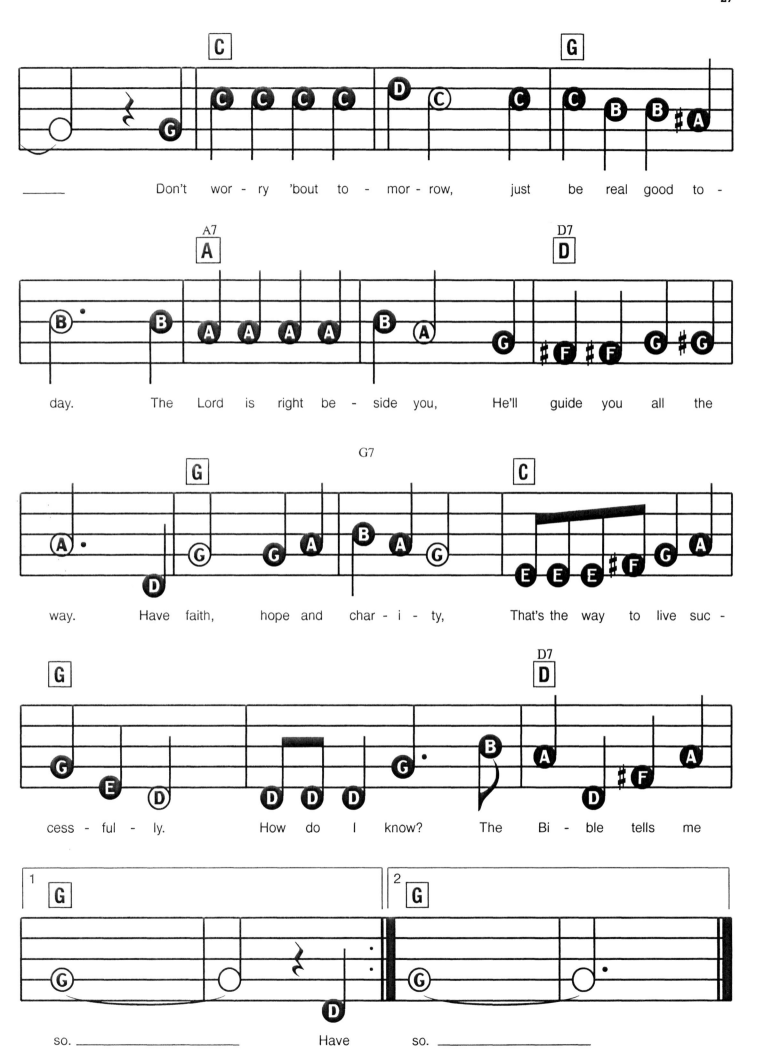

The Brady Bunch
Theme from the Paramount Television Series THE BRADY BUNCH

Registration 7
Rhythm: Rock or Pops

Words and Music by Sherwood Schwartz
and Frank Devol

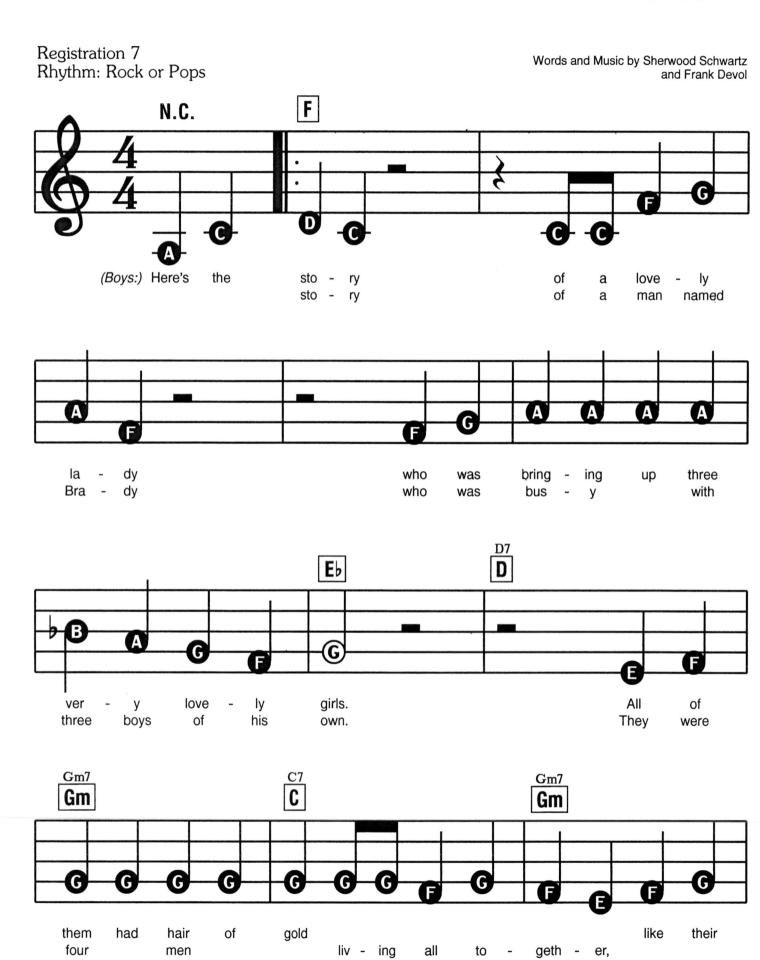

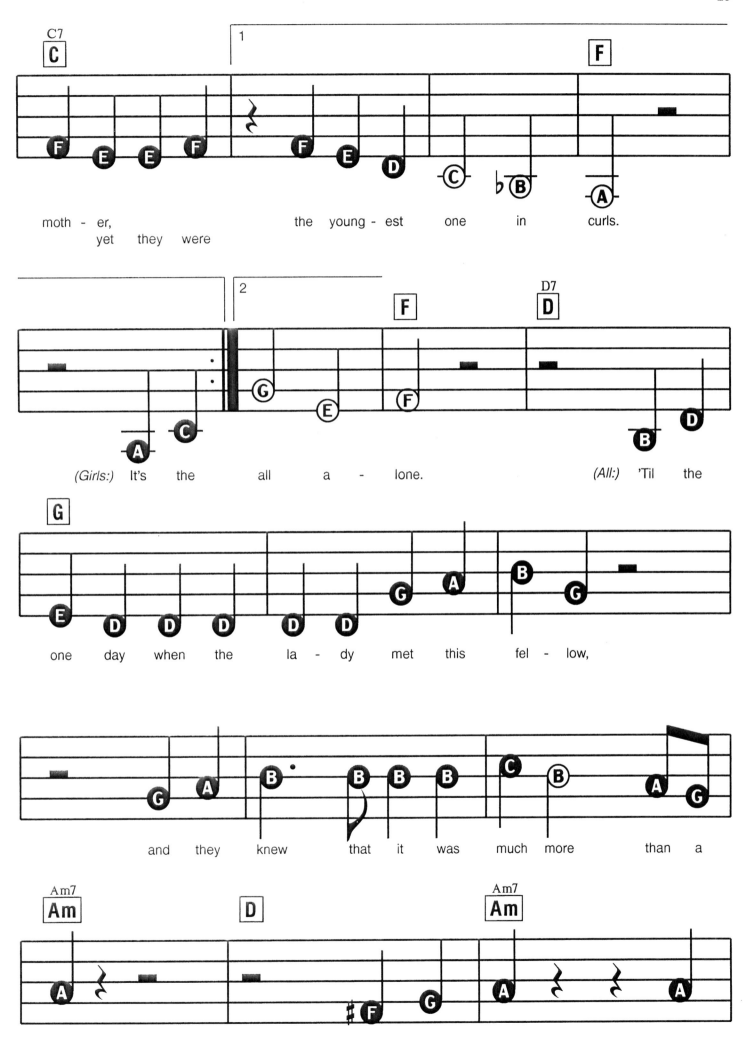

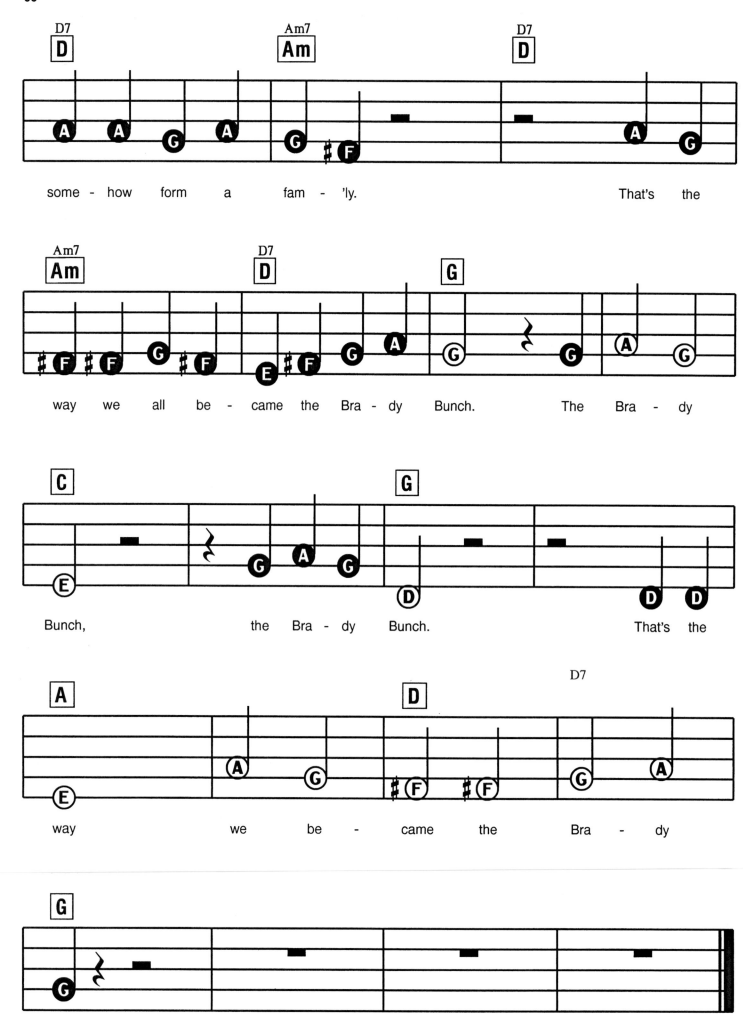

some - how form a fam - 'ly. That's the

way we all be - came the Bra - dy Bunch. The Bra - dy

Bunch, the Bra - dy Bunch. That's the

way we be - came the Bra - dy

Bunch.

The Crawdad Song

Registration 8
Rhythm: Country or Rock

Count 8 and play

Traditional

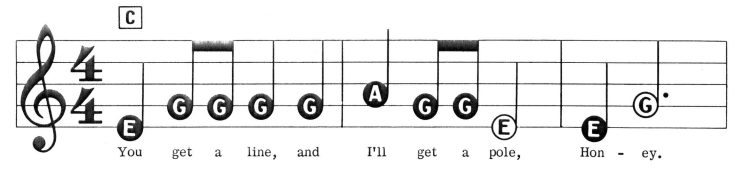

You get a line, and I'll get a pole, Hon - ey.

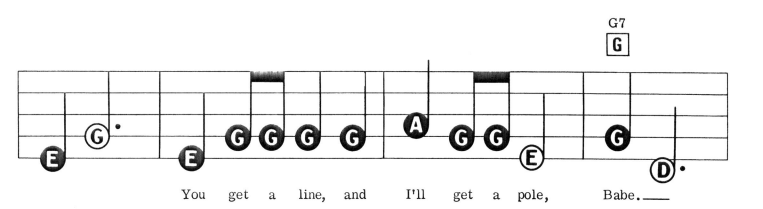

You get a line, and I'll get a pole, Babe.

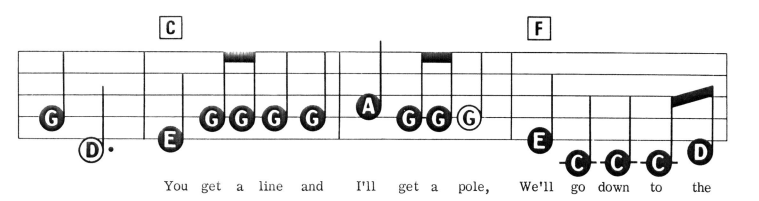

You get a line and I'll get a pole, We'll go down to the

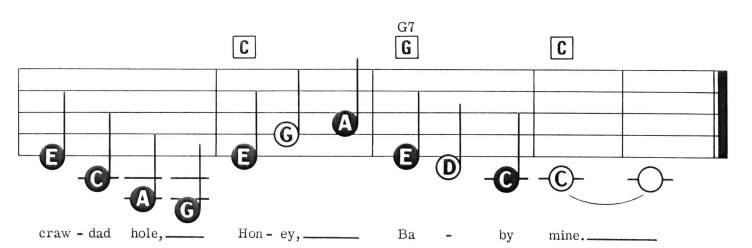

craw - dad hole, Hon - ey, Ba - by mine.

"C" Is For Cookie

Registration 1
Rhythm: Polka, March or Pops

Words and Music by
Joe Raposo

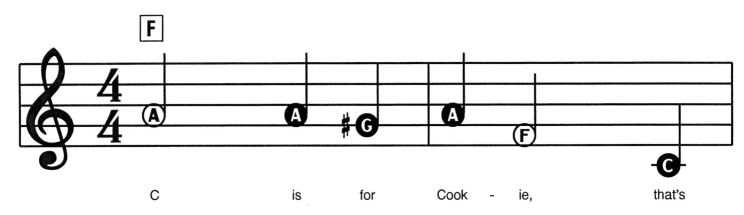

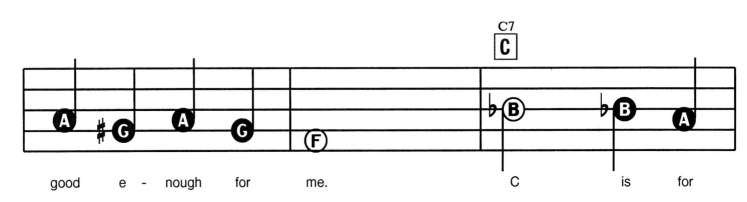

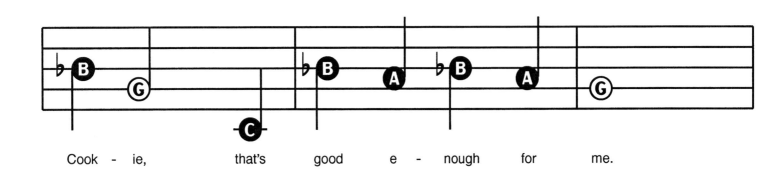

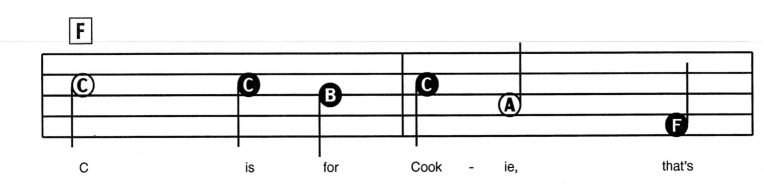

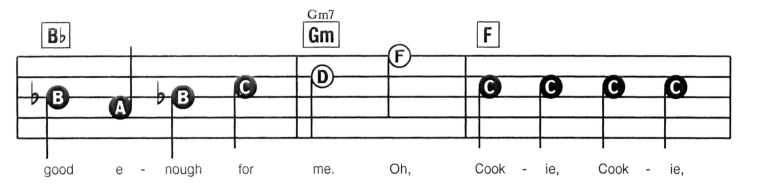

good e - nough for me. Oh, Cook - ie, Cook - ie,

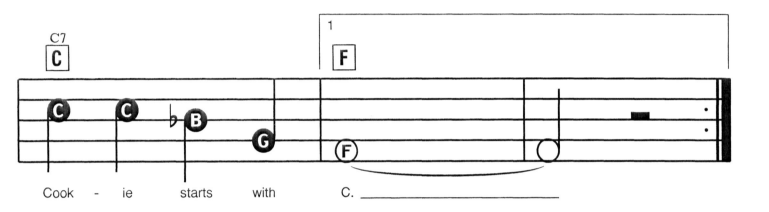

Cook - ie starts with C.

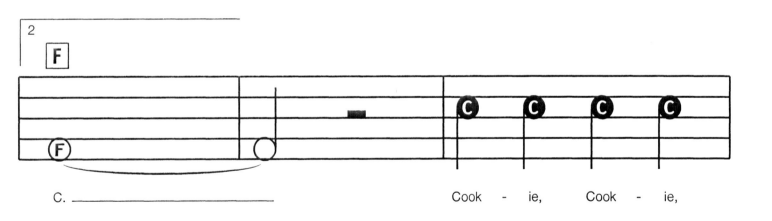

C. Cook - ie, Cook - ie,

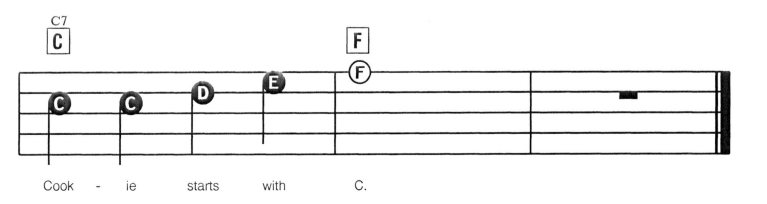

Cook - ie starts with C.

The Candy Man
from WILLY WONKA AND THE CHOCOLATE FACTORY

Registration 5
Rhythm: Swing or Jazz

Words and Music by Leslie Bricusse
and Anthony Newley

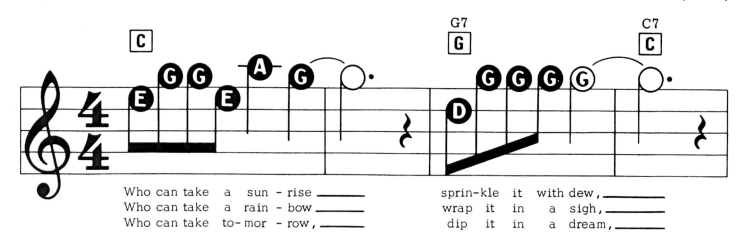

Who can take a sun - rise _____ sprin-kle it with dew, _____
Who can take a rain - bow _____ wrap it in a sigh, _____
Who can take to-mor - row, _____ dip it in a dream, _____

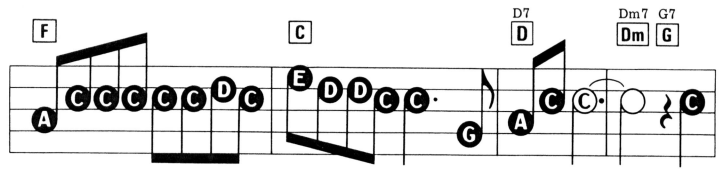

cov - er it in choc-'late and a mir - a - cle or two?
soak it in the sun and make a straw-b'ry le-mon pie? } The can-dy man, _____ the
sep-ar -ate the sor - row and col - lect up all the cream?

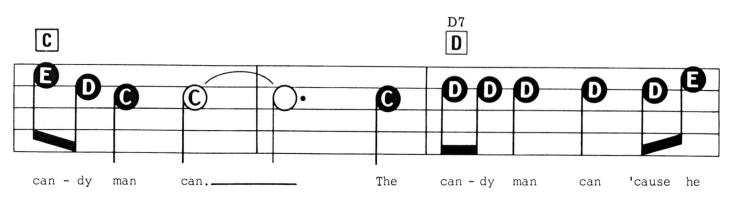

can - dy man can. _____ The can-dy man can 'cause he

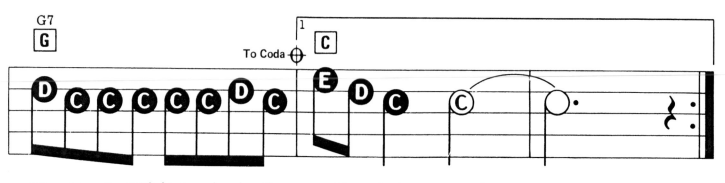

mix - es it with love and makes the world _ taste good. _____

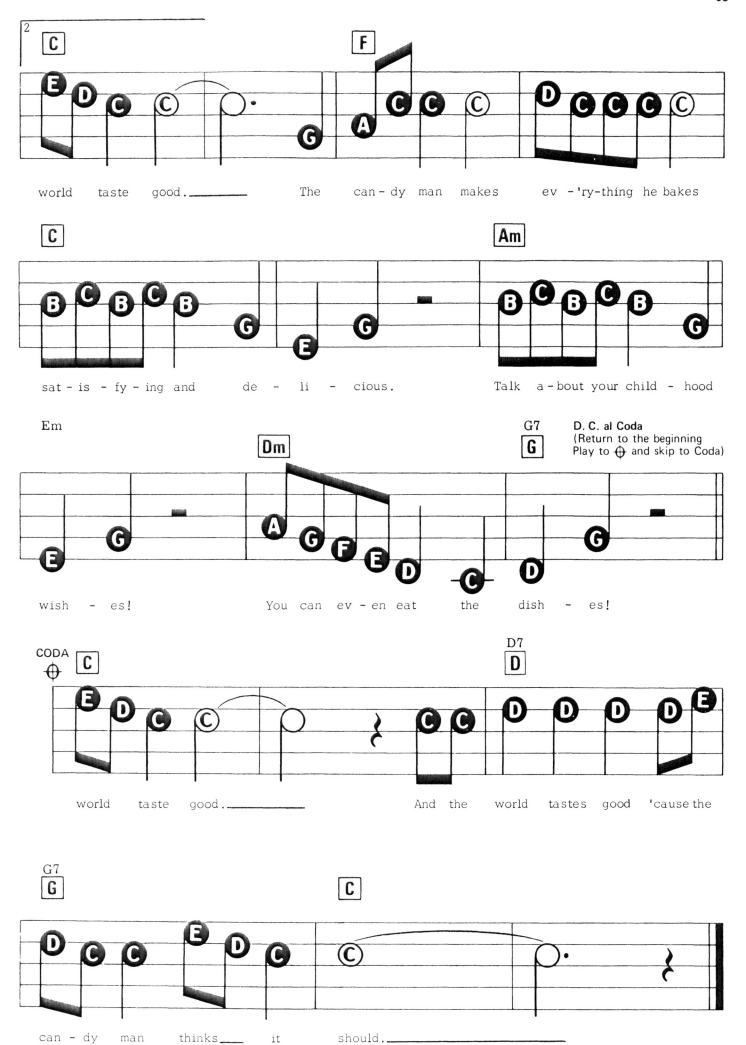

Casper The Friendly Ghost
from the Paramount Cartoon

Registration 1
Rhythm: Polka, Rock or March

Words by Mack David
Music by Jerry Livingston

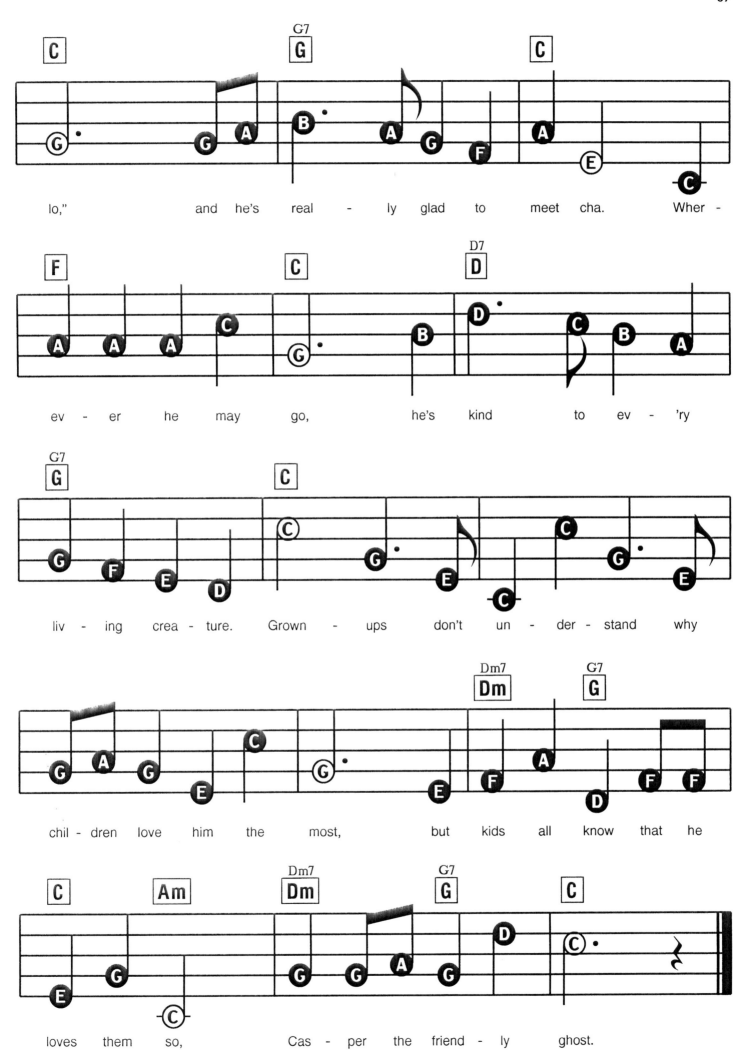

Chim Chim Cher-ee
from Walt Disney's MARY POPPINS

Registration 3
Rhythm: Waltz

Words and Music by Richard M. Sherman
and Robert B. Sherman

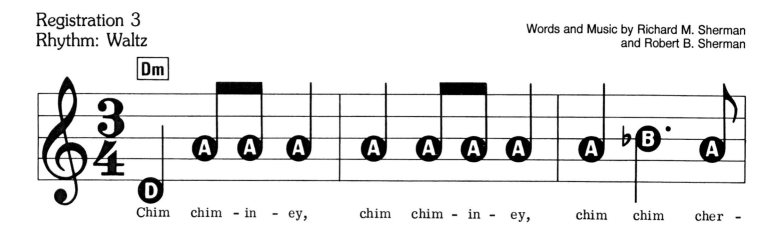

Chim chim - in - ey, chim chim - in - ey, chim chim cher -

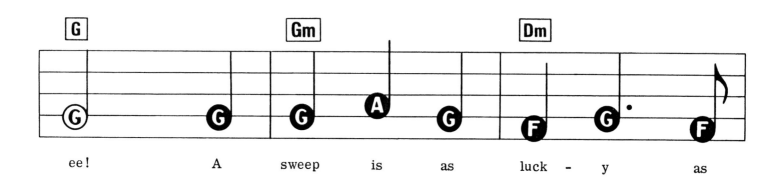

ee! A sweep is as luck - y as

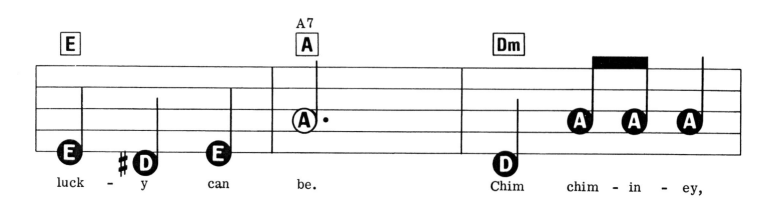

luck - y can be. Chim chim - in - ey,

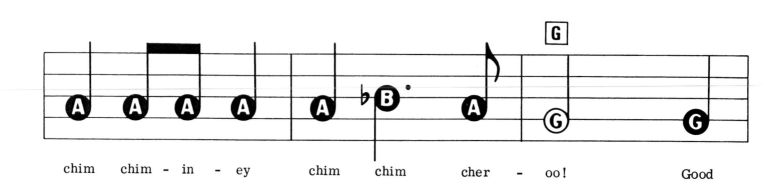

chim chim - in - ey chim chim cher - oo! Good

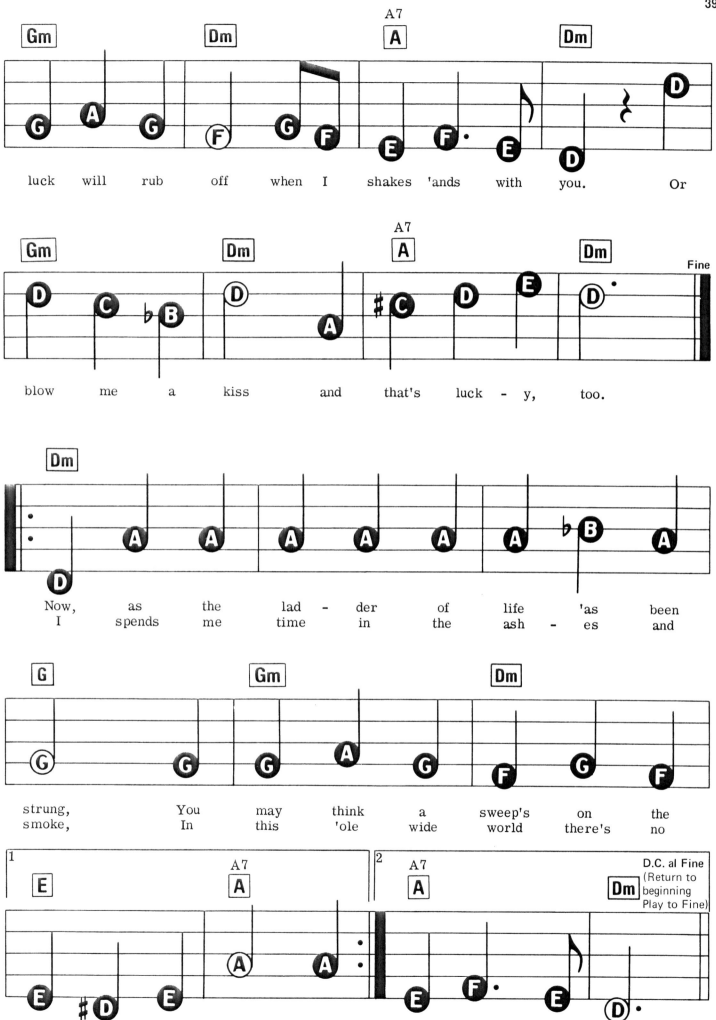

Circle Of Life
from Walt Disney Pictures' THE LION KING

Registration 2
Rhythm: Calypso or Reggae

Music by Elton John
Lyrics by Tim Rice

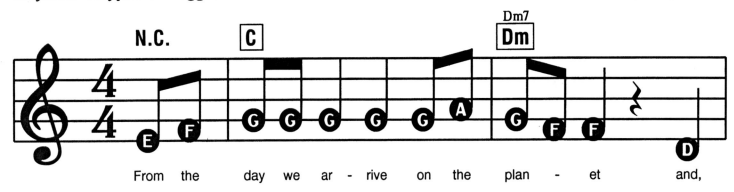

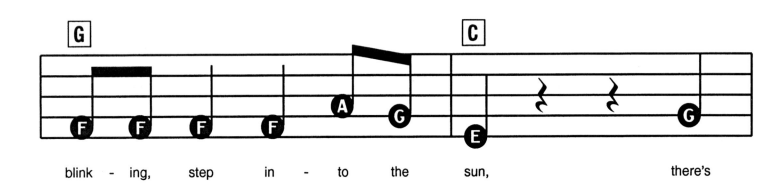

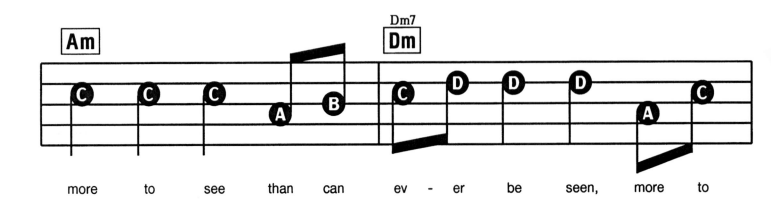

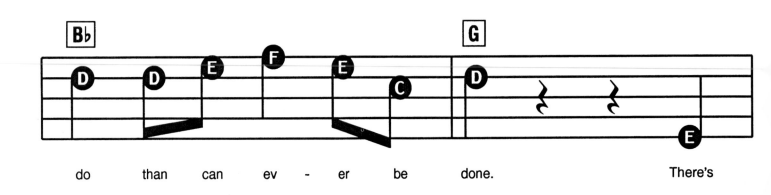

far too much to take in here,   more to

find   than   can   ev - er   be   found.   But   the

sun   roll - ing   high   through   the   sap - phi _ re   sky   keeps   great   and

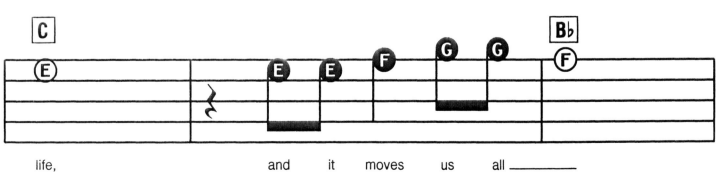

small   on   the   end - less   round. _____   It's   the   cir - cle   of

life,   and   it   moves   us   all _____

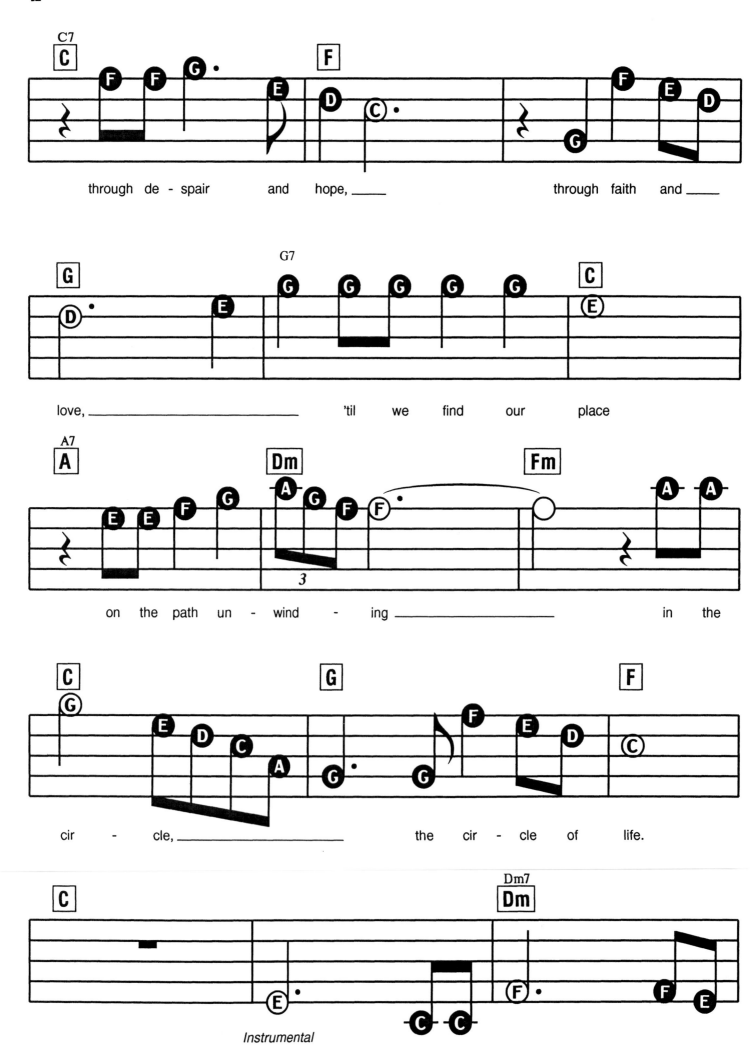

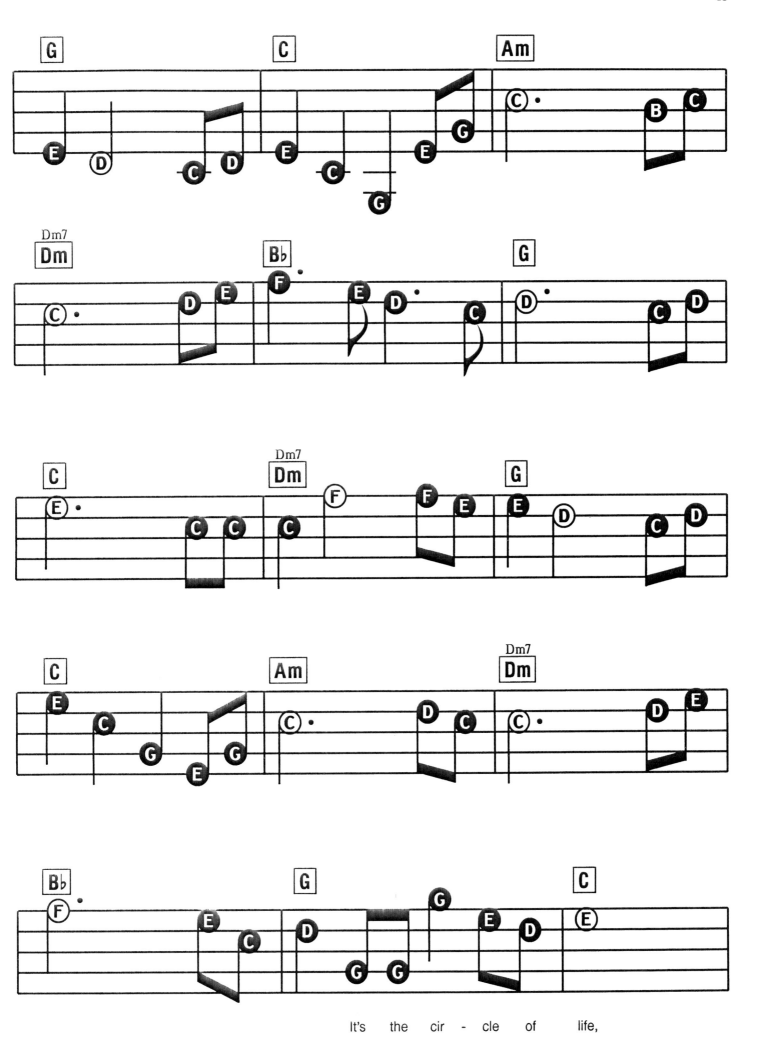

It's the cir - cle of life,

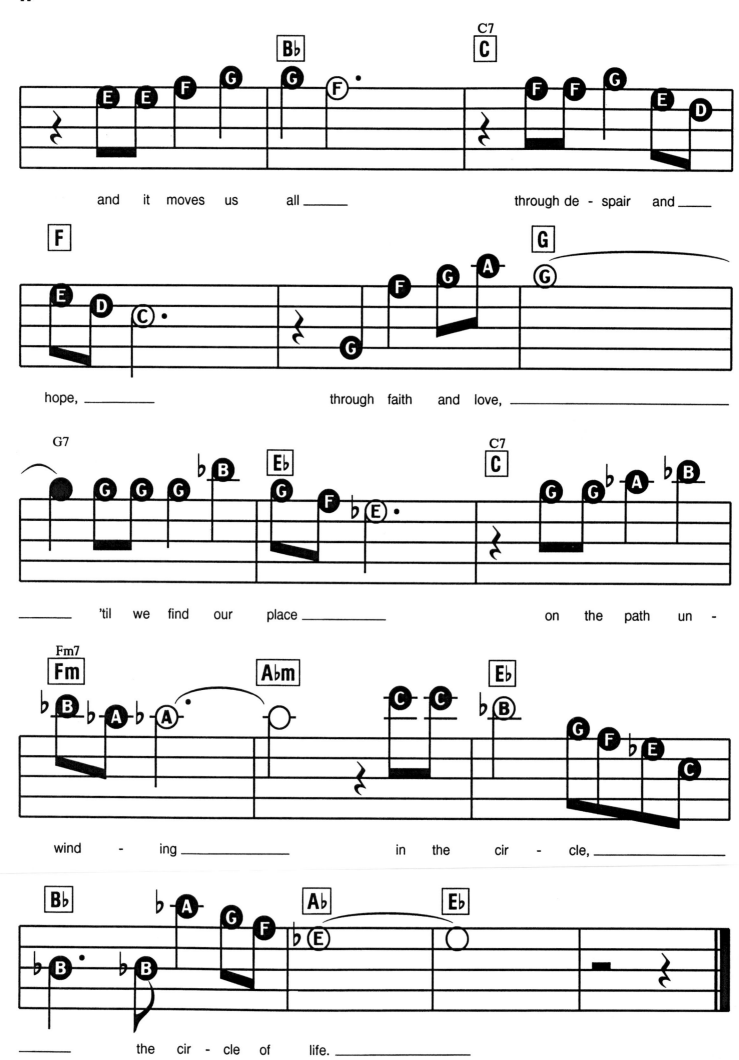

Cruella de Vil
from Walt Disney's 101 DALMATIONS

Registration 9
Rhythm: Swing

Words and Music by
Mel Leven

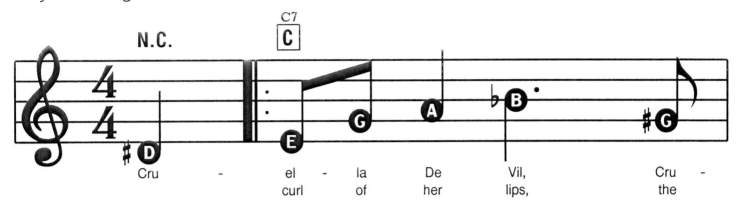

Cru - el - la De Vil, Cru -
curl of her lips, the

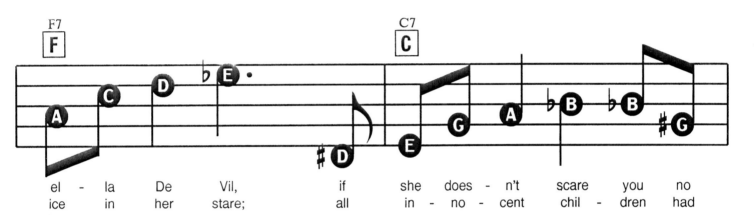

el - la De Vil, if she does - n't scare you no
ice in her stare; all in - no - cent chil - dren had

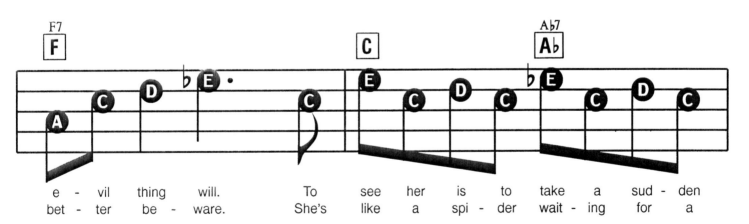

e - vil thing will. To see her is to take a sud - den
bet - ter be - ware. She's like a spi - der wait - ing for a

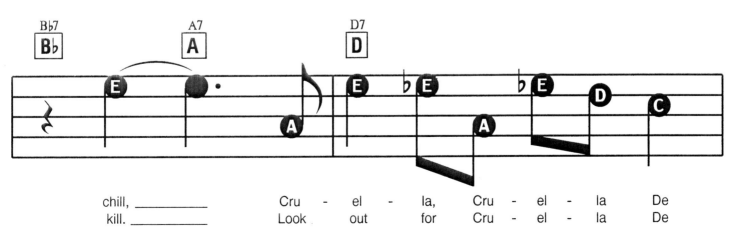

chill, _____ Cru - el - la, Cru - el - la De
kill. _____ Look out for Cru - el - la De

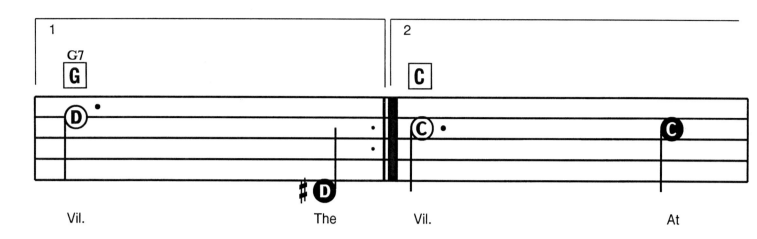

Vil.   The   Vil.   At

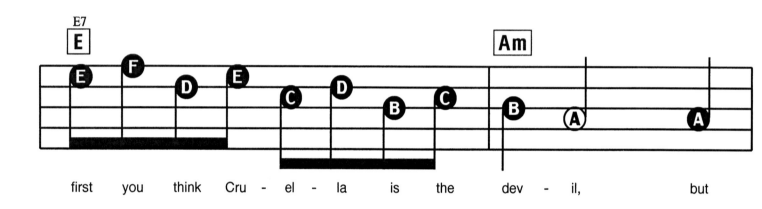

first   you   think   Cru - el - la   is   the   dev - il,   but

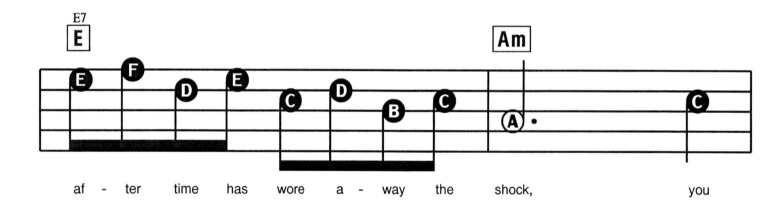

af - ter   time   has   wore   a - way   the   shock,   you

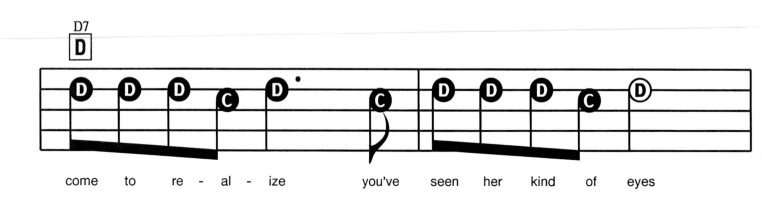

come   to   re - al - ize   you've   seen   her   kind   of   eyes

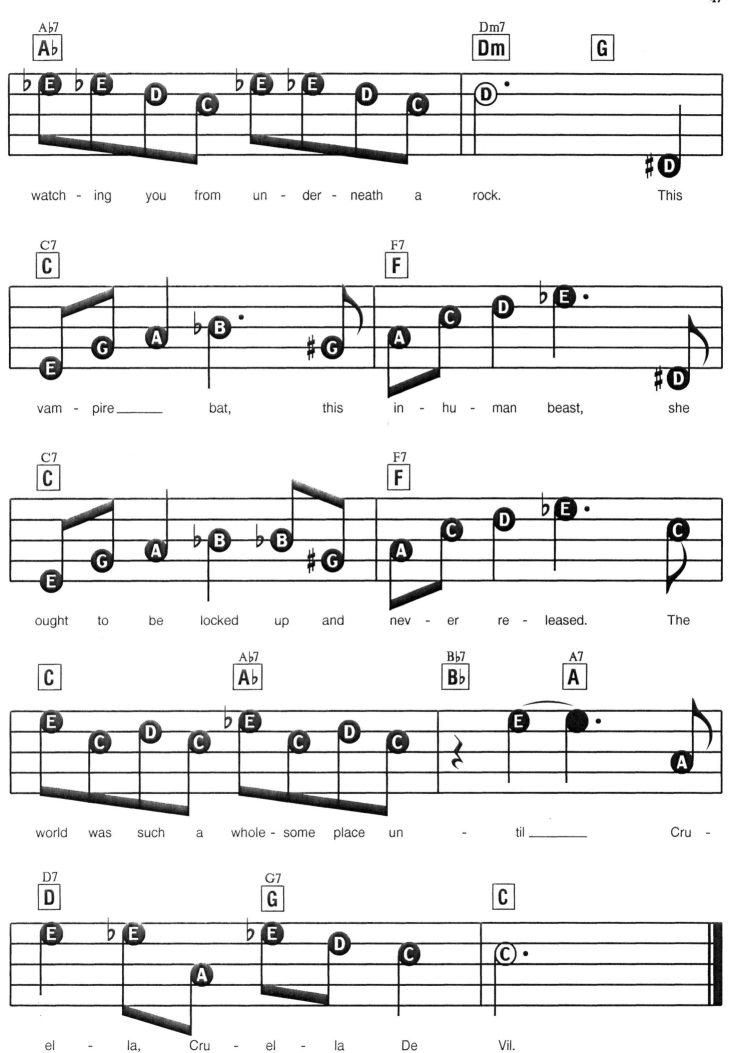

Did You Ever See A Lassie?

Registration 3
Rhythm: Waltz

Anonymous

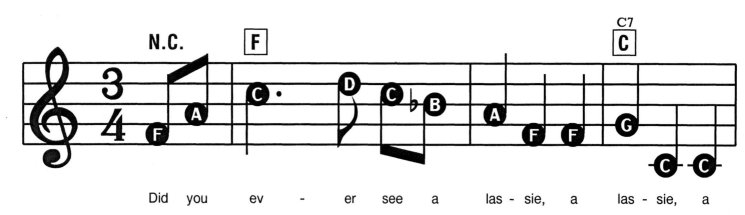

Did you ev - er see a las - sie, a las - sie, a

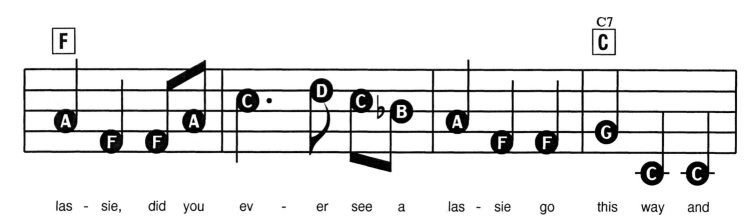

las - sie, did you ev - er see a las - sie go this way and

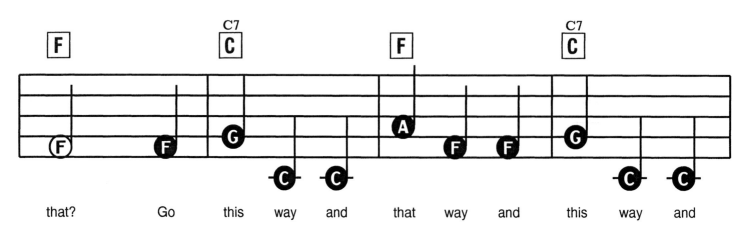

that? Go this way and that way and this way and

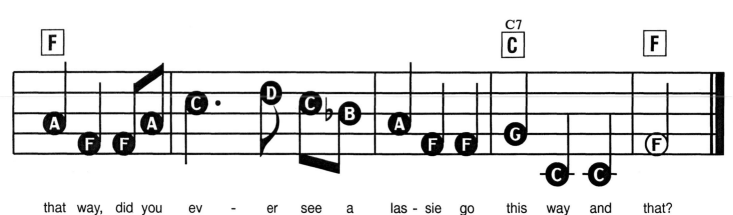

that way, did you ev - er see a las - sie go this way and that?

Dites-Moi
(Tell Me Why)
from SOUTH PACIFIC

Registration 1
Rhythm: Fox Trot

Lyrics by Oscar Hammerstein II
Music by Richard Rodgers

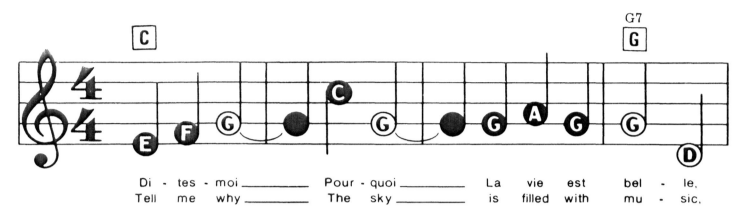

Di - tes - moi _____ Pour - quoi _____ La vie est bel - le,
Tell me why _____ The sky _____ is filled with mu - sic,

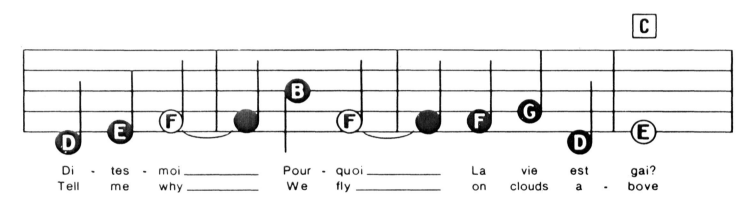

Di - tes - moi _____ Pour - quoi _____ La vie est gai?
Tell me why _____ We fly _____ on clouds a - bove

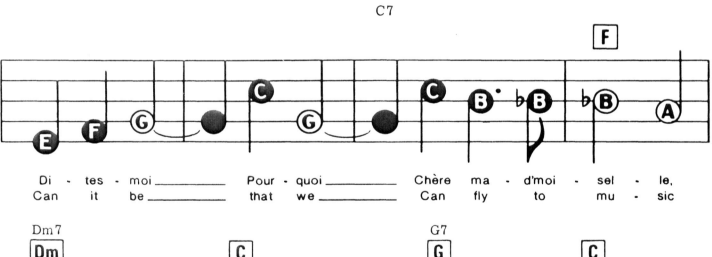

Di - tes - moi _____ Pour - quoi _____ Chère ma - d'moi - sel - le,
Can it be _____ that we _____ Can fly to mu - sic

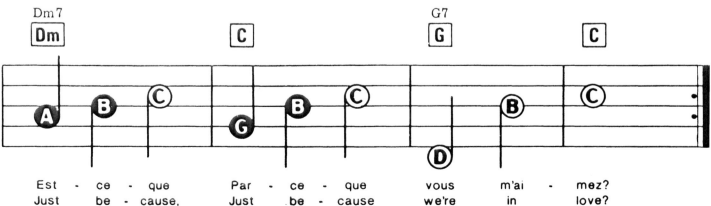

Est - ce - que Par - ce - que vous m'ai - mez?
Just be - cause, Just be - cause we're in love?

Do-Re-Mi
from THE SOUND OF MUSIC

Registration 4
Rhythm: March

Lyrics by Oscar Hammerstein II
Music by Richard Rodgers

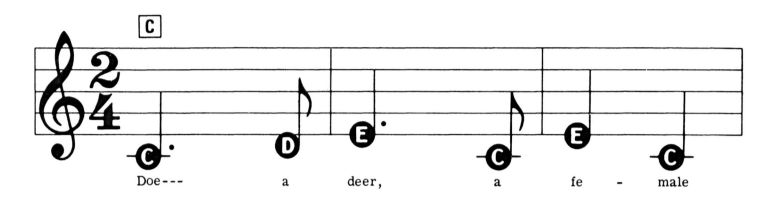

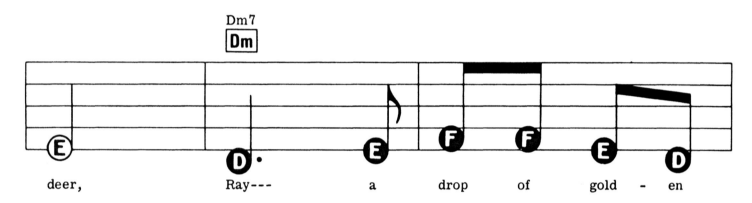

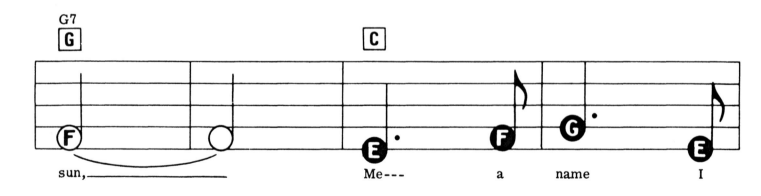

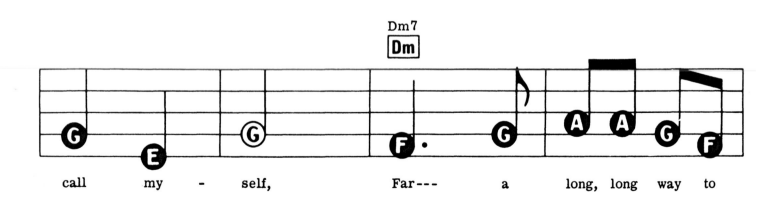

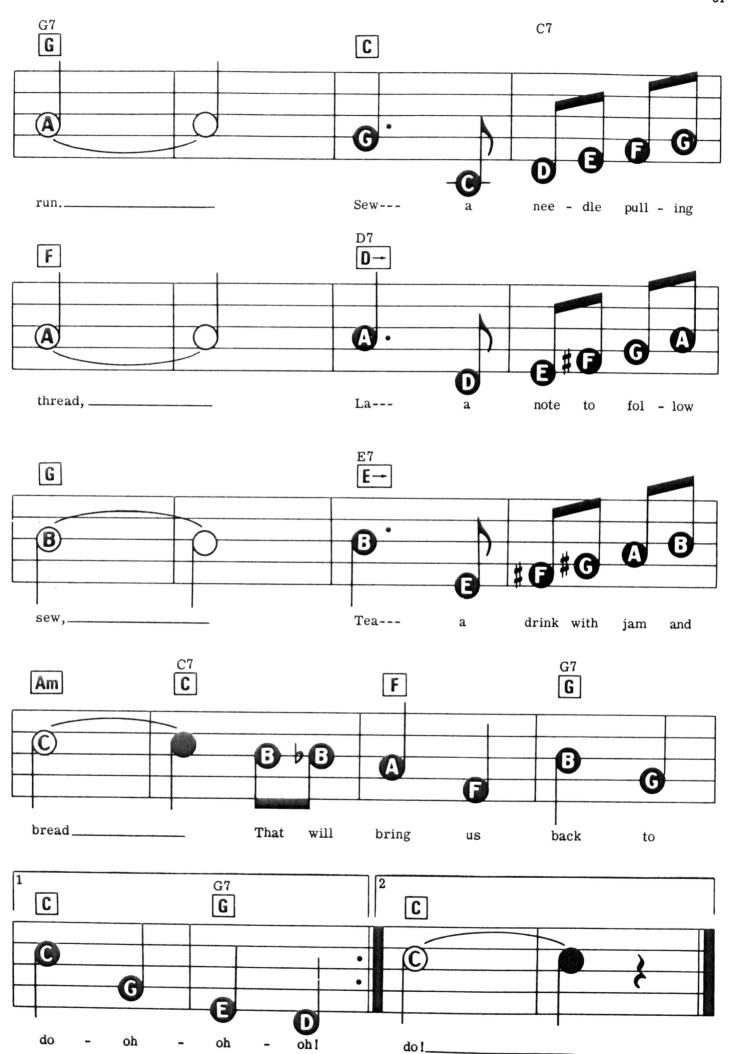

A Dream Is A Wish Your Heart Makes

from Walt Disney's CINDERELLA

Registration 1
Rhythm: Ballad or Fox Trot

Words and Music by Mack David,
Al Hoffman and Jerry Livingston

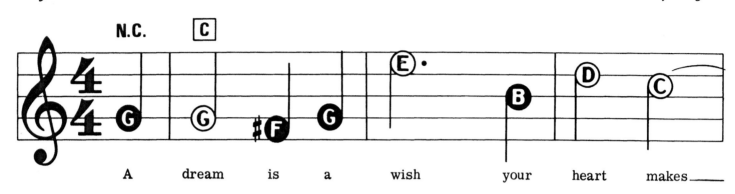

A   dream   is   a   wish   your   heart   makes____

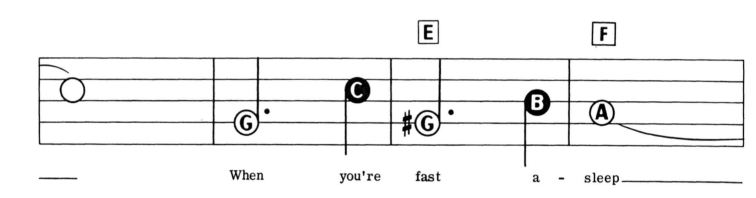

When   you're   fast   a - sleep____

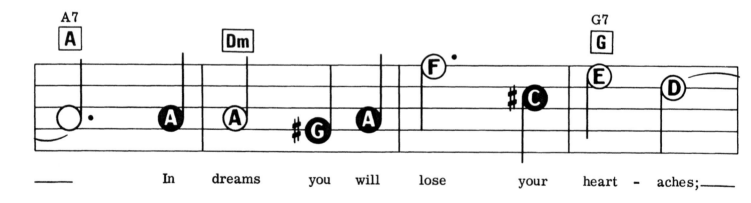

In   dreams   you   will   lose   your   heart - aches;____

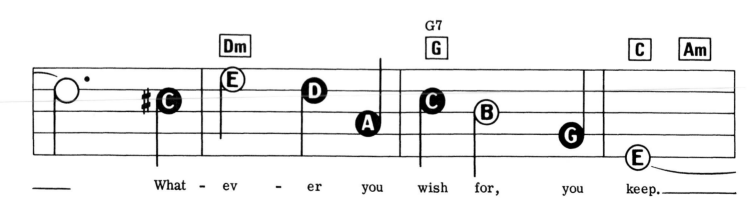

What - ev - er   you   wish   for,   you   keep.____

53

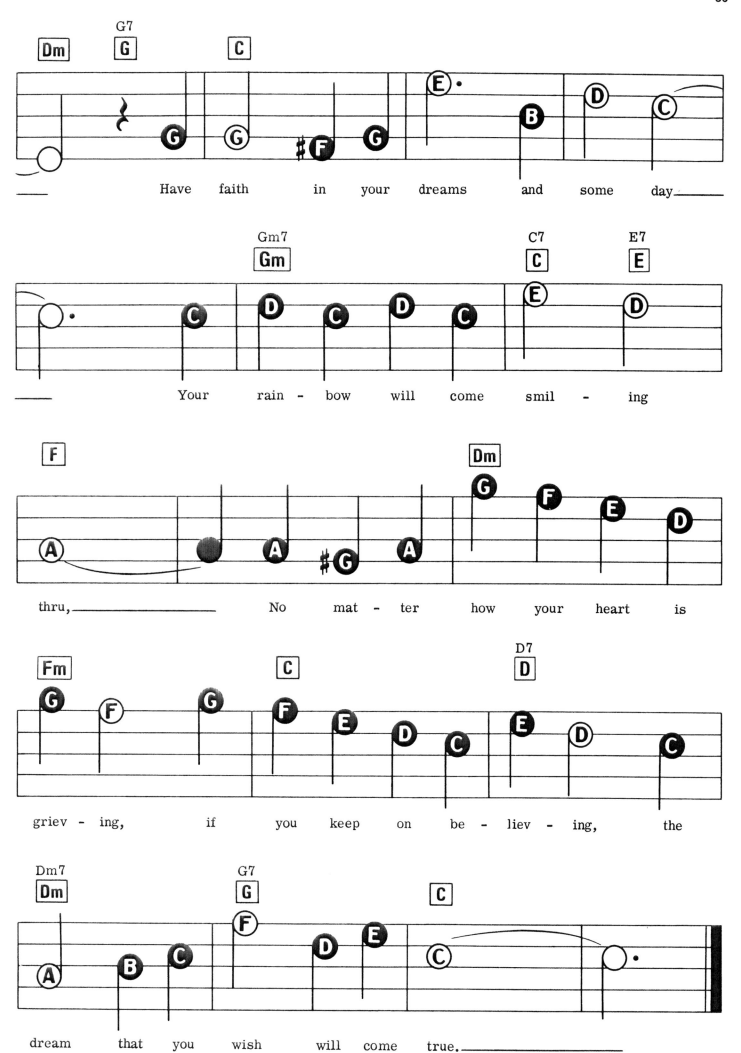

Edelweiss
from THE SOUND OF MUSIC

Registration 1
Rhythm: Waltz

Lyrics by Oscar Hammerstein II
Music by Richard Rodgers

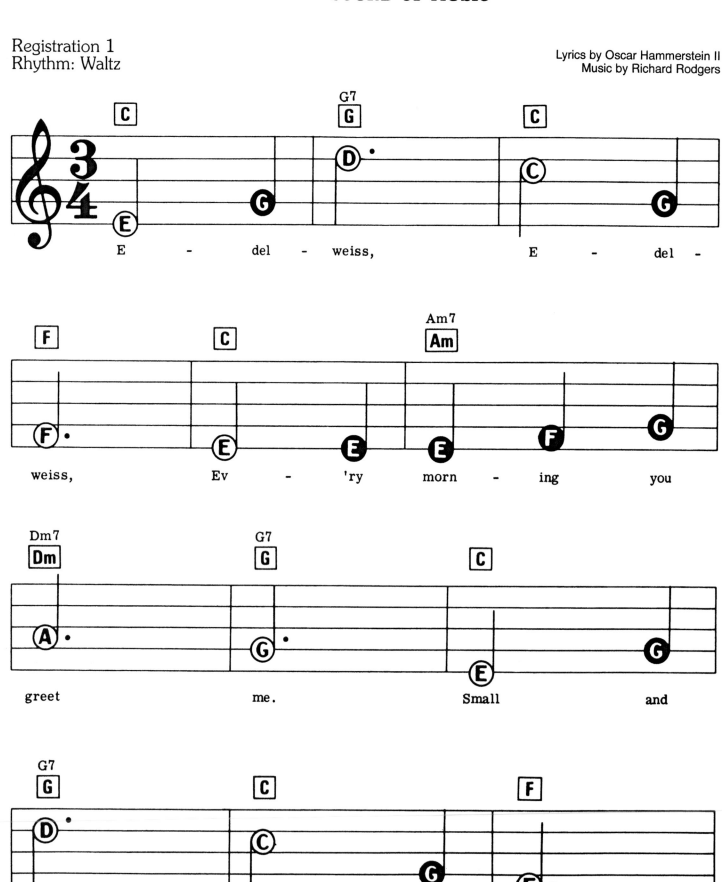

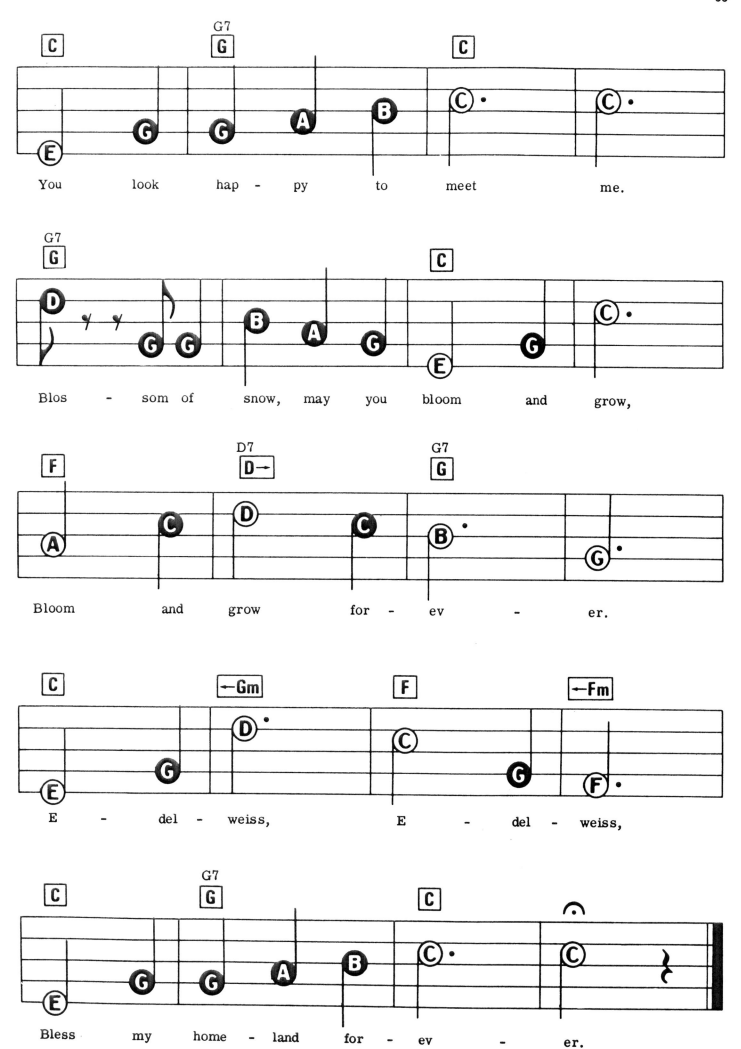

Everything Is Beautiful

Registration 8
Rhythm: Rock or Jazz Rock

Words and Music by
Ray Stevens

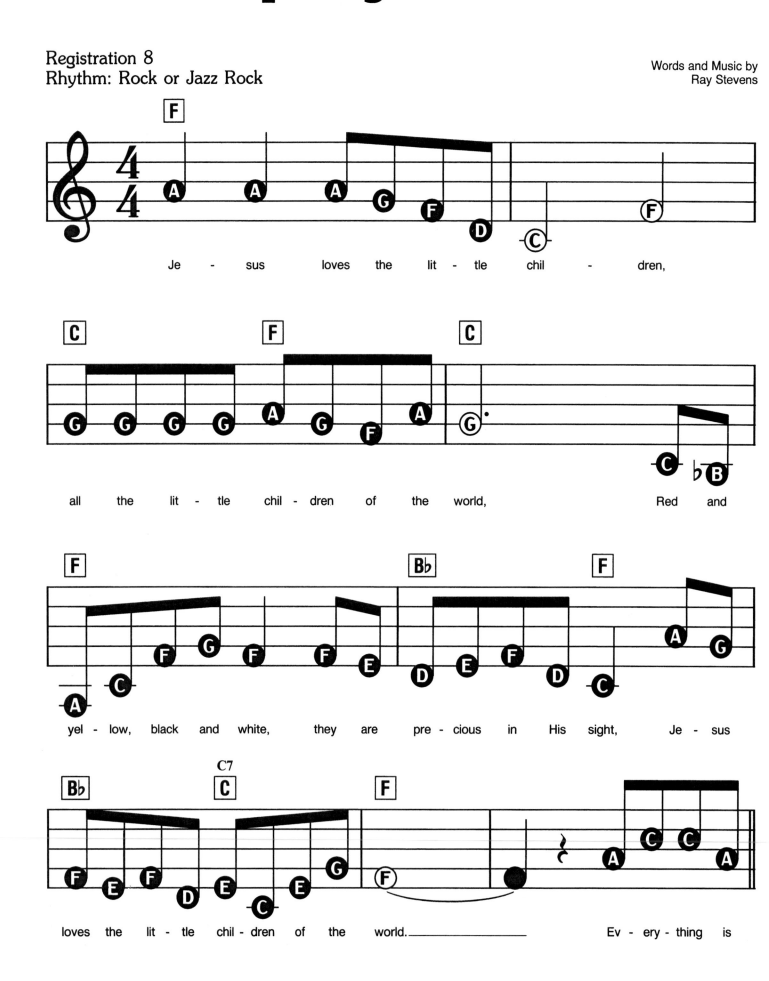

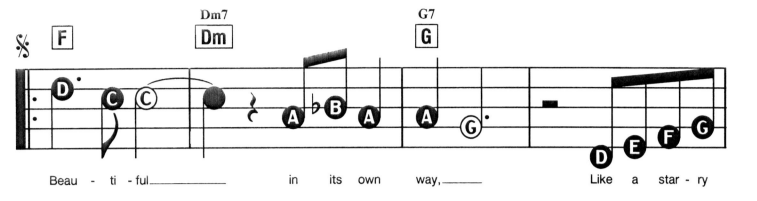

Beau - ti -ful_____ in its own way,_____ Like a star - ry

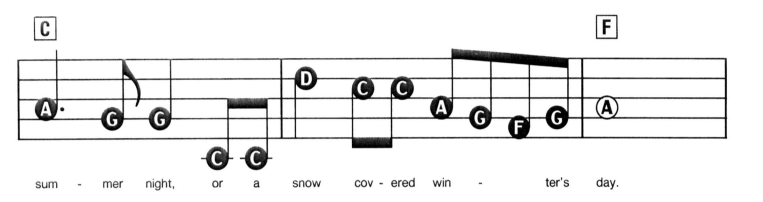

sum - mer night, or a snow cov - ered win - ter's day.

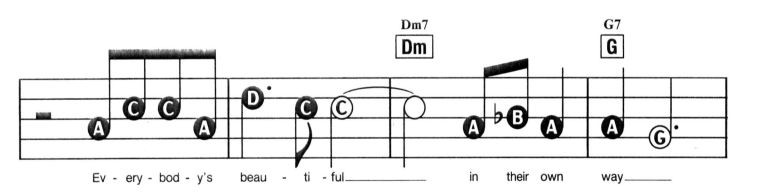

Ev - ery - bod - y's beau - ti -ful_____ in their own way_____

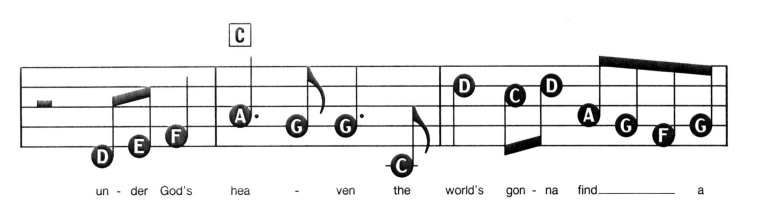

un - der God's hea - ven the world's gon - na find_____ a

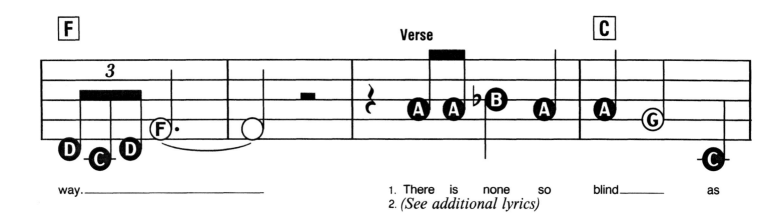

way._____

Verse

1. There   is   none   so   blind_____   as
2. *(See additional lyrics)*

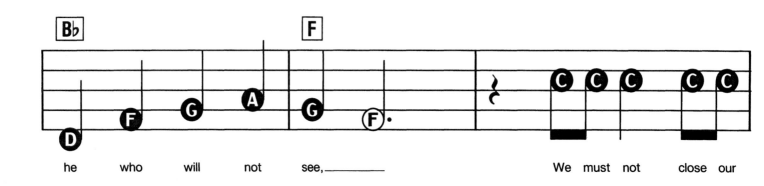

he   who   will   not   see,_____   We   must   not   close   our

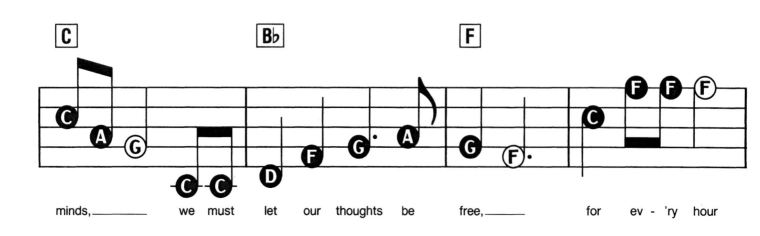

minds,_____   we   must   let   our   thoughts   be   free,_____   for   ev - 'ry   hour

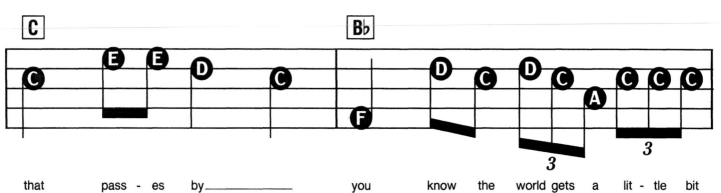

that   pass - es   by_____   you   know   the   world   gets   a   lit - tle   bit

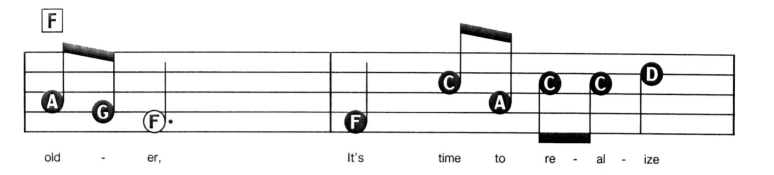

old - er,   It's   time   to   re - al - ize

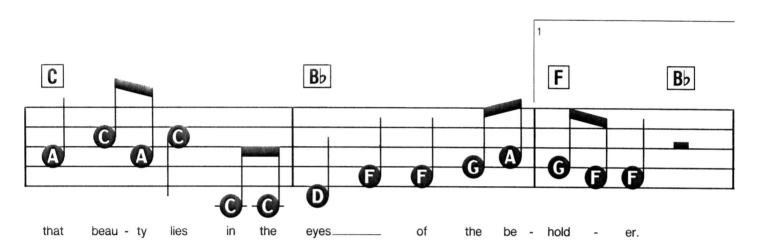

that   beau - ty   lies   in   the   eyes_____   of   the   be - hold - er.

D.S. and Fade
(Return to % and Fade)

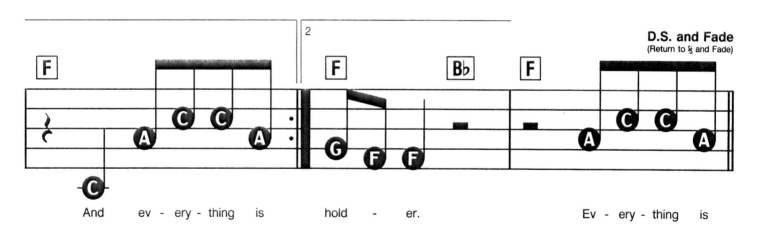

And   ev - ery - thing   is   hold - er.   Ev - ery - thing   is

Additional Lyrics

2. We shouldn't care about the length of his hair or the color of his skin,
   Don't worry about what shows from without but the love that lives within,
   We gonna get it all together now and everything gonna work out fine,
   Just take a little time to look on the good side my friend and straighten it out in your mind.

Feed The Birds
from Walt Disney's MARY POPPINS

Registration 2
Rhythm: Waltz

Words and Music by Richard M. Sherman
and Robert B. Sherman

Feed _____ the birds, tup - pence _____ a bag,
Though _____ her words are sim - ple _____ and few,

Tup - pence, _____ tup - pence, _____ tup - pence _____ a bag. "Feed _____ the
Lis - ten, _____ lis - ten she's call - ing _____ to you. "Feed _____ the

birds," that's what she cries, While o - ver - head her
birds,

birds fill the skies. All a - round the ca - the - dral, the

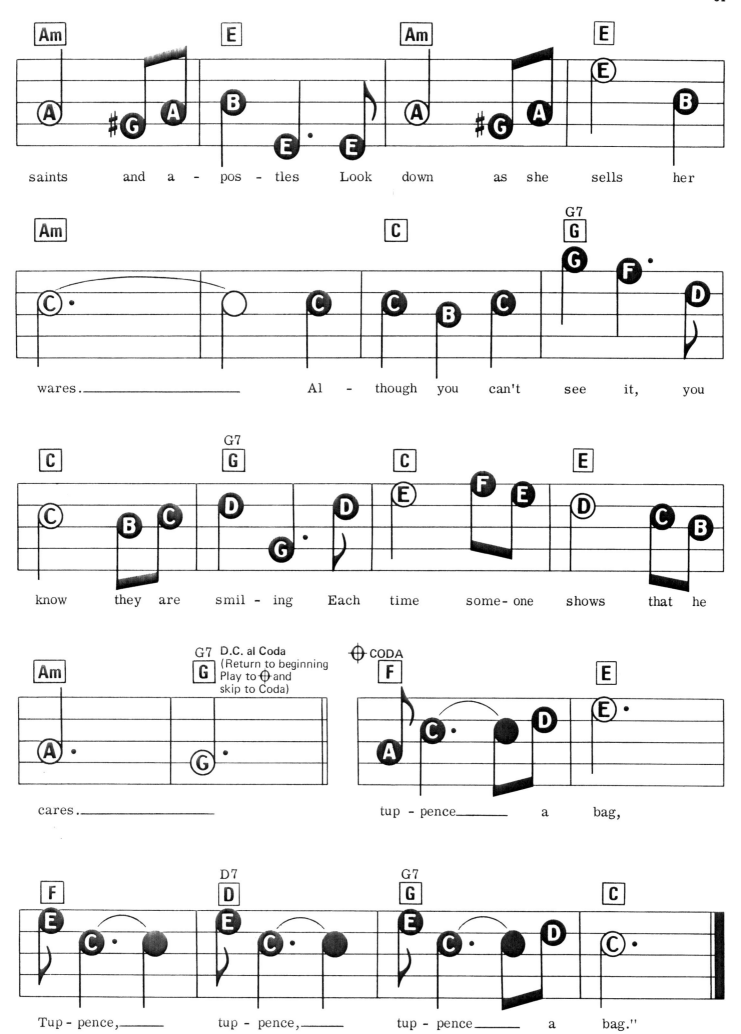

Frog Went A-Courtin'

Registration 2
Rhythm: March, Polka or Pops

Anonymous

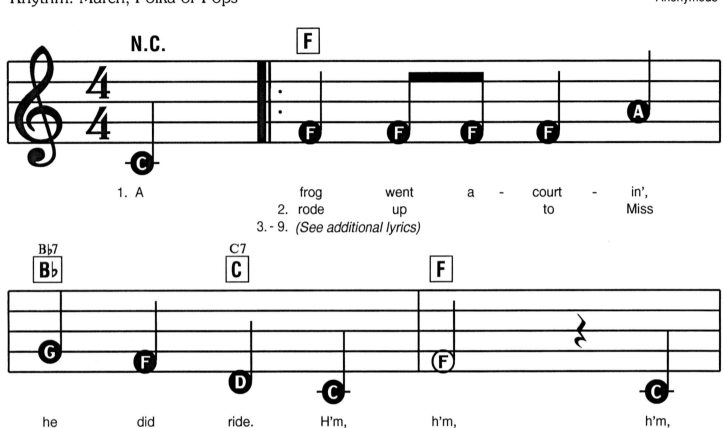

1. A   frog   went   a -   court -   in',
2. rode   up   to   Miss
3. - 9. *(See additional lyrics)*

he   did   ride.   H'm,   h'm,   h'm,
Mous - ie's   den.   H'm,   h'm,   h'm,

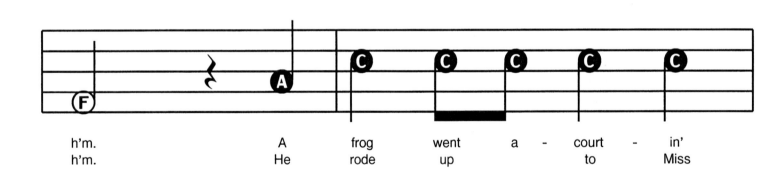

h'm.   A   frog   went   a -   court -   in'
h'm.   He   rode   up   to   Miss

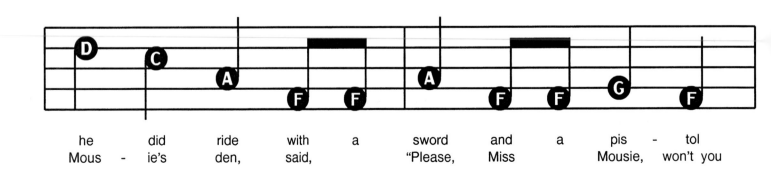

he   did   ride,   with   a   sword   and   a   pis - tol
Mous - ie's   den,   said,   "Please,   Miss   Mousie,   won't   you

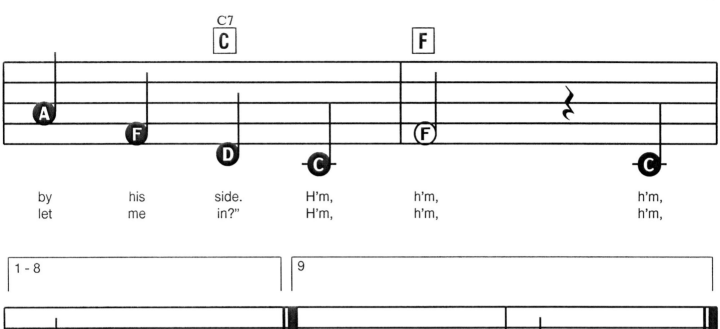

by   his   side.   H'm,   h'm,   h'm,
let   me   in?"   H'm,   h'm,   h'm,

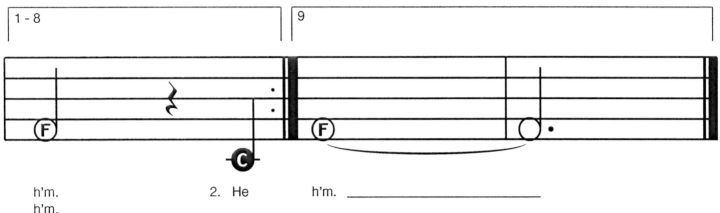

h'm.   2. He   h'm.
h'm.

Additional Lyrics

3. "Yes, Sir Frog, I sit and spin."
H'm, h'm, H'm, h'm.
"Yes, Sir Frog, I sit and spin;
Pray Mister Froggie, won't you walk in?"
H'm, h'm, H'm, h'm.

4. The frog said, "My dear, I've come to see."
H'm, h'm, H'm, h'm.
The frog said, "My dear, I've come to see
If you, Miss Mousie, will marry me."
H'm, h'm, H'm, h'm.

5. "I don't know what to say to that."
H'm, h'm, H'm, h'm.
"I don't know what to say to that
Till I speak with my Uncle Rat."
H'm, h'm, H'm, h'm.

6. When Uncle Rat came riding home,
H'm, h'm, H'm, h'm.
When Uncle Rat came riding home,
Said he, "Who's been here since I've been gone?"
H'm, h'm, H'm, h'm.

7. "A fine young froggie has been here."
H'm, h'm, H'm, h'm.
"A fine young froggie has been here;
He means to marry me, it's clear."
H'm, h'm, H'm, h'm.

8. So Uncle Rat, he rode to town.
H'm, h'm, H'm, h'm.
So Uncle Rat, he rode to town
And bought his niece a wedding gown.
H'm, h'm, H'm, h'm.

9. The frog and mouse they went to France.
H'm, h'm, H'm, h'm.
The frog and mouse they went to France,
And that's the end of my romance.
H'm, h'm, H'm, h'm.

(Meet) The Flintstones
from THE FLINTSTONES

Registration 5
Rhythm: Swing

Words and Music by W. Hanna,
J. Barbera and H. Curtin

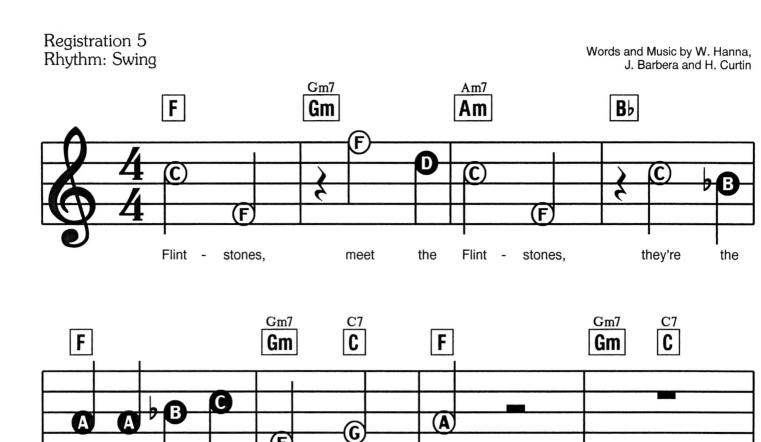

Flint - stones, meet the Flint - stones, they're the

mod - ern stone - age fam - i - ly.

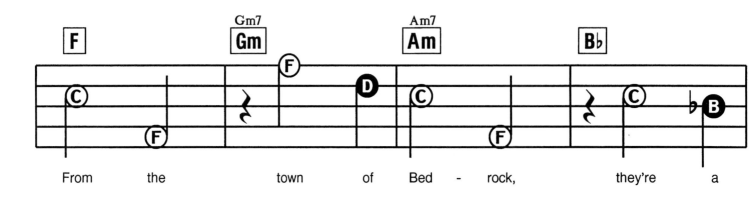

From the town of Bed - rock, they're a

place right out of his - to - ry.

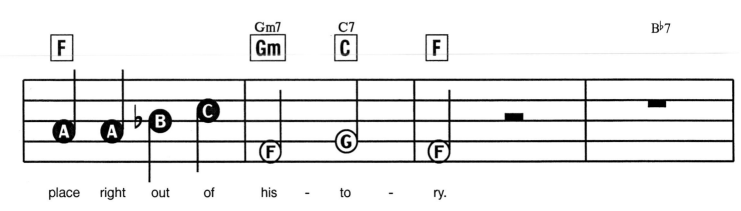

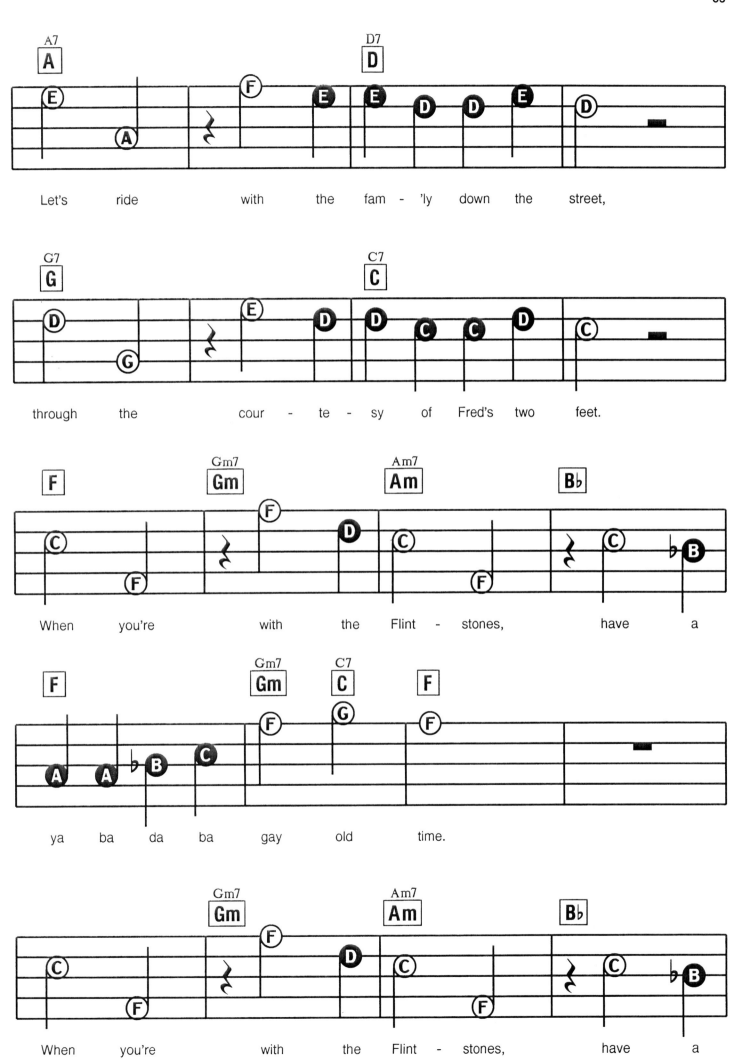

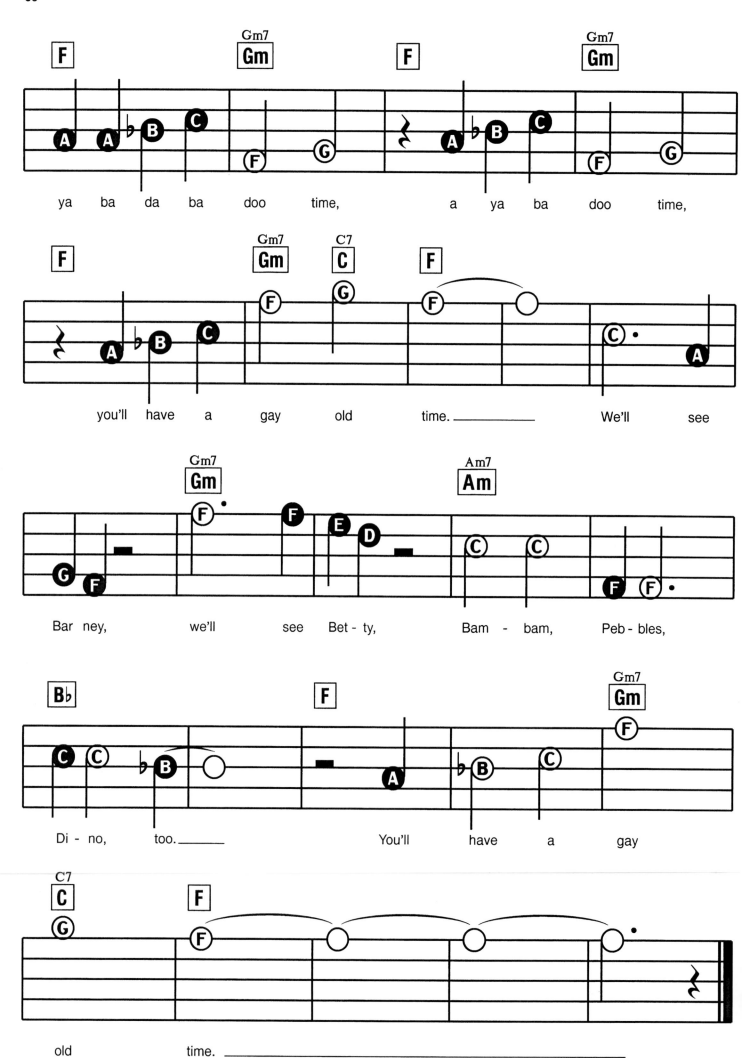

Go In And Out The Window

Registration 8
Rhythm: March, Polka or Rock

Traditional

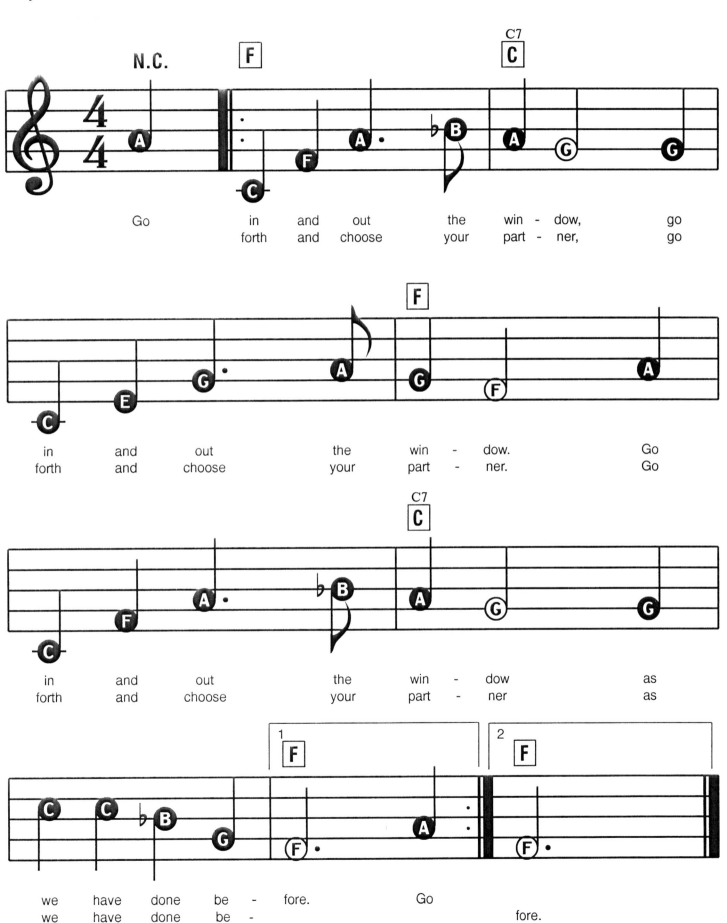

Getting To Know You

from THE KING AND I

Registration 8
Rhythm: Fox Trot or Swing

Lyrics by Oscar Hammerstein II
Music by Richard Rodgers

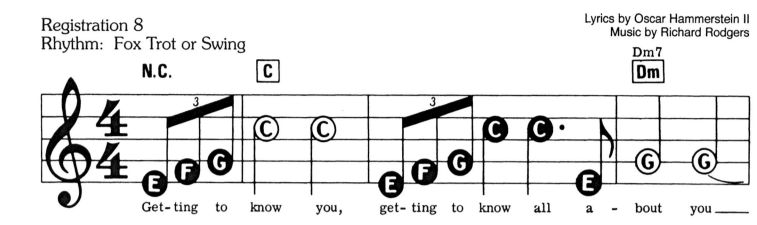

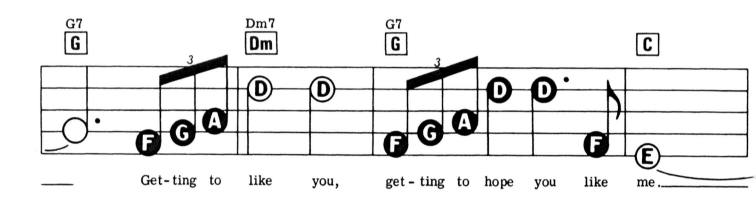

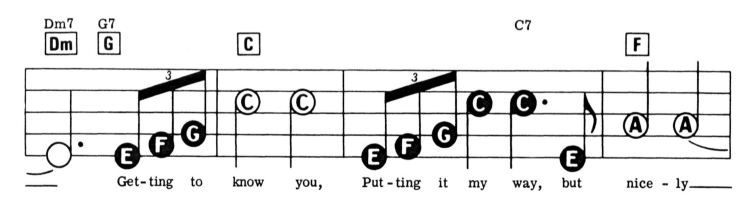

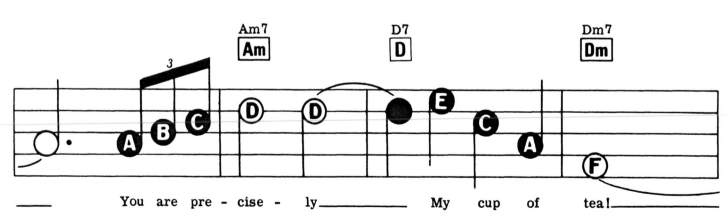

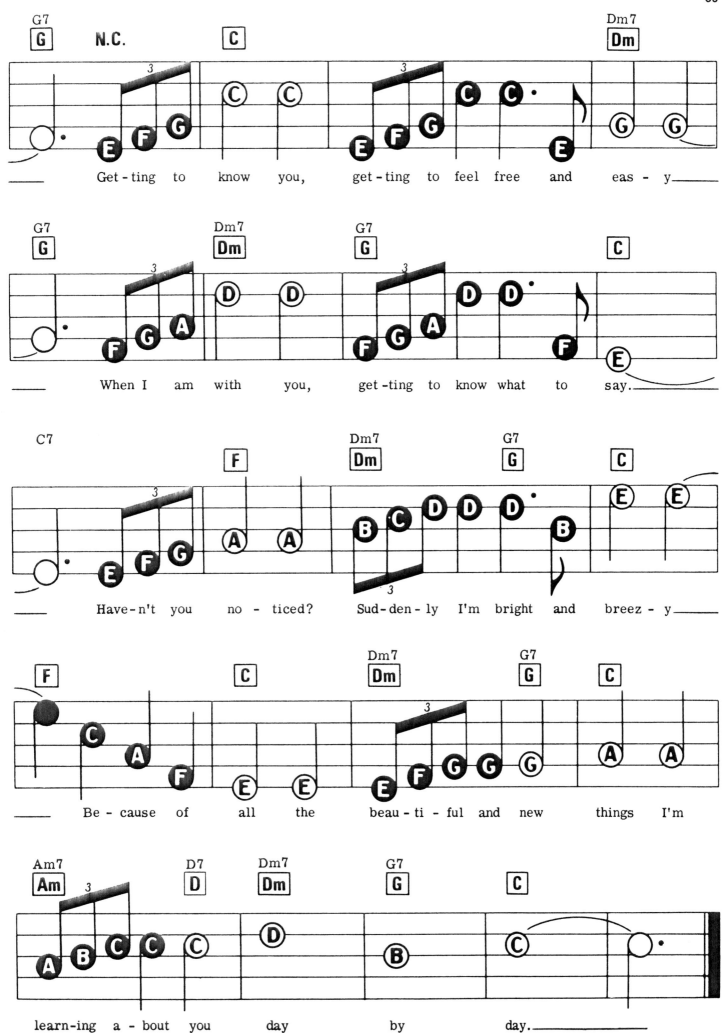

Happy Trails
from the Television Series THE ROY ROGERS SHOW

Registration 5
Rhythm: Swing or Pops

Words and Music by
Dale Evans

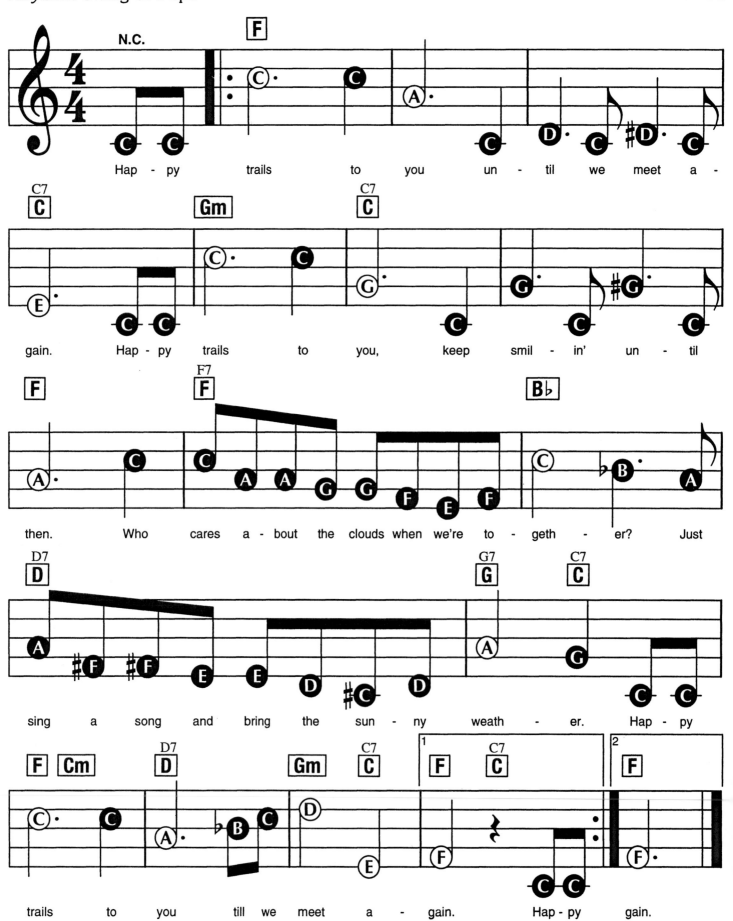

Heart And Soul
from the Paramount Short Subject A SONG IS BORN

Registration 8
Rhythm: Swing

Words by Frank Loesser
Music by Hoagy Carmichael

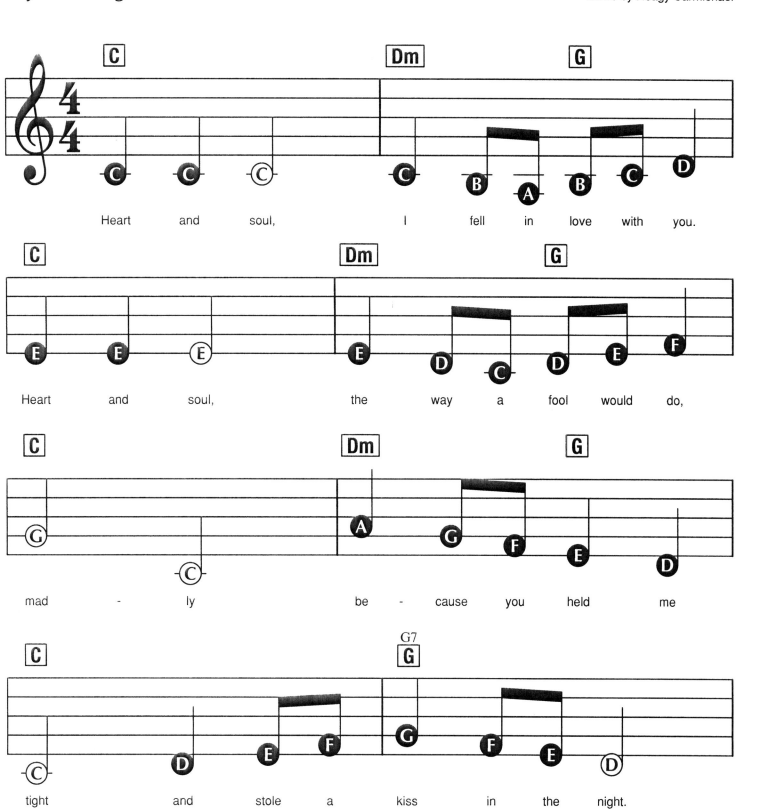

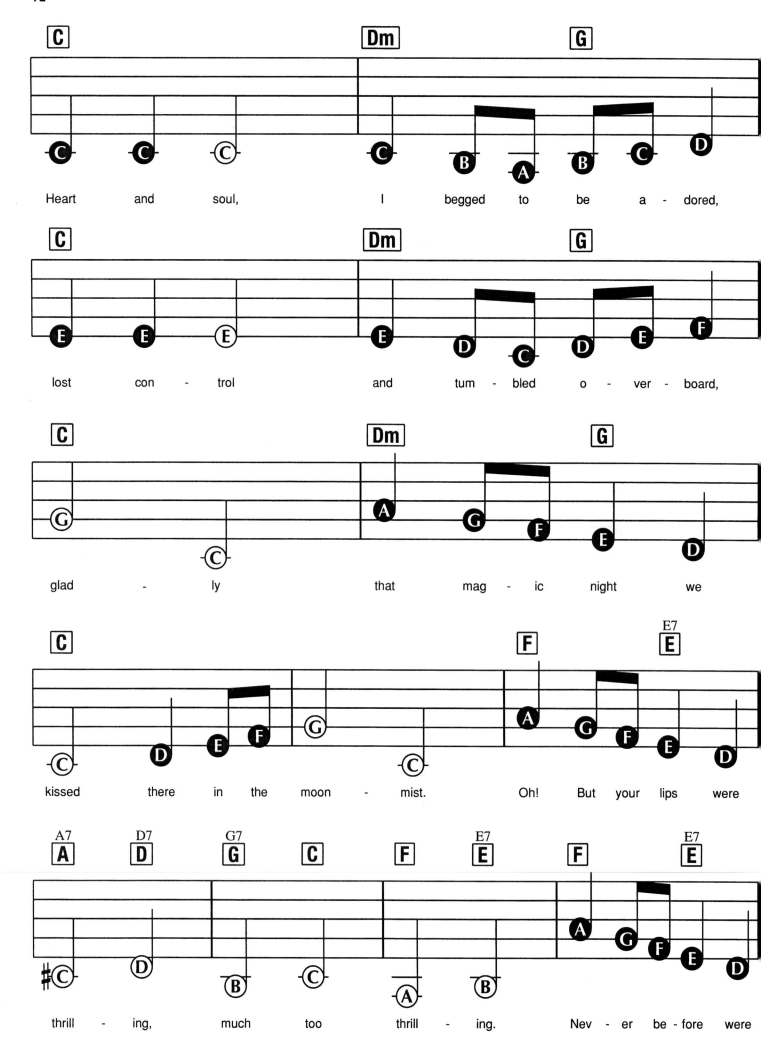

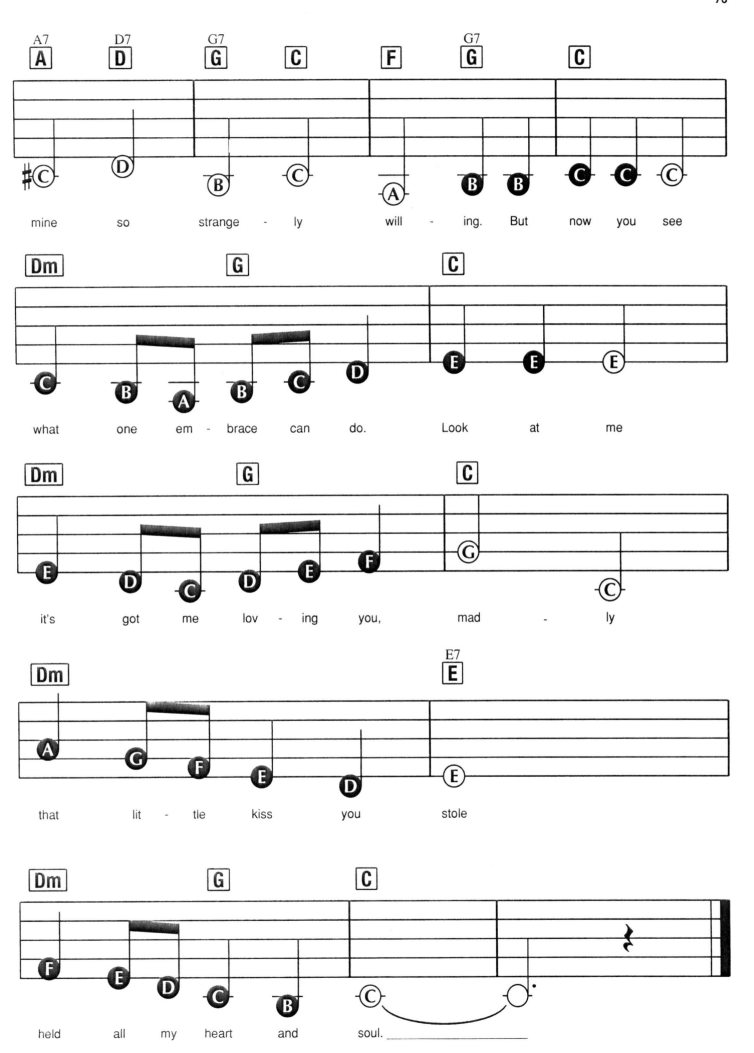

Heigh-Ho
the Dwarfs' Marching Song from SNOW WHITE AND THE SEVEN DWARFS

Registration 4
Rhythm: March

Words by Larry Morey
Music by Frank Churchill

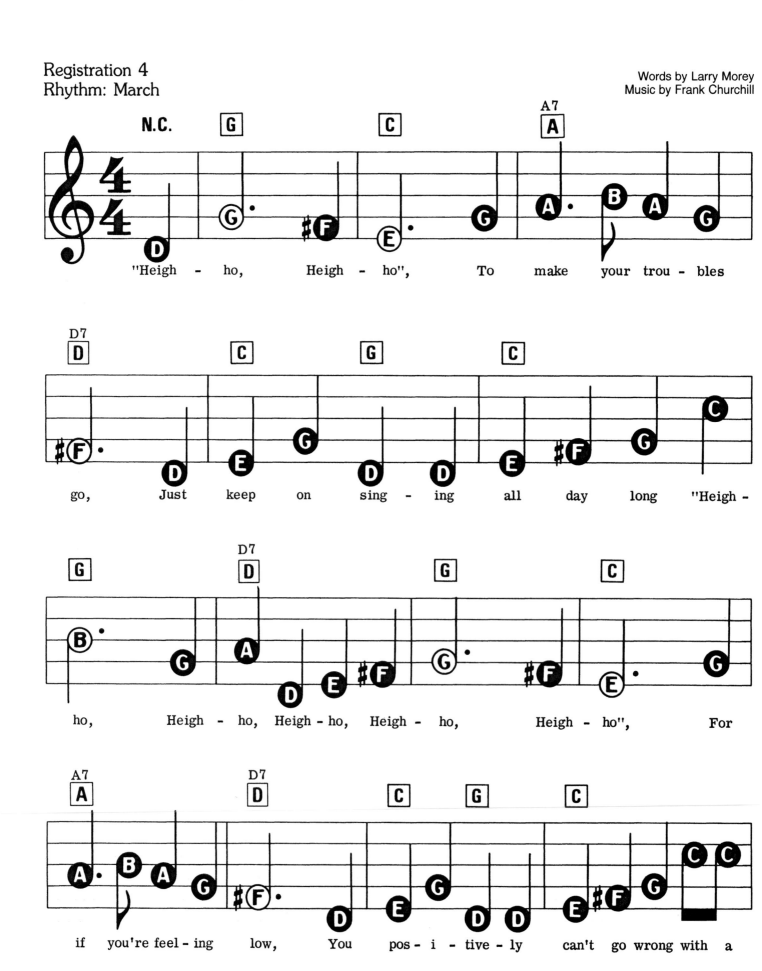

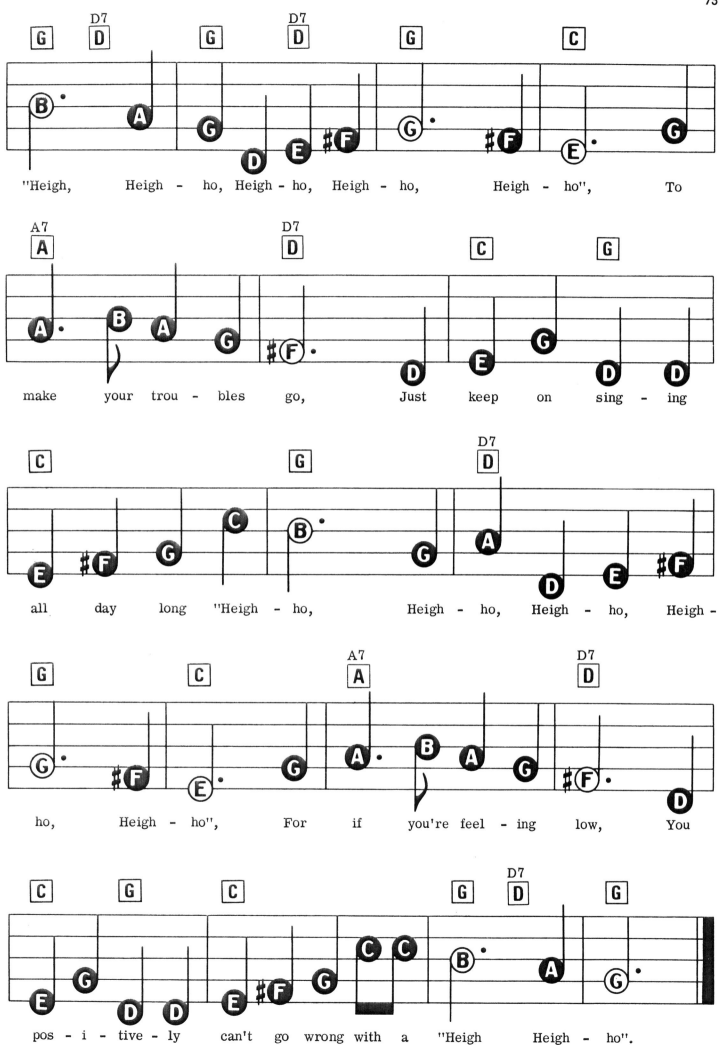

Hi-Diddle-Dee-Dee
(An Actor's Life For Me)
from Walt Disney's PINOCCHIO

Registration 1
Rhythm: Waltz

Words by Ned Washington
Music by Leigh Harline

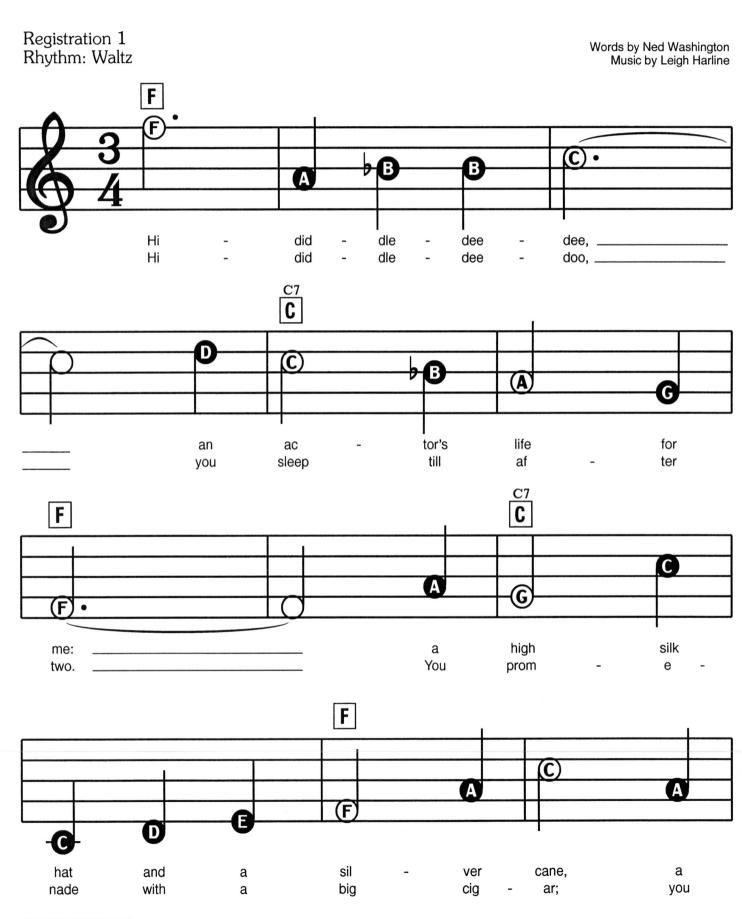

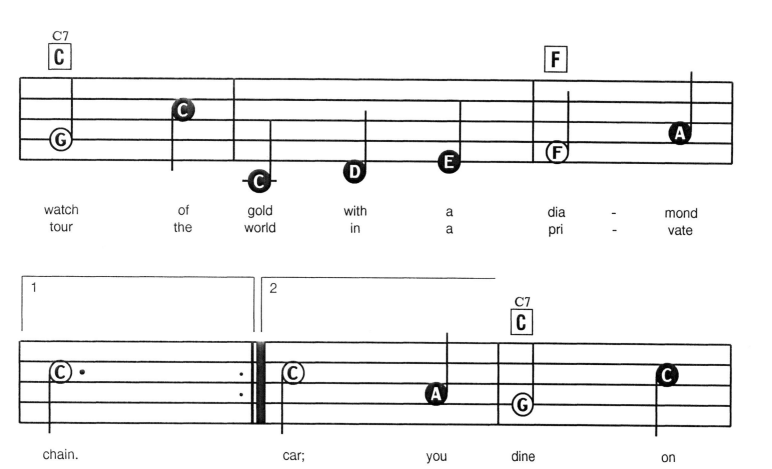

watch   of   gold   with   a   dia - mond
tour   the   world   in   a   pri - vate

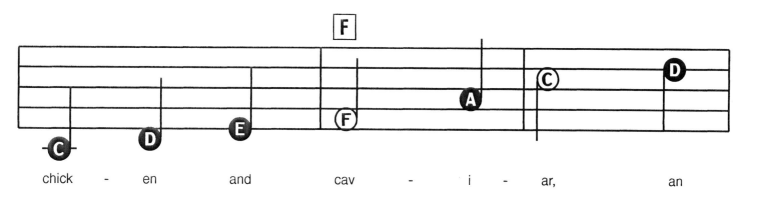

chain.   car;   you   dine   on

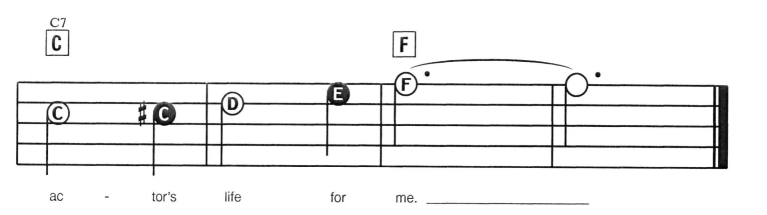

chick - en   and   cav - i - ar,   an

ac - tor's   life   for   me. _____

House At Pooh Corner

Registration 7
Rhythm: Pops

Words and Music by
Kenny Loggins

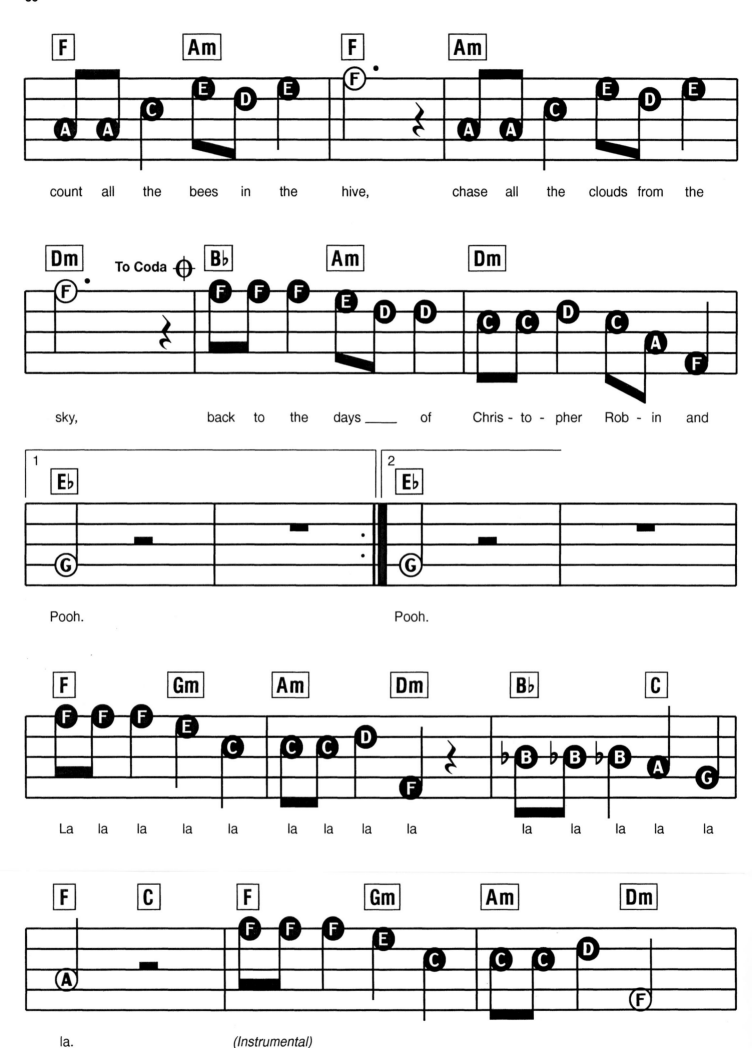

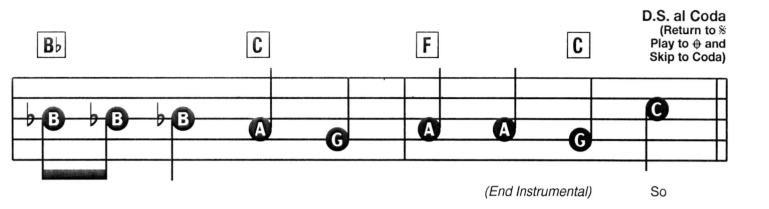

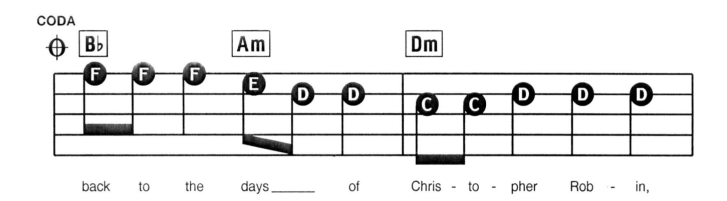

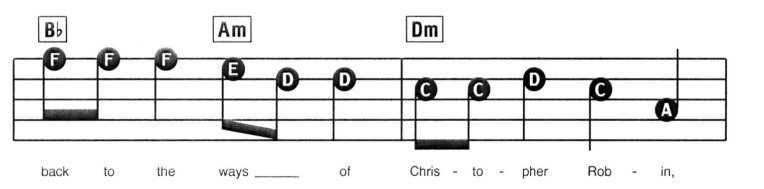

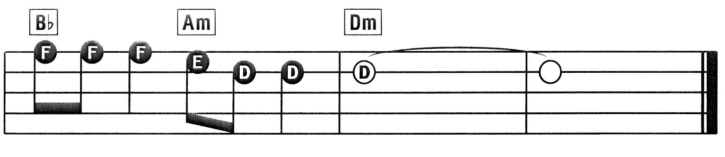

I Don't Want To Live On The Moon

from the Television Series SESAME STREET

Registration 2
Rhythm: Pops or Rock

Words and Music by
Jeff Moss

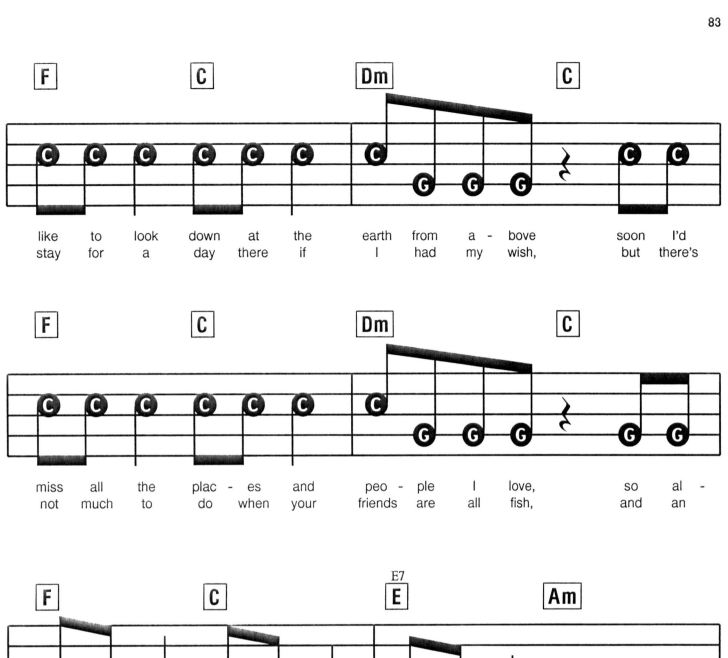

like to look down at the earth from a - bove soon I'd
stay for a day there if I had my wish, but there's

miss all the plac - es and peo - ple I love, so al -
not much to do when your friends are all fish, and an

though I might like it for one af - ter - noon I
oy - ster and clam are - n't real fam - i - ly. So I

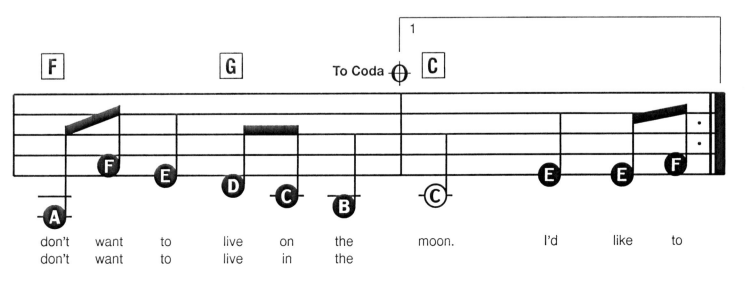

don't want to live on the moon. I'd like to
don't want to live in the

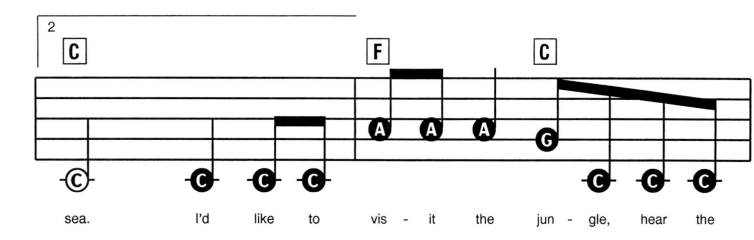

sea.   I'd   like to vis - it the jun - gle, hear the

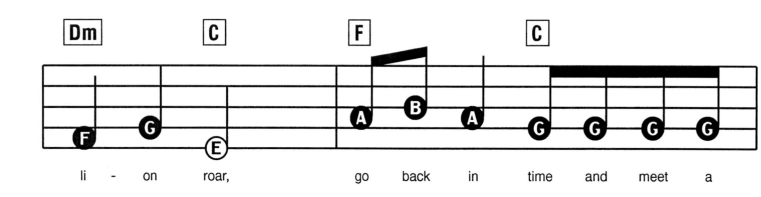

li - on roar,   go back in time and meet a

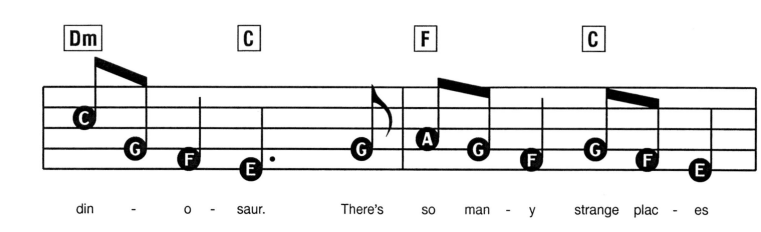

din - o - saur. There's so man - y strange plac - es

D.S. al Coda
(Return to %
Play to ⊕ and
Skip to Coda)

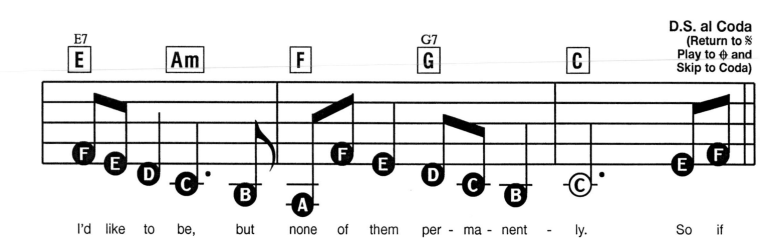

I'd like to be,   but none of them per - ma - nent - ly.   So if

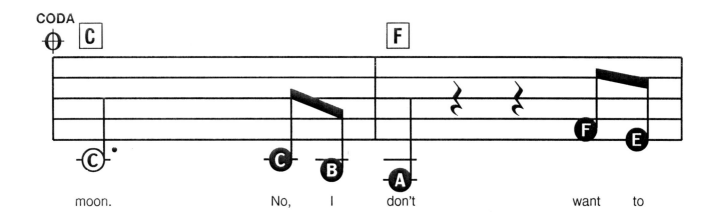

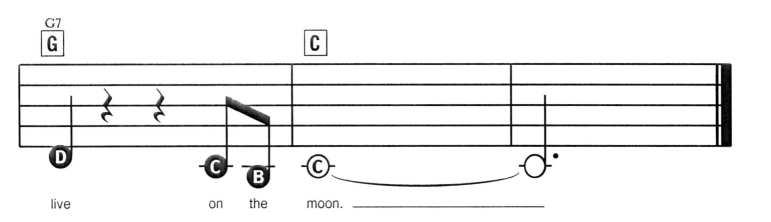

Additional Lyrics

D.S. So if I should visit the moon,
Well, I'll dance on a moonbeam and then
I will make a wish on a star
And I'll wish I was home once again;
Though I'd like to look down at the earth from above,
Soon I'd miss all the places and people I love,
So although I may go, I'll be coming home soon
'Cause I don't want to live on the moon.
No, I don't want to live on the moon.

I Whistle A Happy Tune
from THE KING AND I

Registration 10
Rhythm: Swing

Lyrics by Oscar Hammerstein II
Music by Richard Rodgers

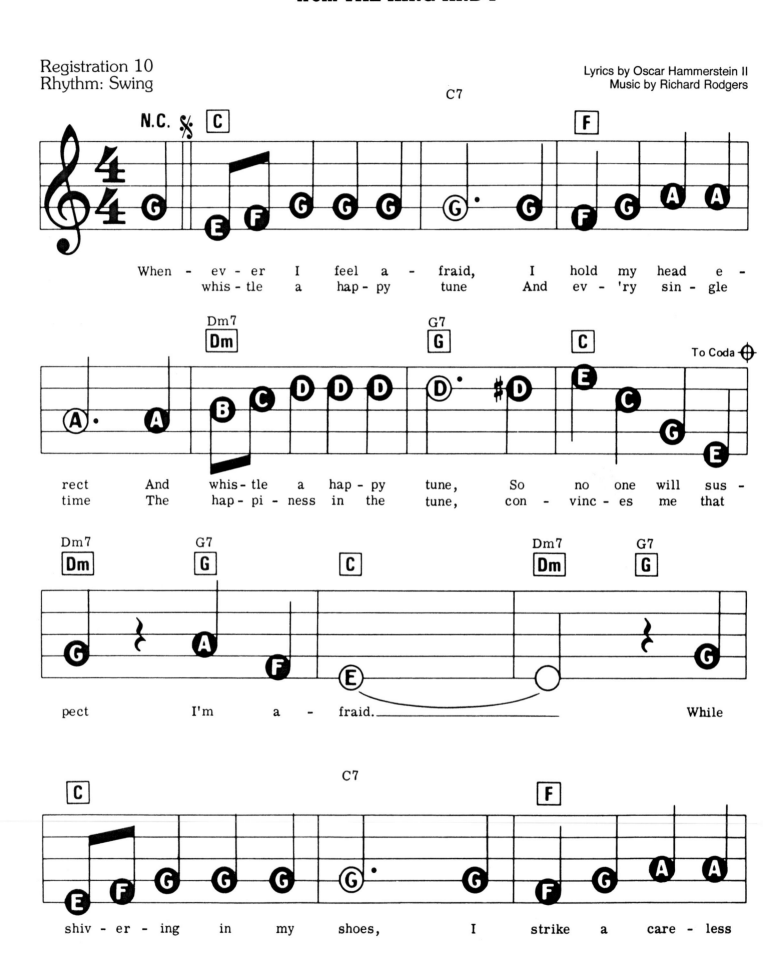

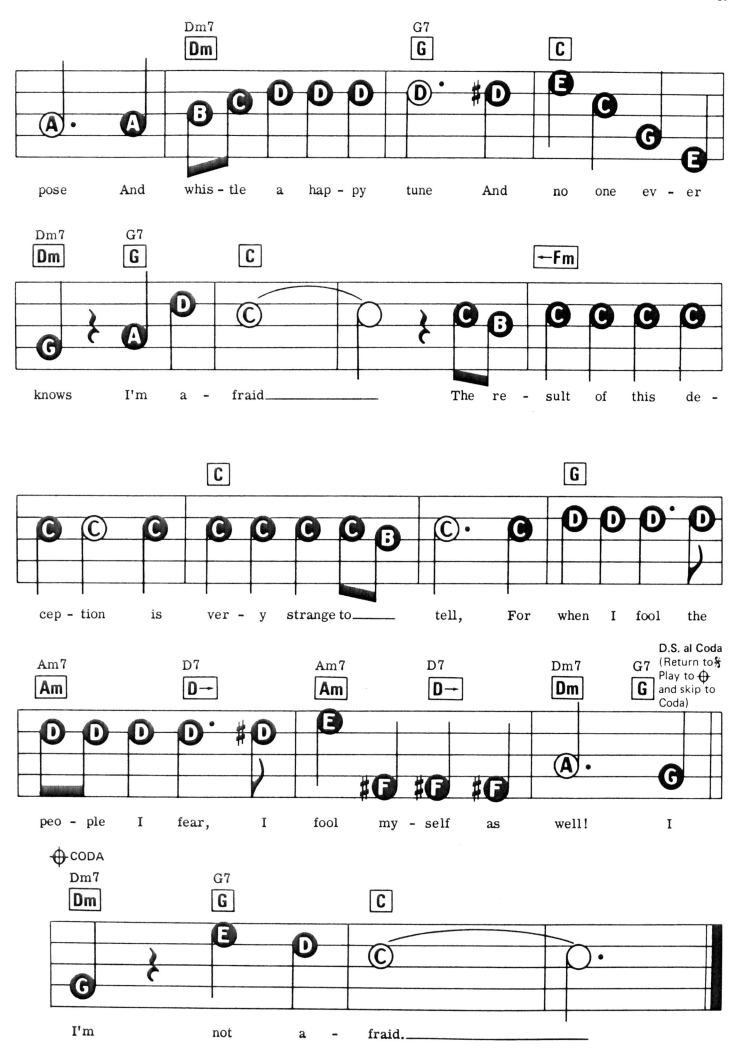

I Love Trash
from the Television Series SESAME STREET

Registration 3
Rhythm: Waltz

Words and Music by
Jeff Moss

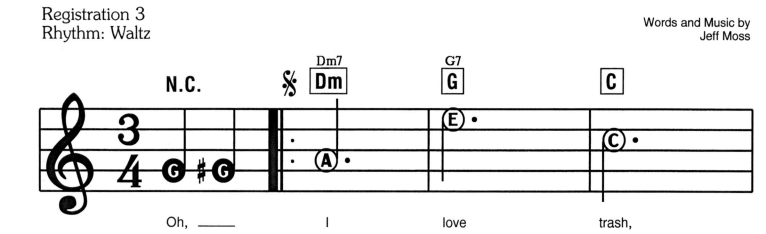

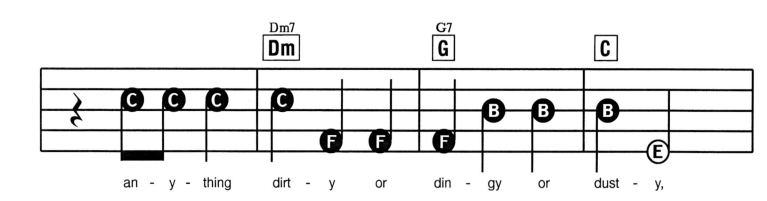

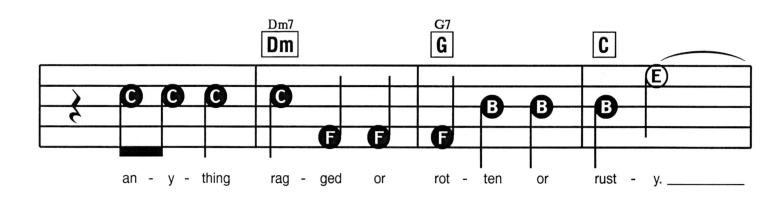

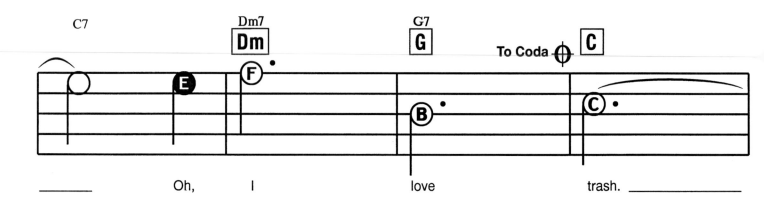

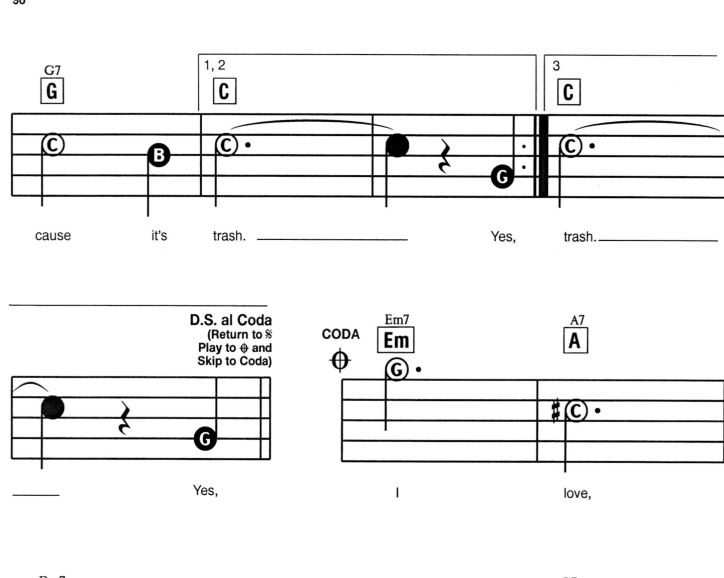

cause   it's   trash. ——————————— Yes,   trash.———————

D.S. al Coda
(Return to ℅
Play to ⊕ and
Skip to Coda)

——————   Yes,   I   love,

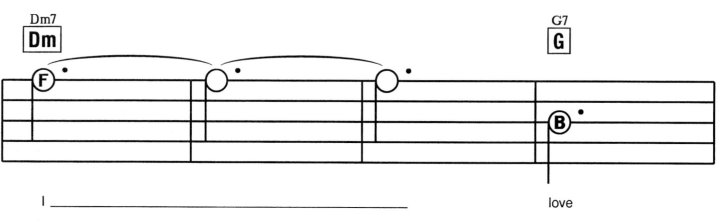

I —————————————————   love

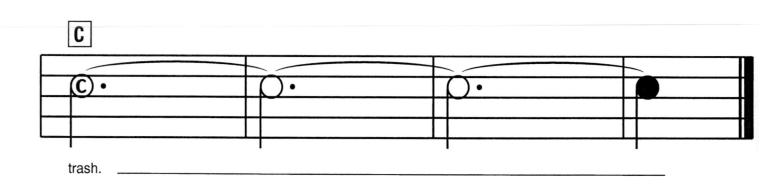

trash. ——————————————————

I'm Popeye The Sailor Man
Theme from the Paramount Cartoon POPEYE THE SAILOR

Registration 9
Rhythm: Waltz

Words and Music by
Sammy Lerner

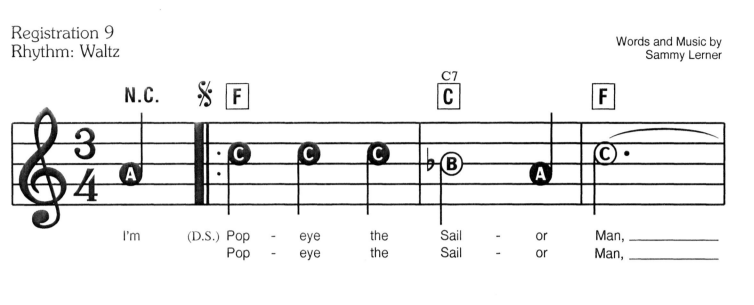

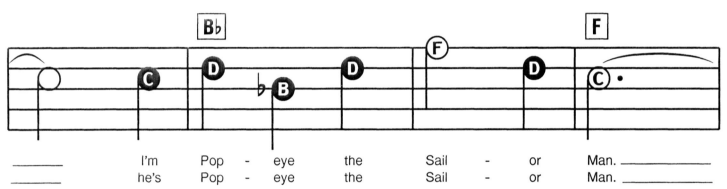

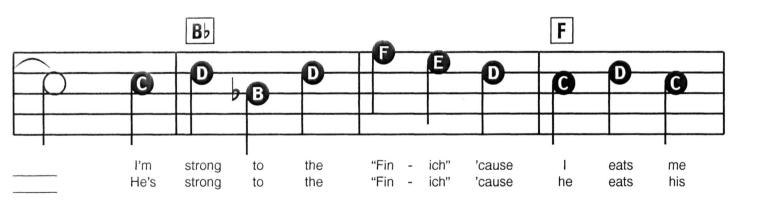

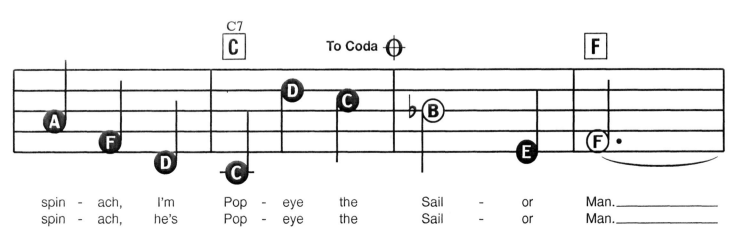

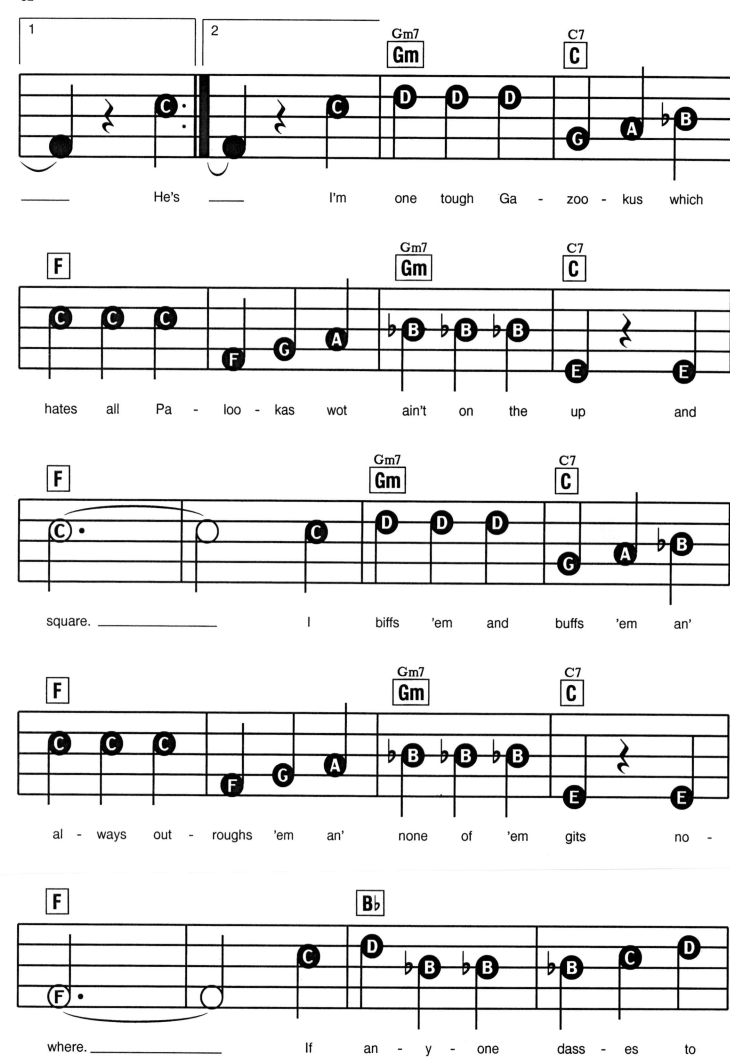

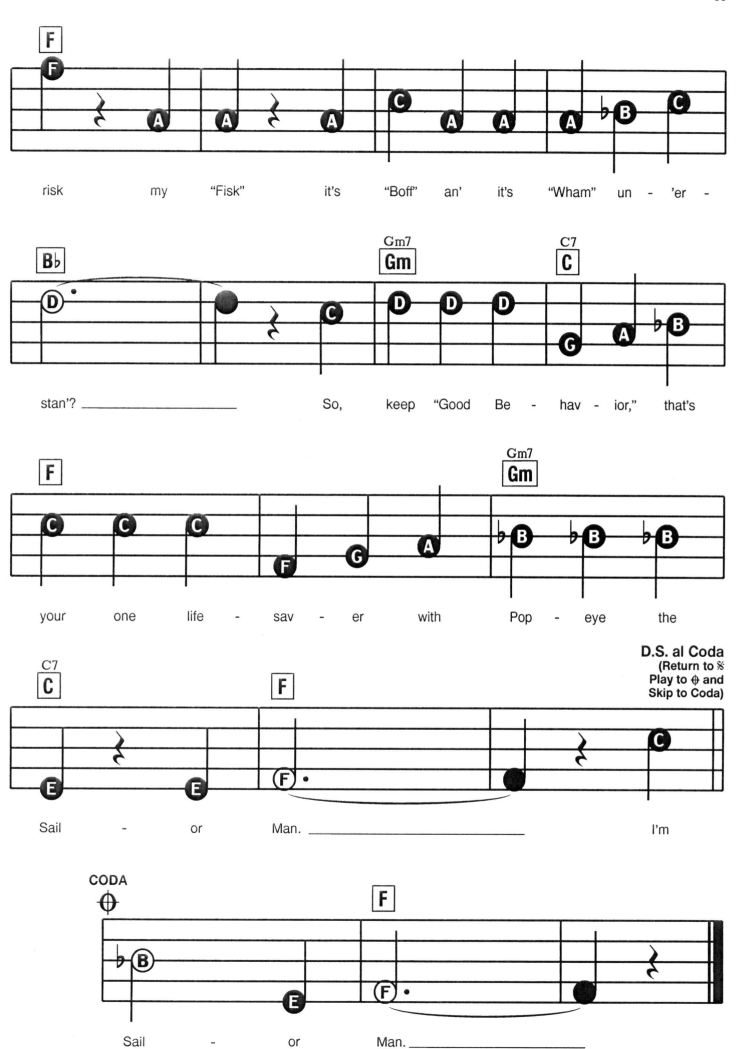

risk my "Fisk" it's "Boff" an' it's "Wham" un - 'er -

stan'? _____ So, keep "Good Be - hav - ior," that's

your one life - sav - er with Pop - eye the

Sail - or Man. _____ I'm

Sail - or Man. _____

I've Got No Strings
from Walt Disney's PINOCCHIO

Registration 2
Rhythm: Fox Trot or Swing

Words by Ned Washington
Music by Leigh Harline

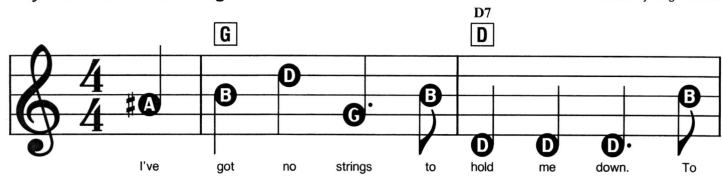

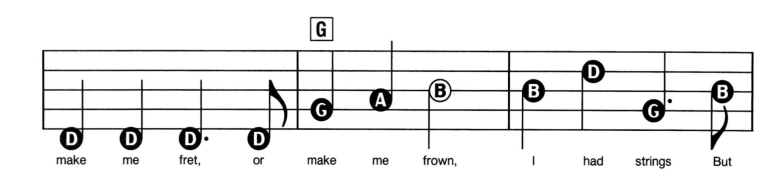

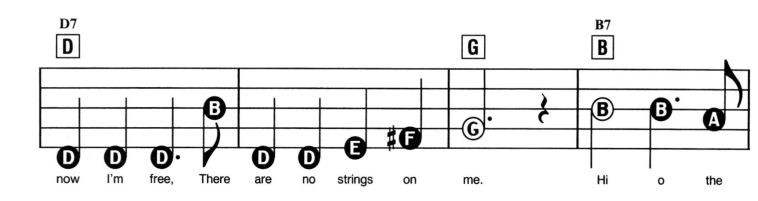

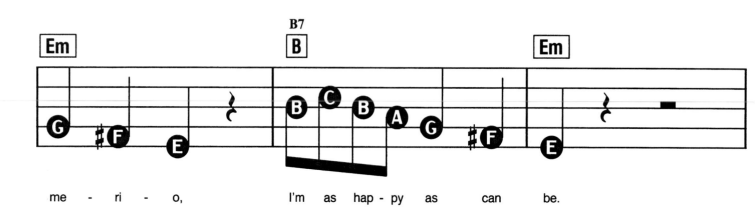

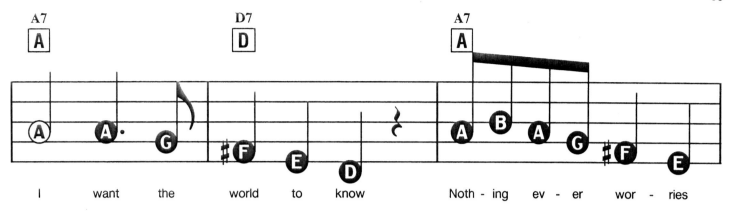

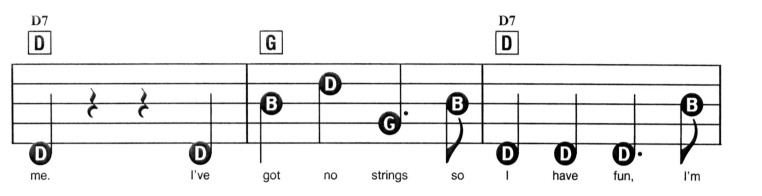

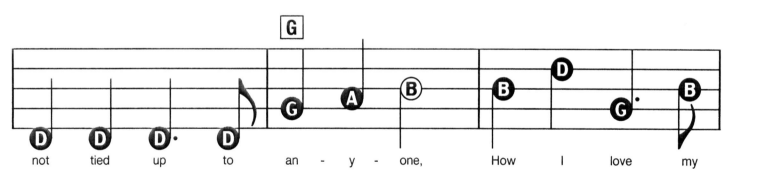

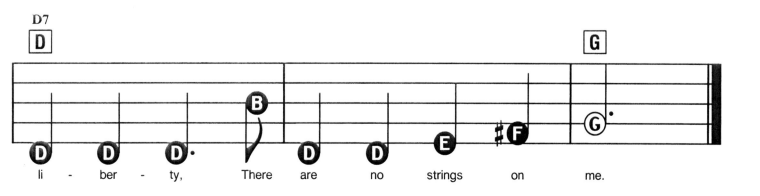

It's A Small World

Registration 2
Rhythm: March

Words and Music by Richard M. Sherman
and Robert B. Sherman

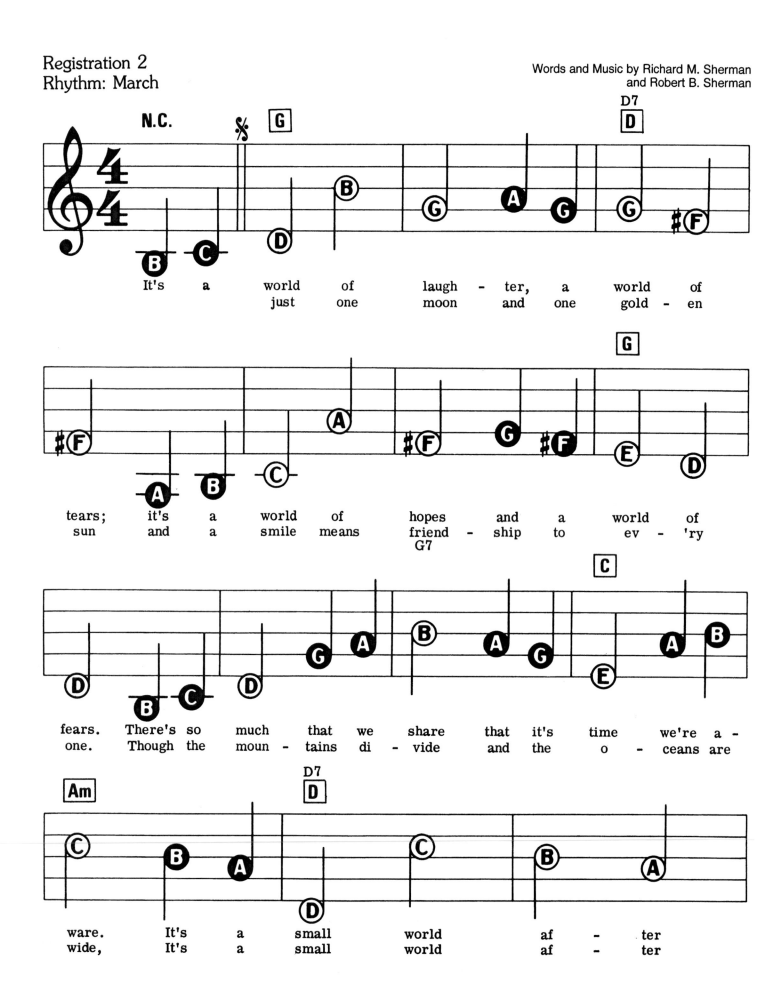

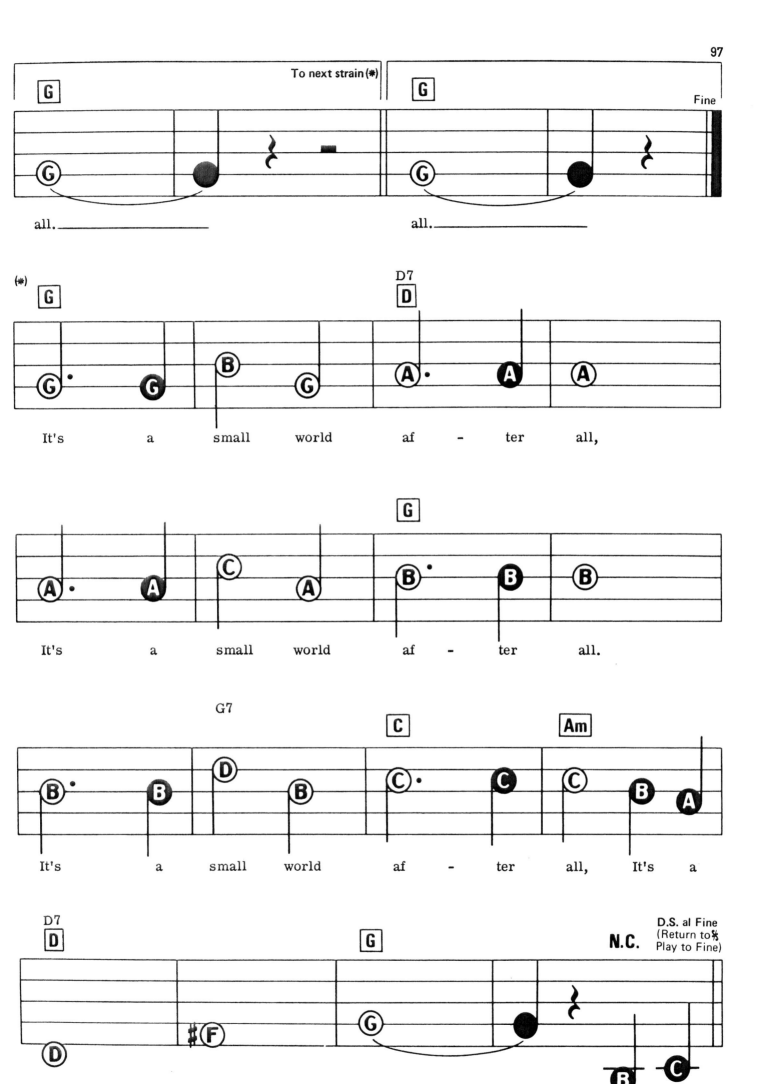

Jesus Loves Me

Registration 2
Rhythm: Swing

Traditional

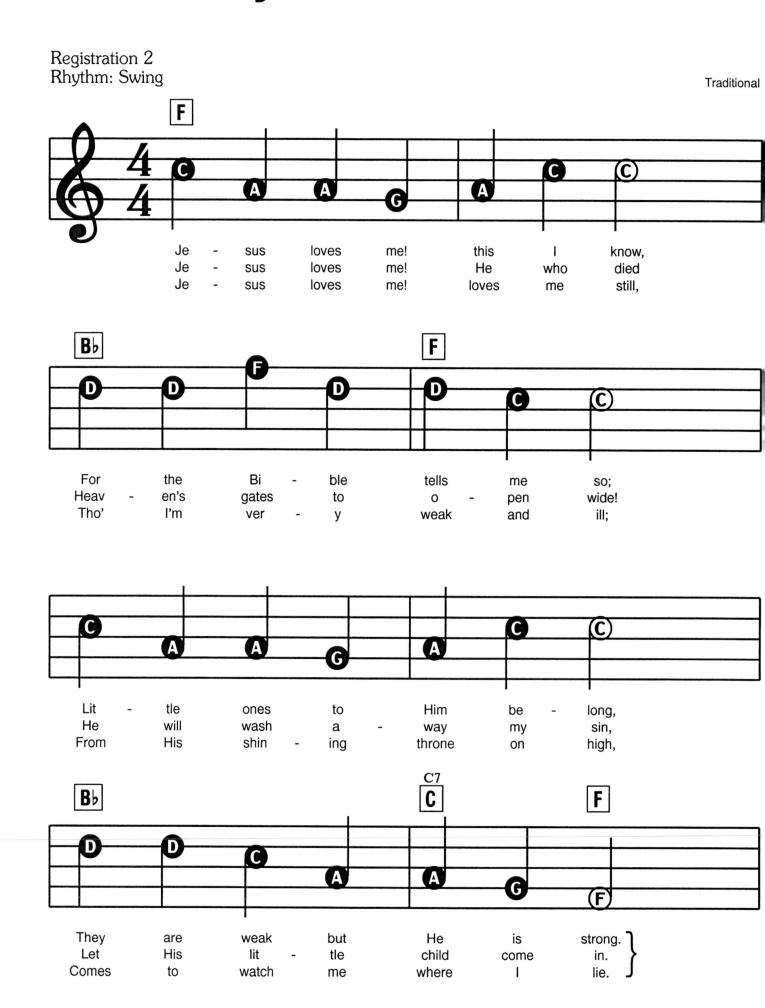

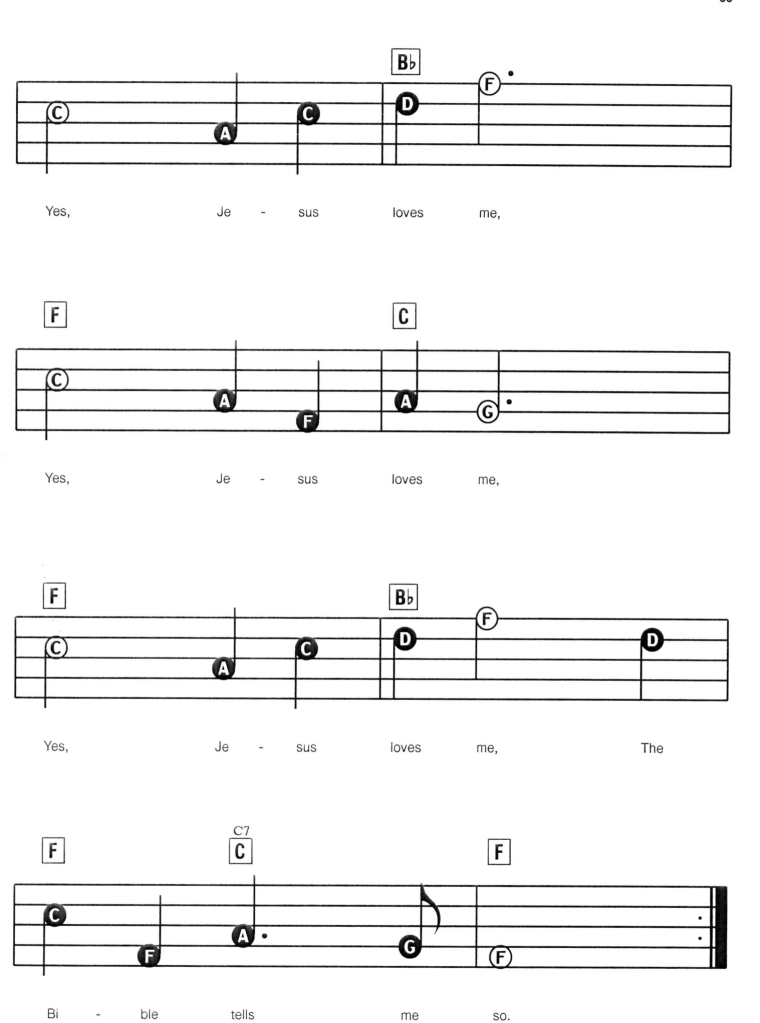

Yes, Je - sus loves me,

Yes, Je - sus loves me,

Yes, Je - sus loves me, The

Bi - ble tells me so.

Kum Ba Yah

Registration 3
Rhythm: 8 Beat or Rock

Traditional

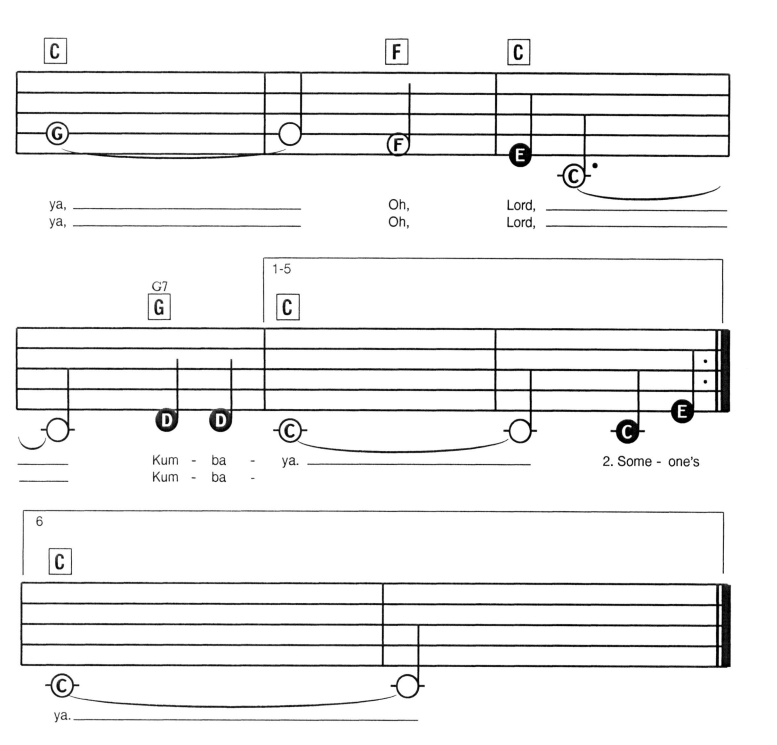

ya, _____ Oh, Lord, _____
ya, _____ Oh, Lord, _____

_____ Kum - ba - ya. _____ 2. Some - one's
_____ Kum - ba -

ya. _____

Additional Lyrics

3. Someone's singin', Lord, Kum-bah-ya...
4. Someone's cryin', Lord, Kum-bah-ya...
5. Someone's dancin', Lord, Kum-bah-ya...
6 Someone's shoutin', Lord, Kum-bah-ya...

Let's Go Fly A Kite
from Walt Disney's MARY POPPINS

Registration 4
Rhythm: Waltz

Words and Music by Richard M. Sherman
and Robert B. Sherman

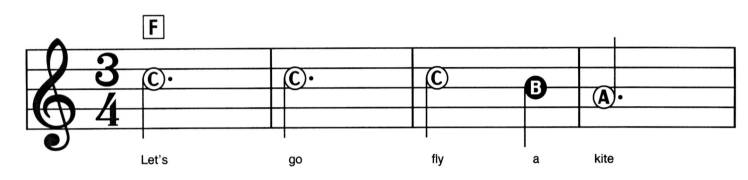

Let's go fly a kite

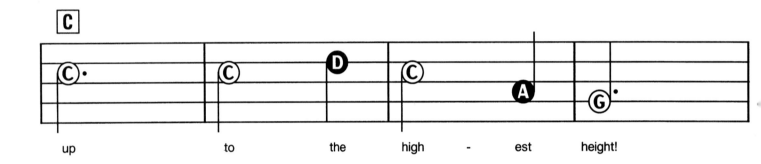

up to the high - est height!

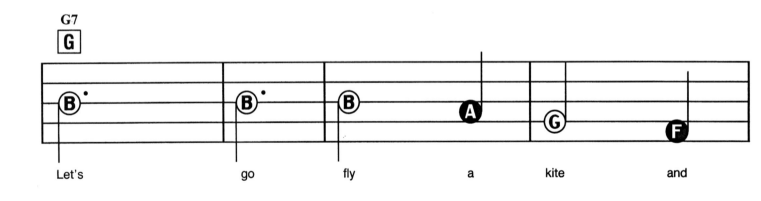

Let's go fly a kite and

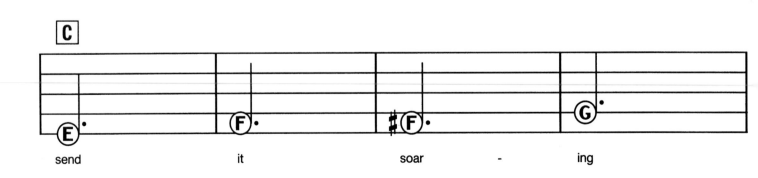

send it soar - ing

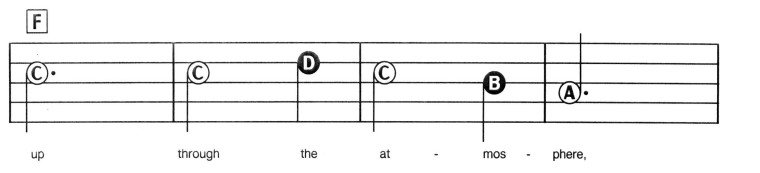

up   through   the   at - mos - phere,

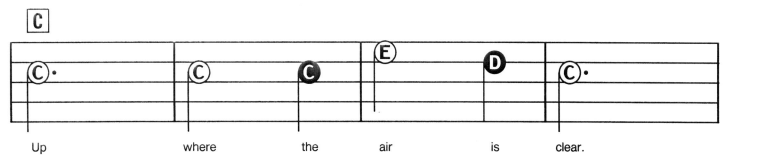

Up   where   the   air   is   clear.

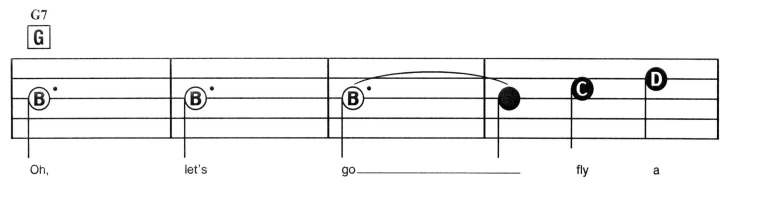

Oh,   let's   go⎯⎯⎯ fly   a

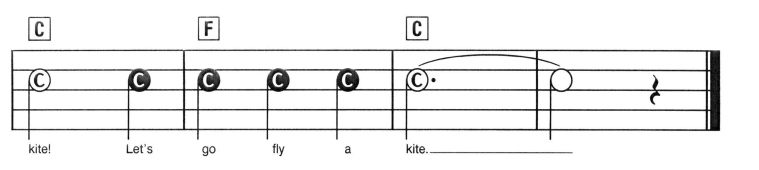

kite!   Let's   go   fly   a   kite.⎯⎯⎯

Lazy Mary, Will You Get Up?

Registration 6
Rhythm: Waltz

Traditional

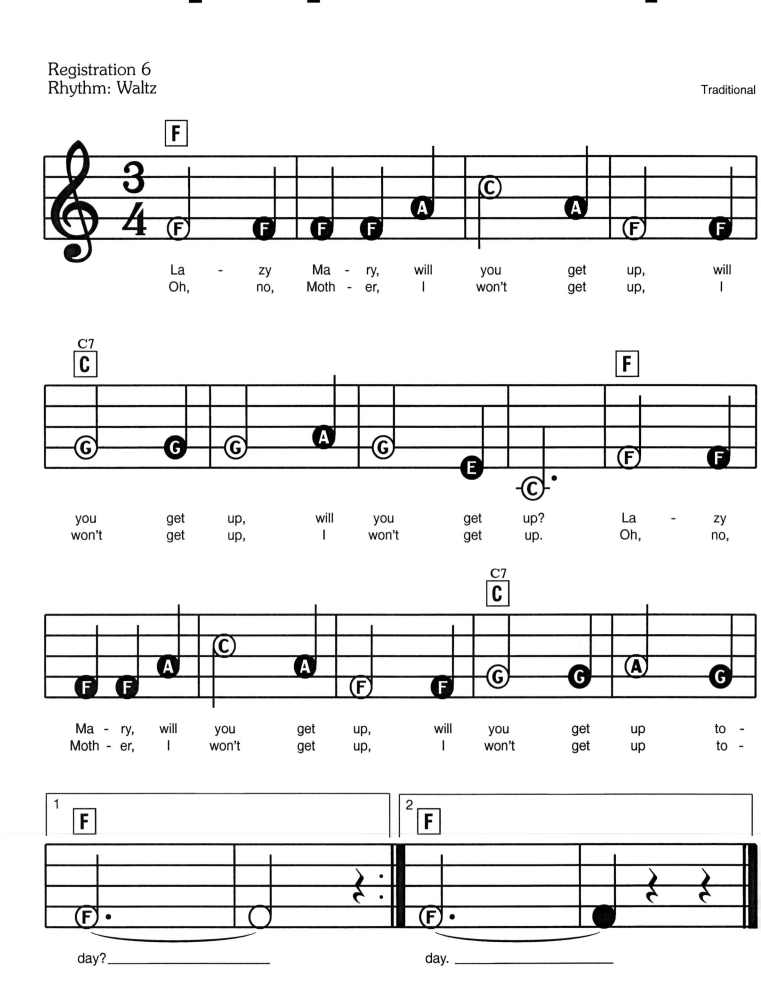

Magic Penny

Registration 8
Rhythm: Pops, Rock or Calypso

Words and Music by
Malvina Reynolds

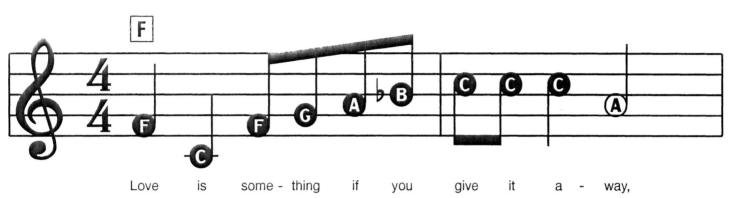

Love is some - thing if you give it a - way,

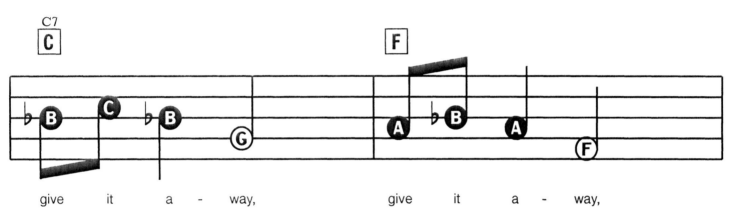

give it a - way, give it a - way,

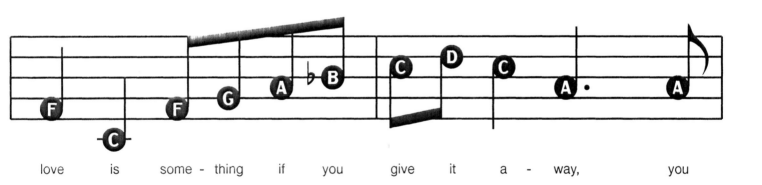

love is some - thing if you give it a - way, you

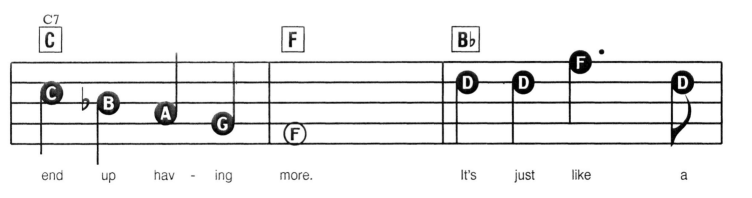

end up hav - ing more. It's just like a

MCA music publishing

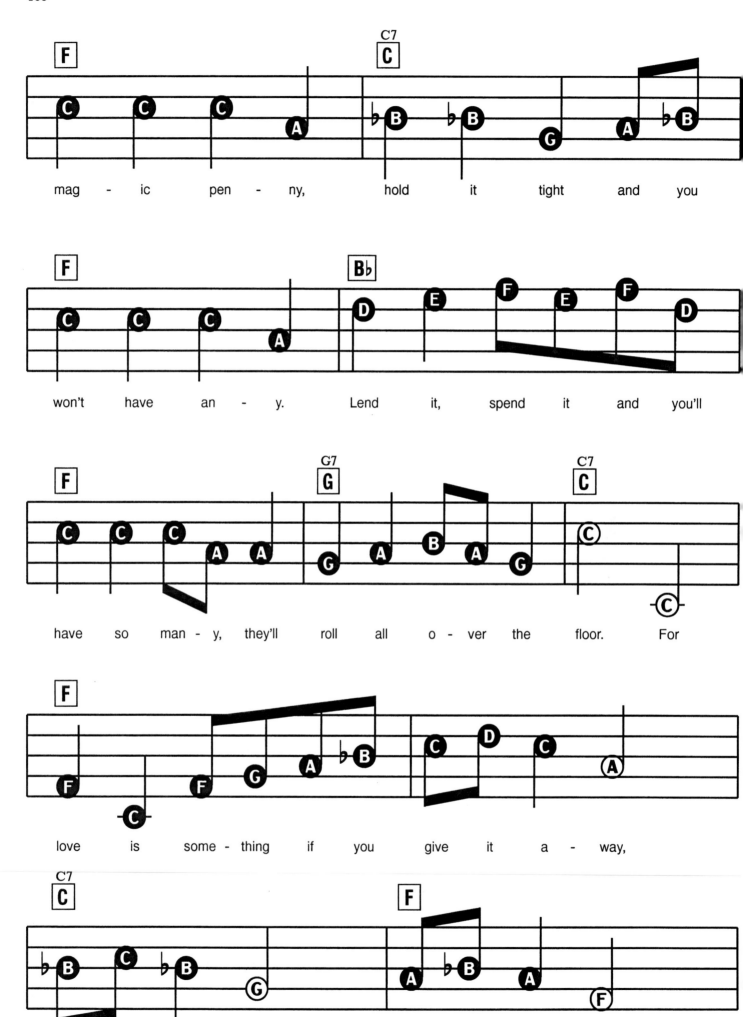

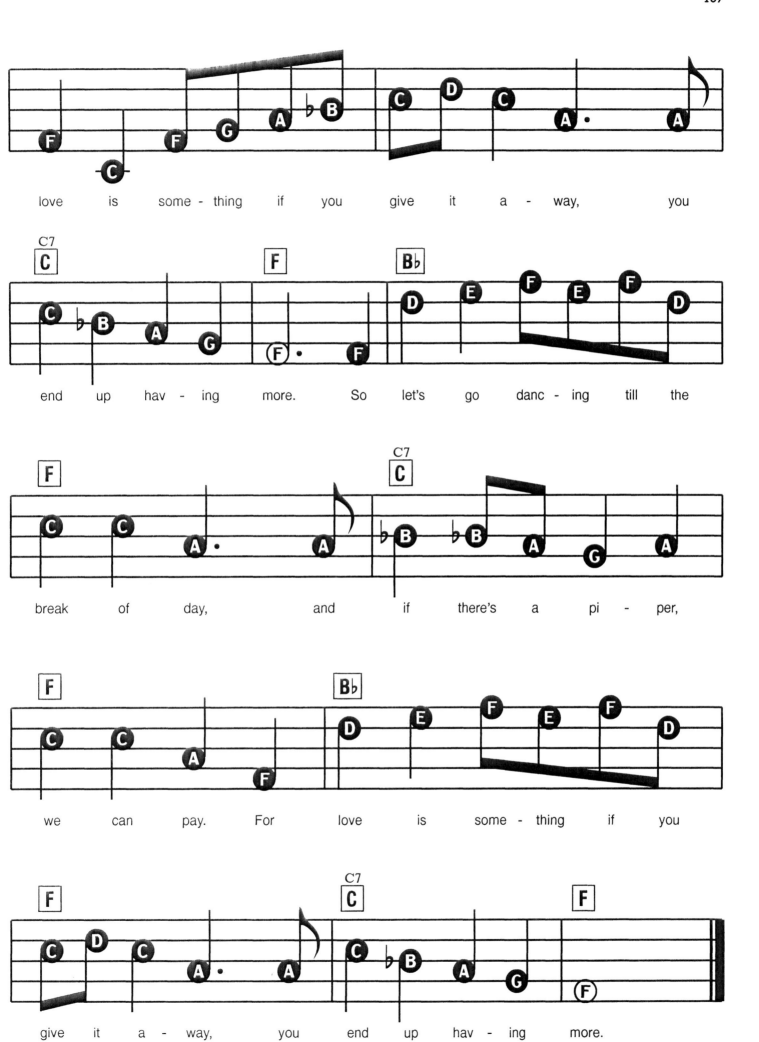

Mah-na Mah-na

Registration 9
Rhythm: Rock

By Piero Umiliani

109

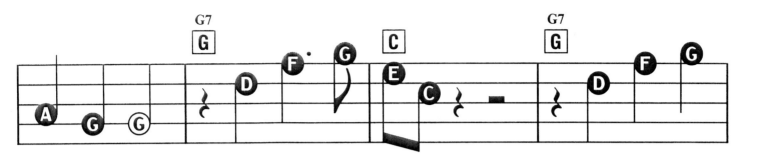

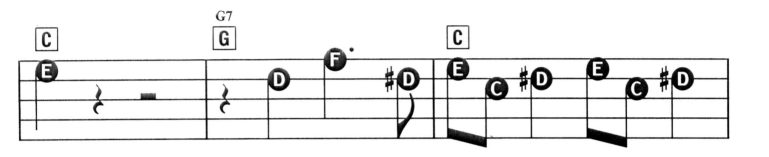

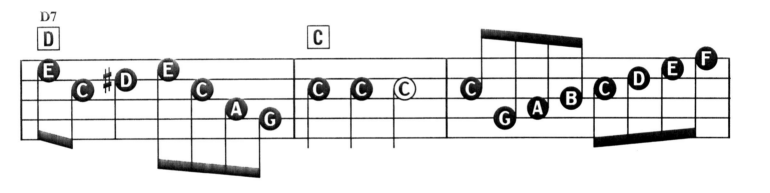

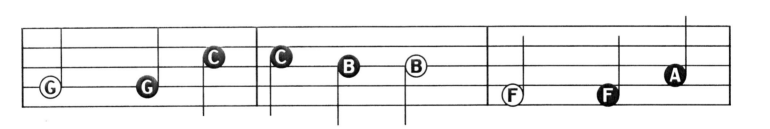

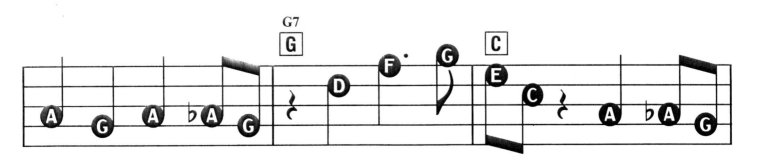

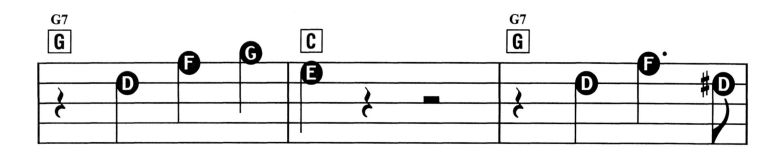

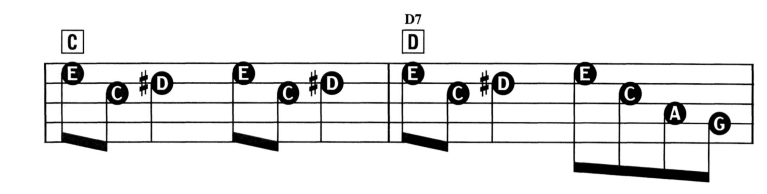

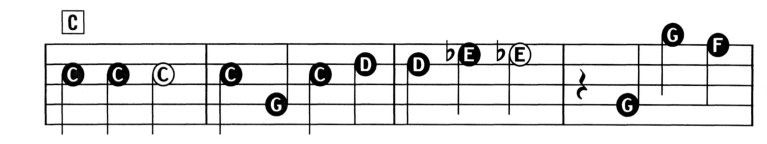

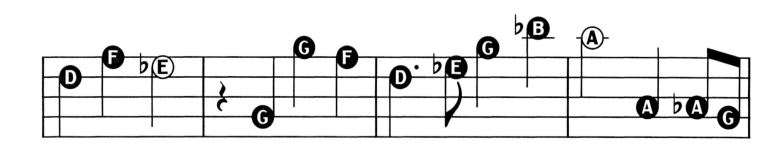

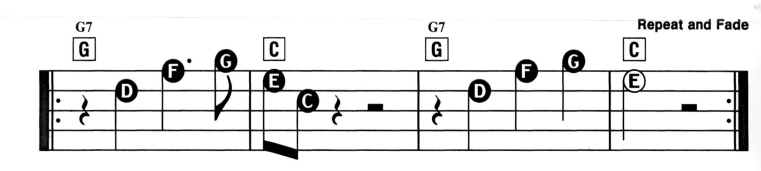

The Marvelous Toy

Registration 5
Rhythm: Pops, Fox Trot or March

Words and Music by
Tom Paxton

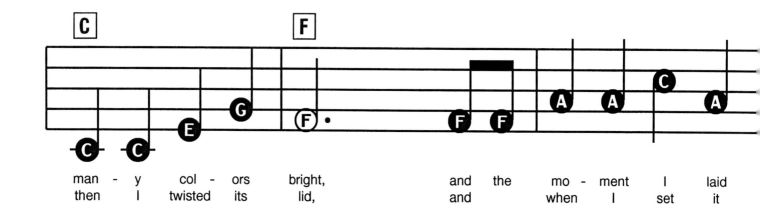

man - y col - ors bright, and the mo - ment I laid
then I twisted its lid, and when I set it

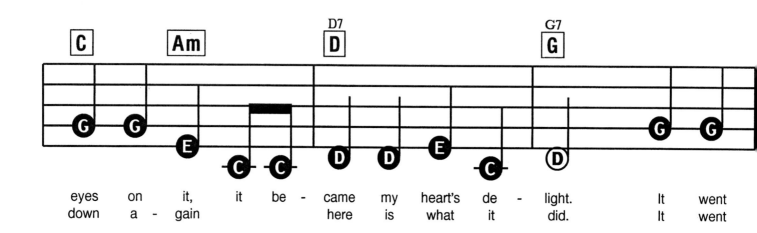

eyes on it, it be - came my heart's de - light. It went
down a - gain here is what it did. It went

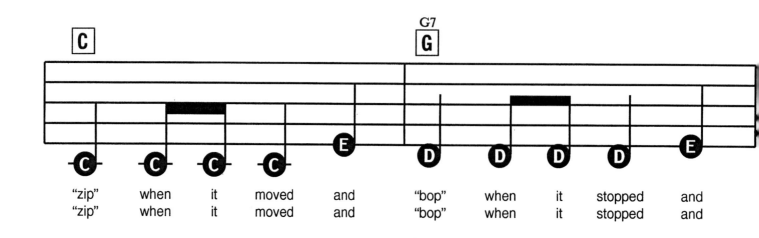

"zip" when it moved and "bop" when it stopped and
"zip" when it moved and "bop" when it stopped and

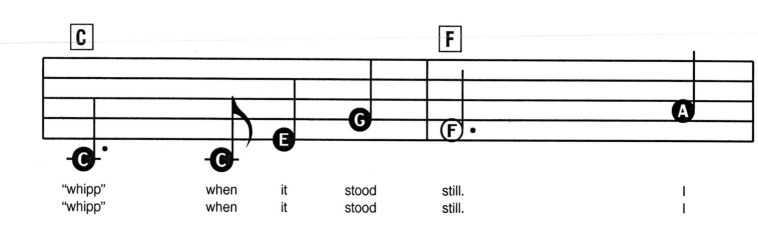

"whipp" when it stood still. I
"whipp" when it stood still. I

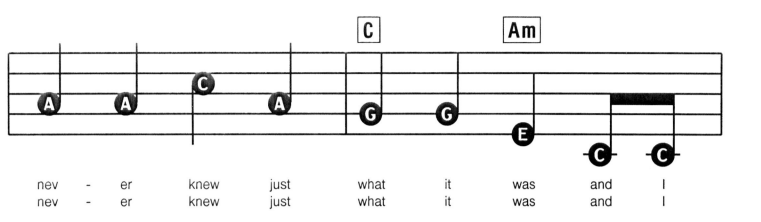

nev - er knew just what it was and I
nev - er knew just what it was and I

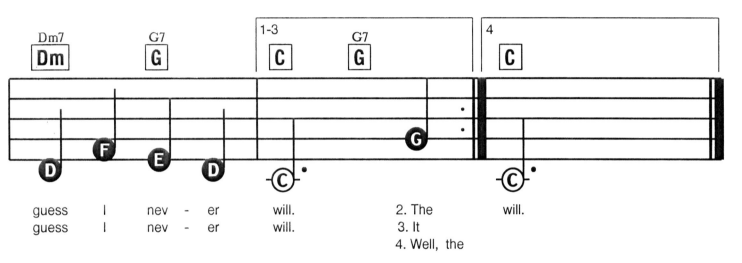

guess I nev - er will. 2. The will.
guess I nev - er will. 3. It
                        4. Well, the

Additional Lyrics

3. It first marched left and then marched right,
   And then marched under a chair,
   And when I looked where it had gone,
   It wasn't even there!
   I started to sob and my daddy laughed,
   For he knew that I would find,
   When I turned around my marvelous toy,
   Chuggin' from behind.
   It went "zip" when it moved and "bop" when it stopped
   And "whirr" when it stood still.
   I never knew just what it was,
   And I guess I never will.

4. Well, the years have gone by too quickly it seems,
   And I have my own little boy,
   And yesterday I gave to him
   My marv'lous little toy.
   His eyes nearly popped right out of his head,
   And he gave a squeal of glee.
   Neither one of us knows just what it is,
   But he loves it just like me.
   It still goes "zip" when it moves and "bop" when it stops
   And "whirr" when it stands still.
   I never knew just what it was,
   And I guess I never will.

Mary Had A Little Lamb

Registration 4
Rhythm: Fox Trot or Swing

Words by Sarah Josepha Hale
Music is Traditional

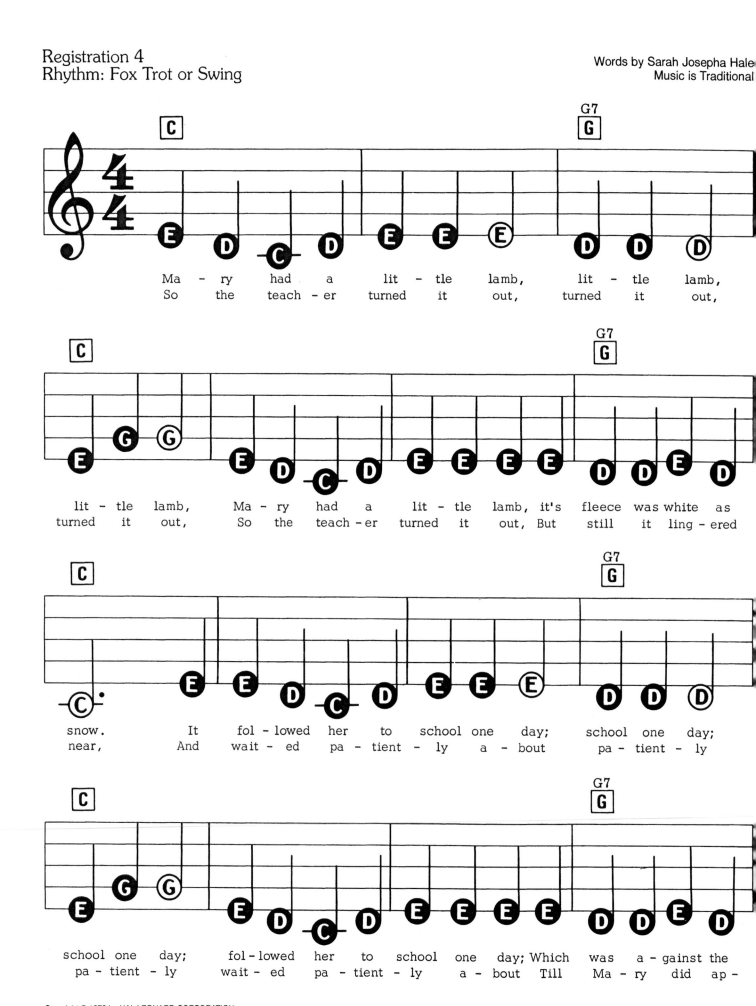

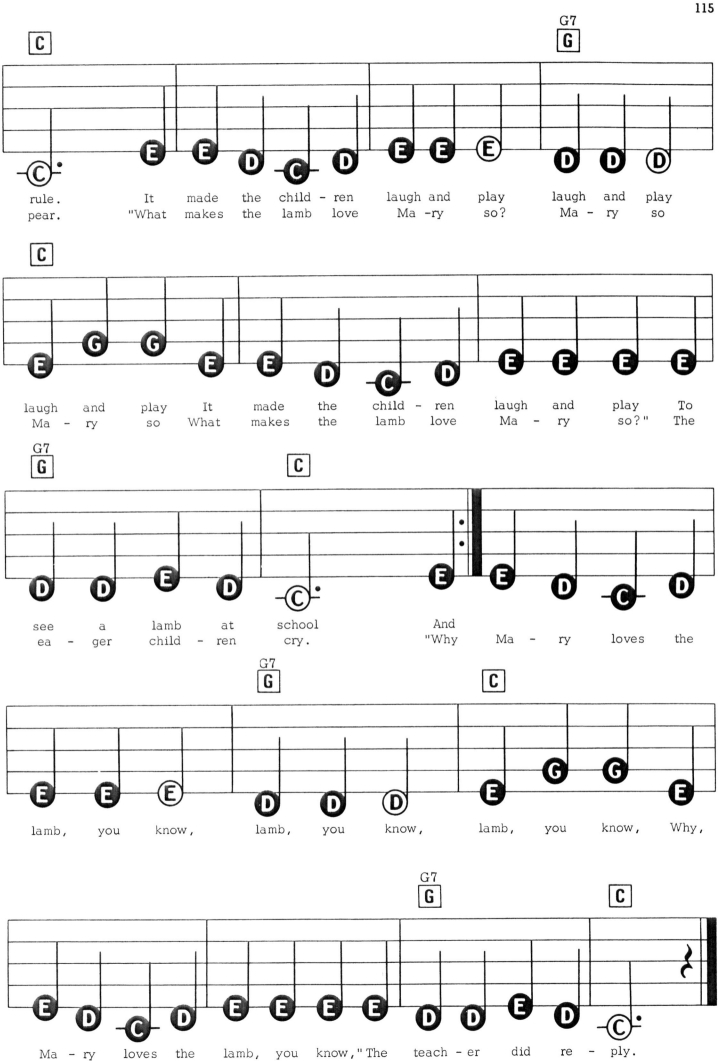

Mickey Mouse March
from Walt Disney's THE MICKEY MOUSE CLUB

Words and Music by
Jimmie Dodd

Registration 5
Rhythm: 6/8 March

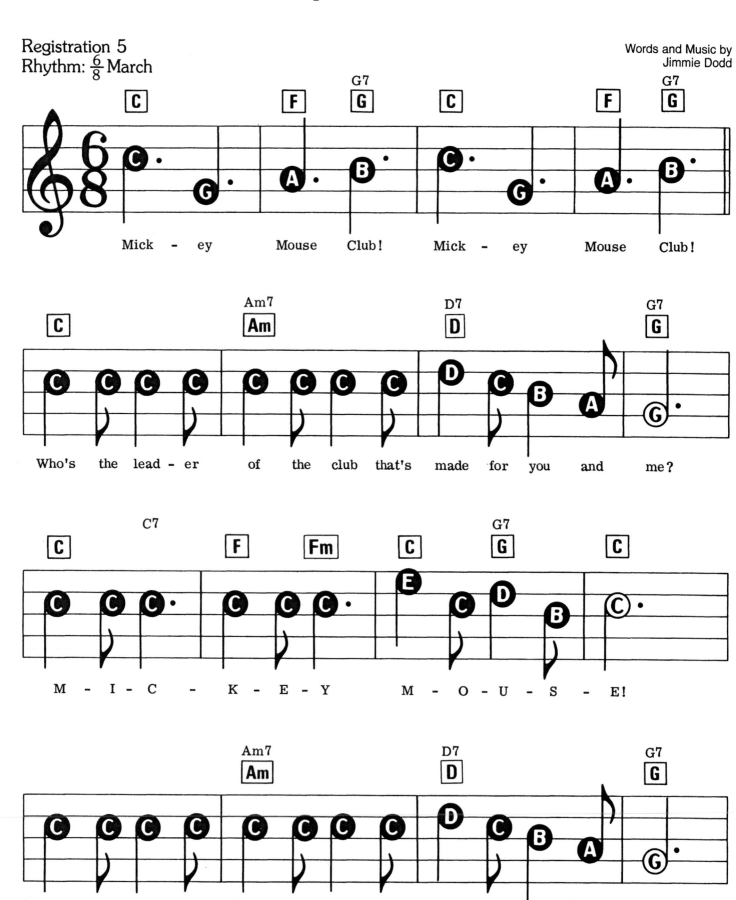

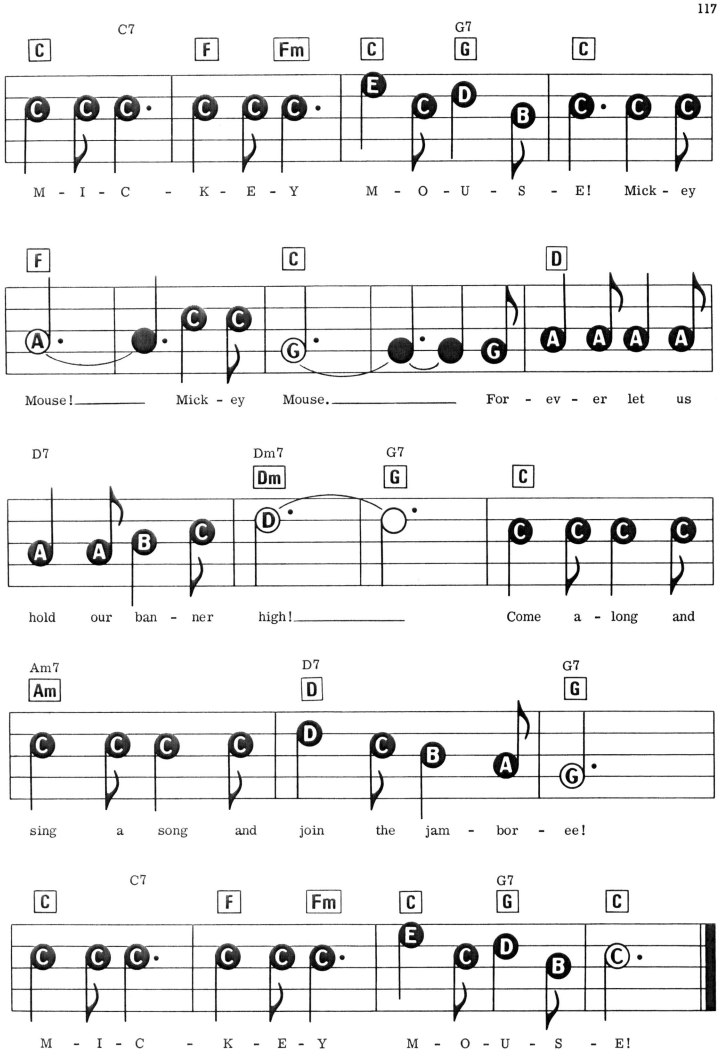

The Muffin Man

Registration 4
Rhythm: March or Polka

Traditional

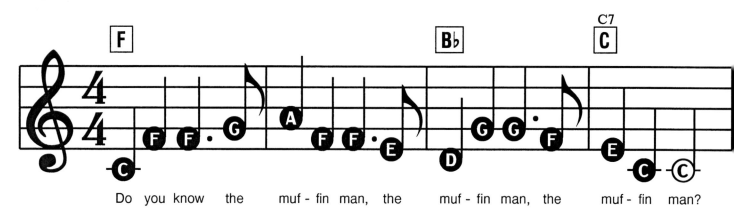

Do you know the muf - fin man, the muf - fin man, the muf - fin man?

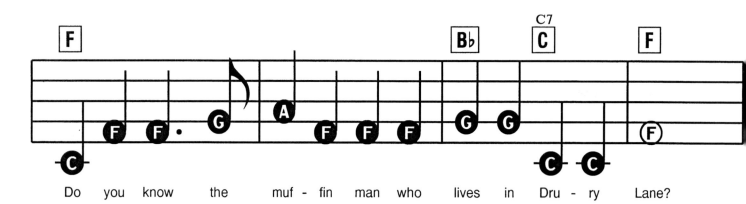

Do you know the muf - fin man who lives in Dru - ry Lane?

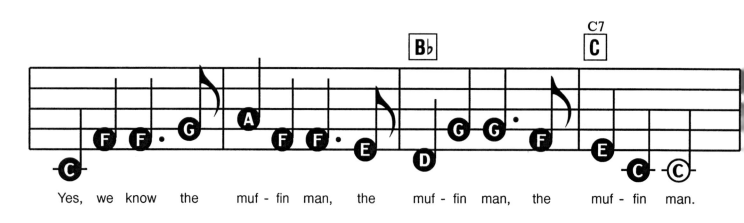

Yes, we know the muf - fin man, the muf - fin man, the muf - fin man.

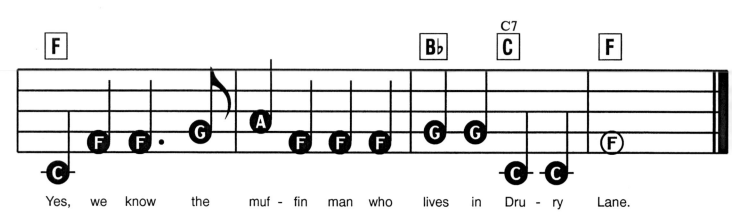

Yes, we know the muf - fin man who lives in Dru - ry Lane.

The Muppet Show Theme

Registration 9
Rhythm: Swing

By Jim Henson
and Sam Pottle

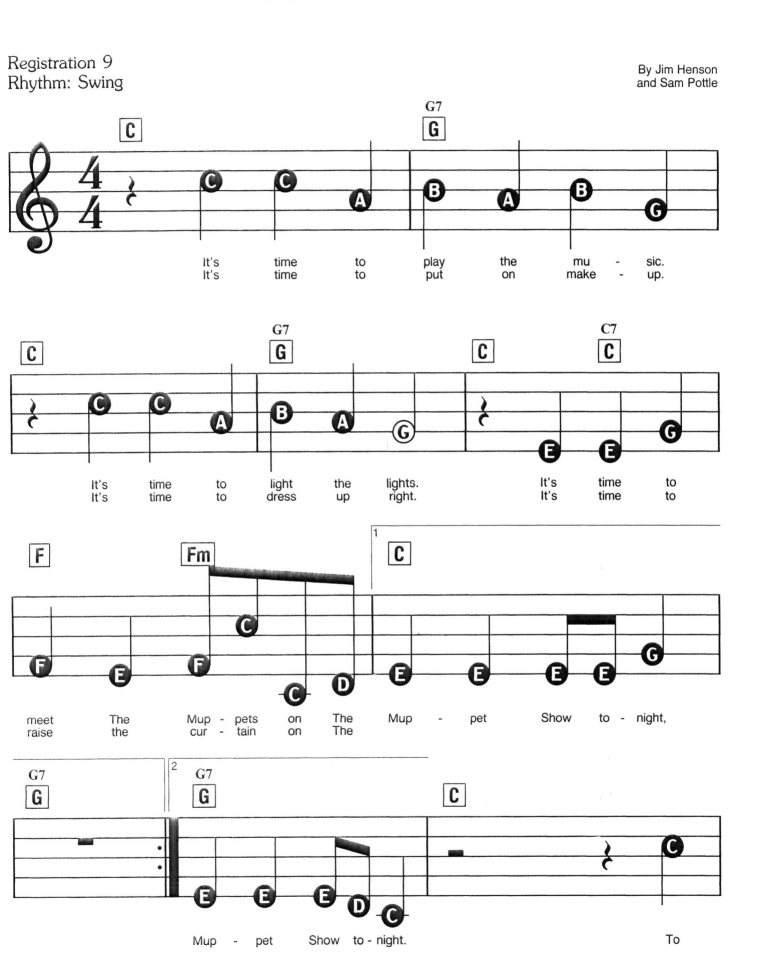

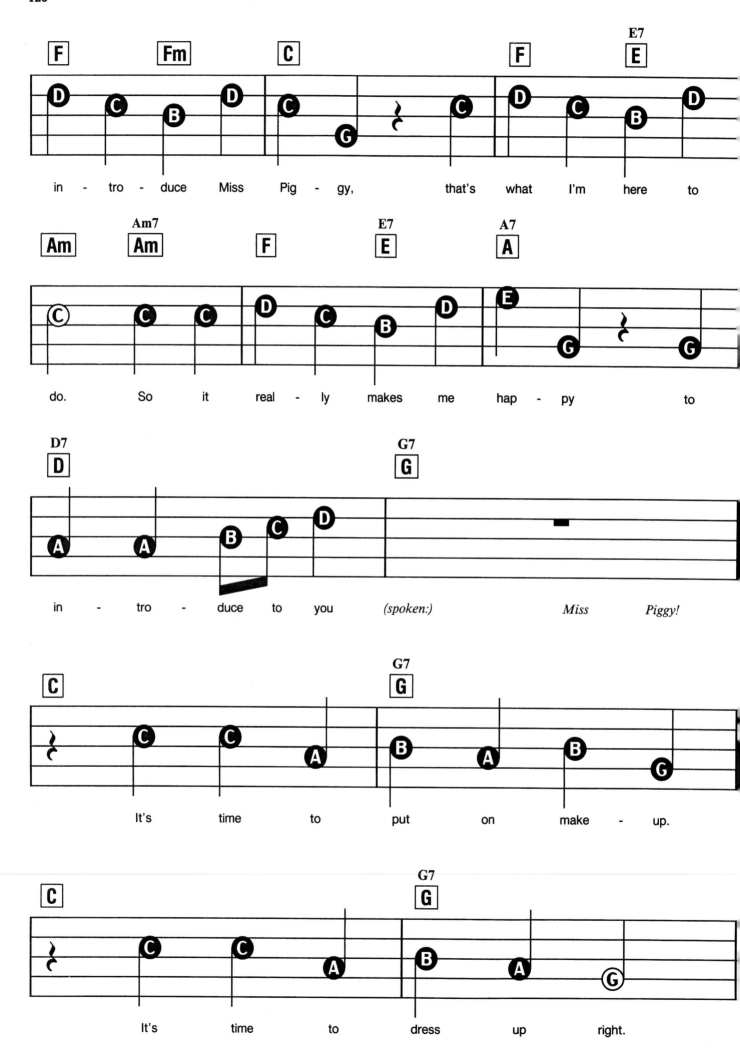

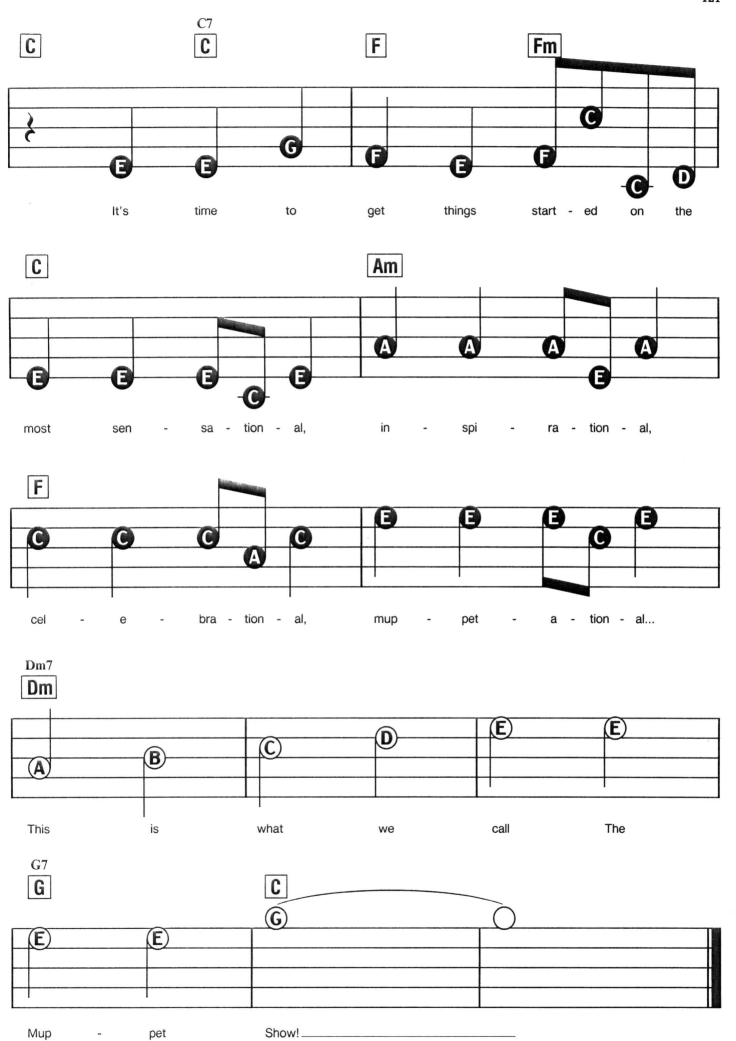

My Favorite Things
from THE SOUND OF MUSIC

Registration 9
Rhythm: Waltz

Lyrics by Oscar Hammerstein II
Music by Richard Rodgers

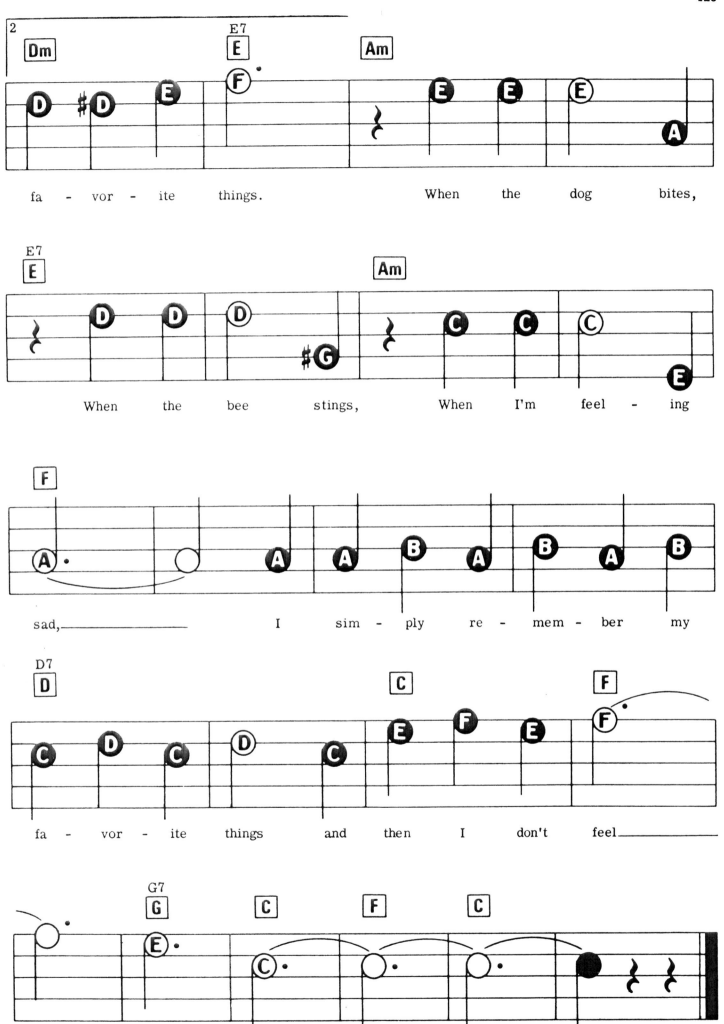

On The Good Ship Lollipop

from BRIGHT EYES

Registration 3
Rhythm: Fox Trot or Swing

Words and Music by Sidney Clare
and Richard A. Whiting

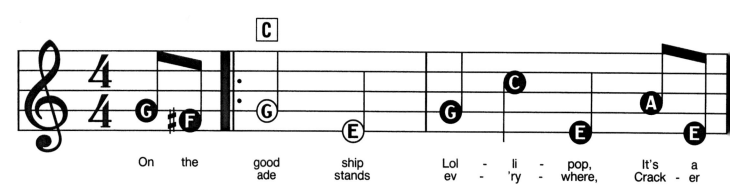

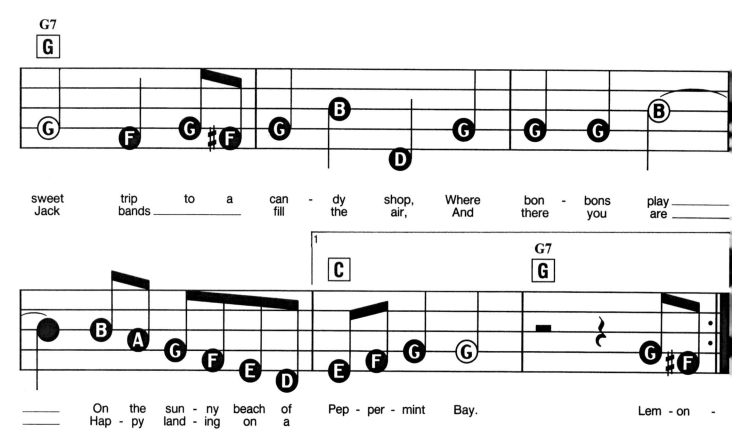

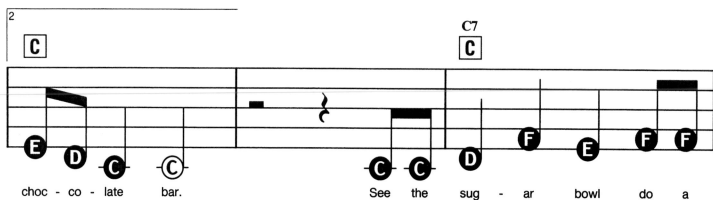

125

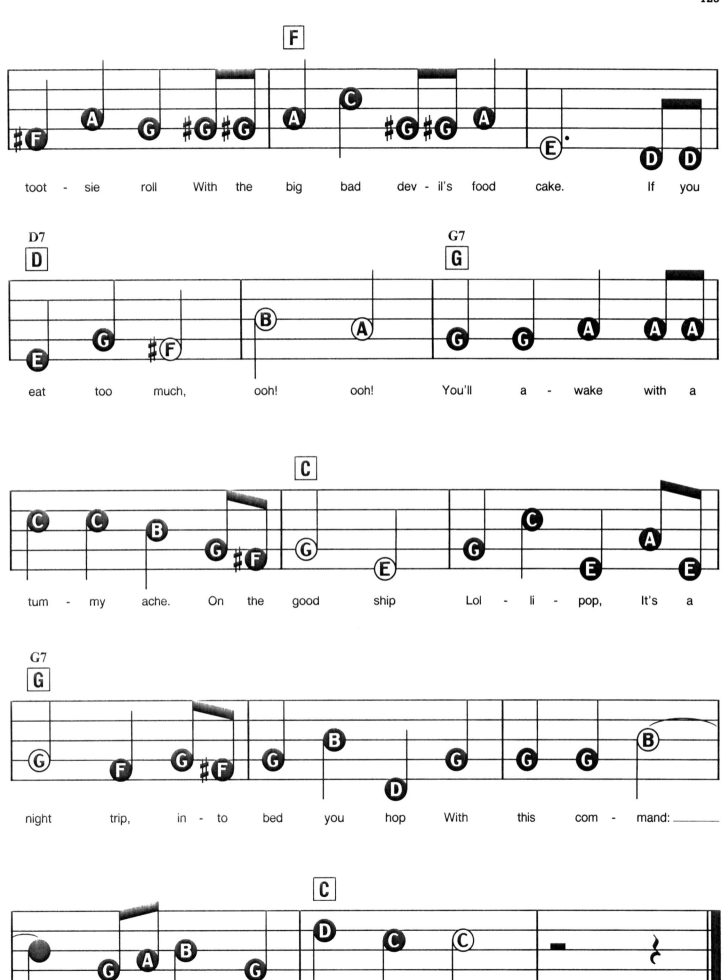

The Paw Paw Patch

Registration 1
Rhythm: Polka, March or Rock

Traditional

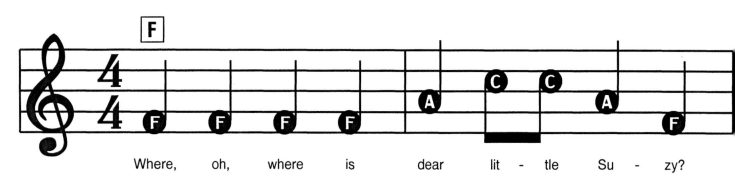

Where, oh, where is dear lit - tle Su - zy?

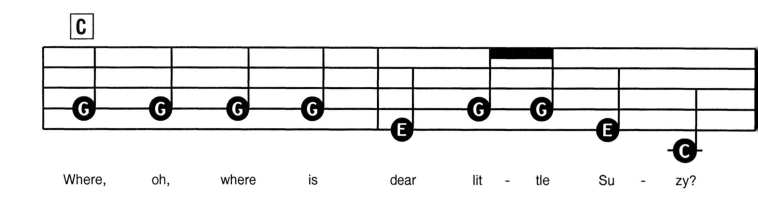

Where, oh, where is dear lit - tle Su - zy?

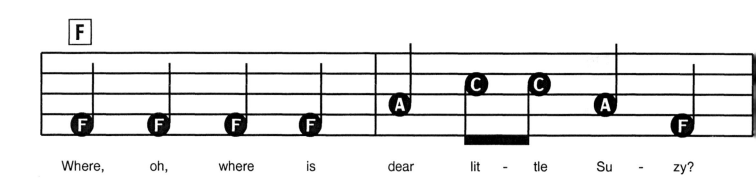

Where, oh, where is dear lit - tle Su - zy?

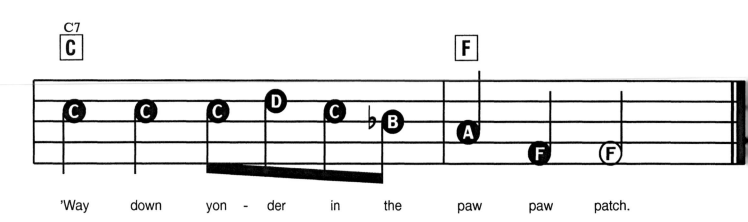

'Way down yon - der in the paw paw patch.

People In Your Neighborhood

from the Television Series SESAME STREET

Registration 8
Rhythm: Swing

Words and Music by
Jeff Moss

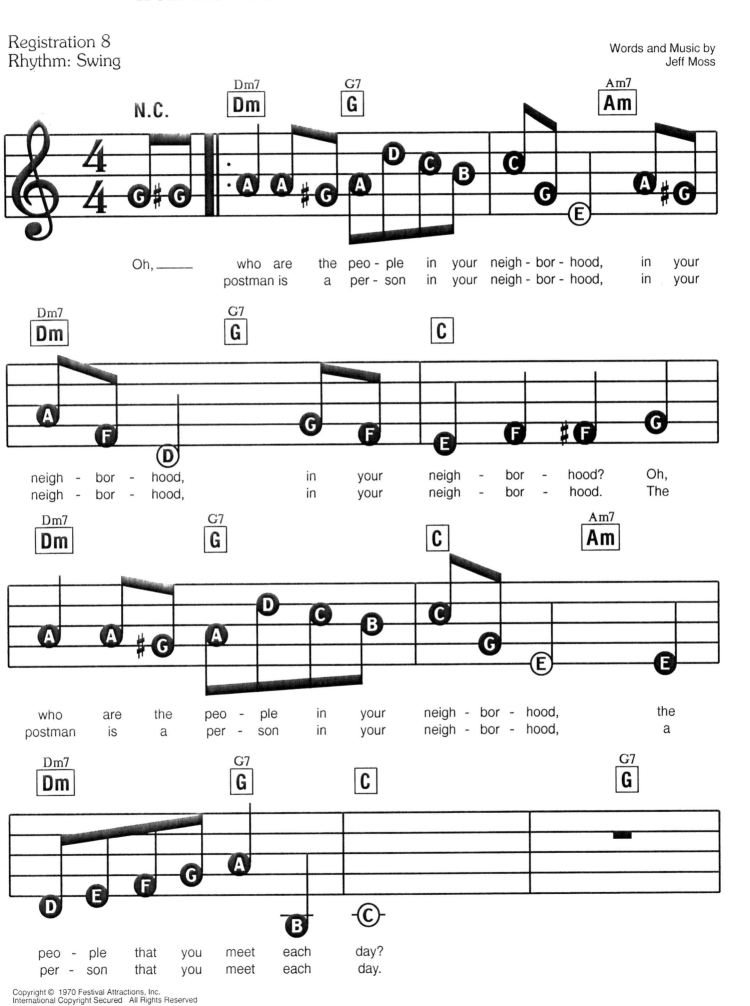

Oh, _____ who are the peo - ple in your neigh - bor - hood, in your
postman is a per - son in your neigh - bor - hood, in your

neigh - bor - hood, in your neigh - bor - hood? Oh,
neigh - bor - hood, in your neigh - bor - hood. The

who are the peo - ple in your neigh - bor - hood, the
postman is a per - son in your neigh - bor - hood, a

peo - ple that you meet each day?
per - son that you meet each day.

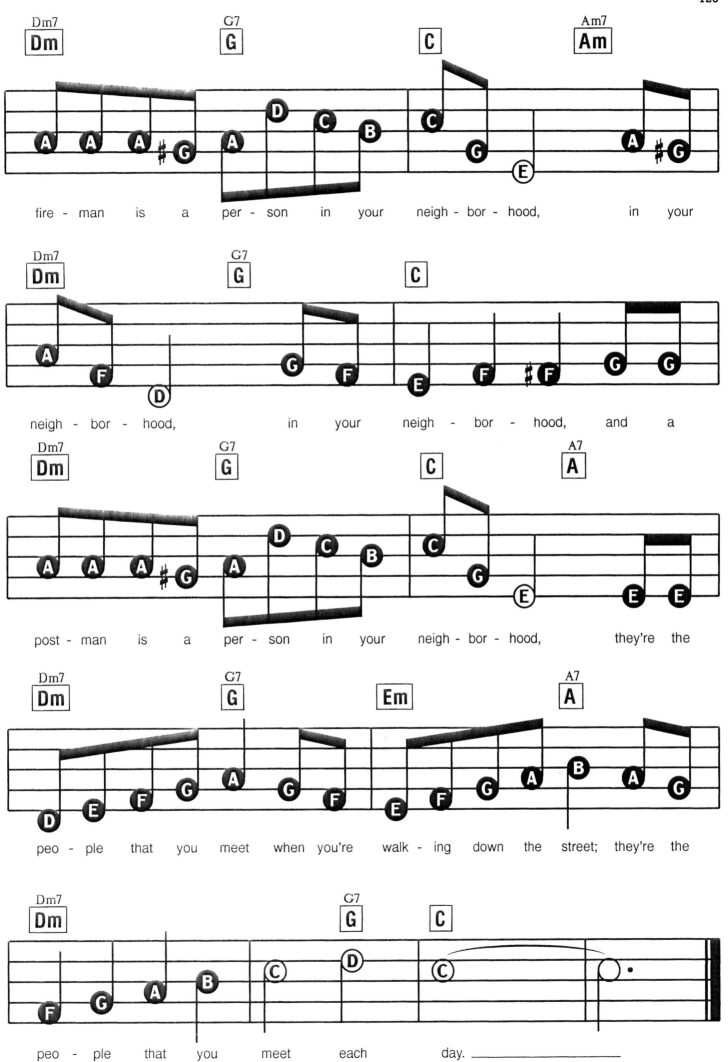

Peter Cottontail

Registration 1
Rhythm: Fox Trot

Words and Music by Steve Nelson
and Jack Rollins

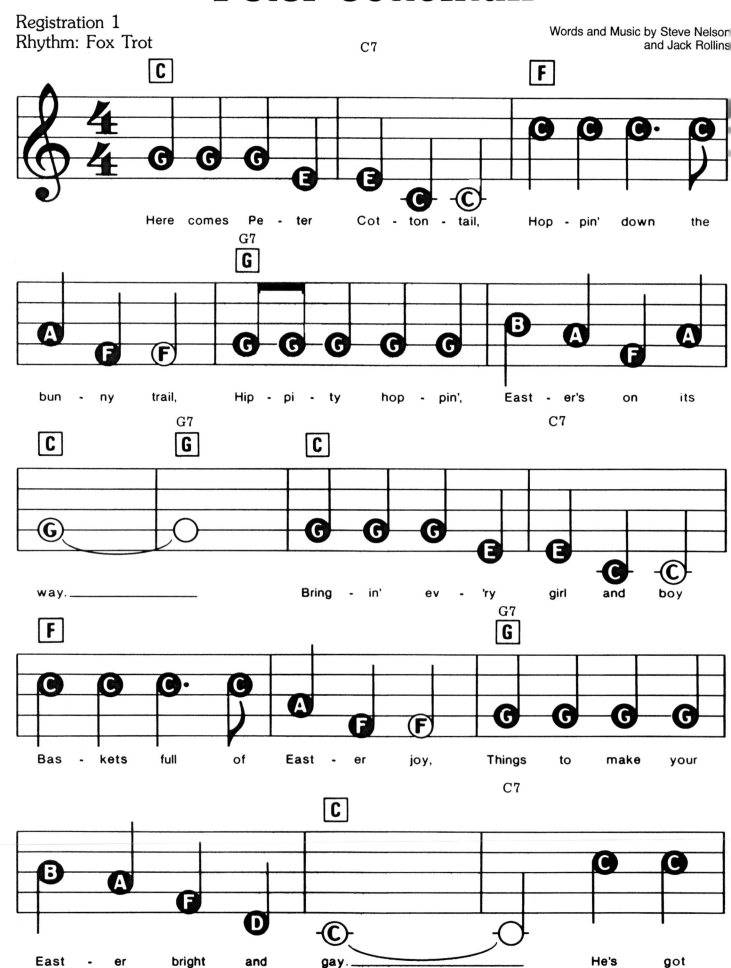

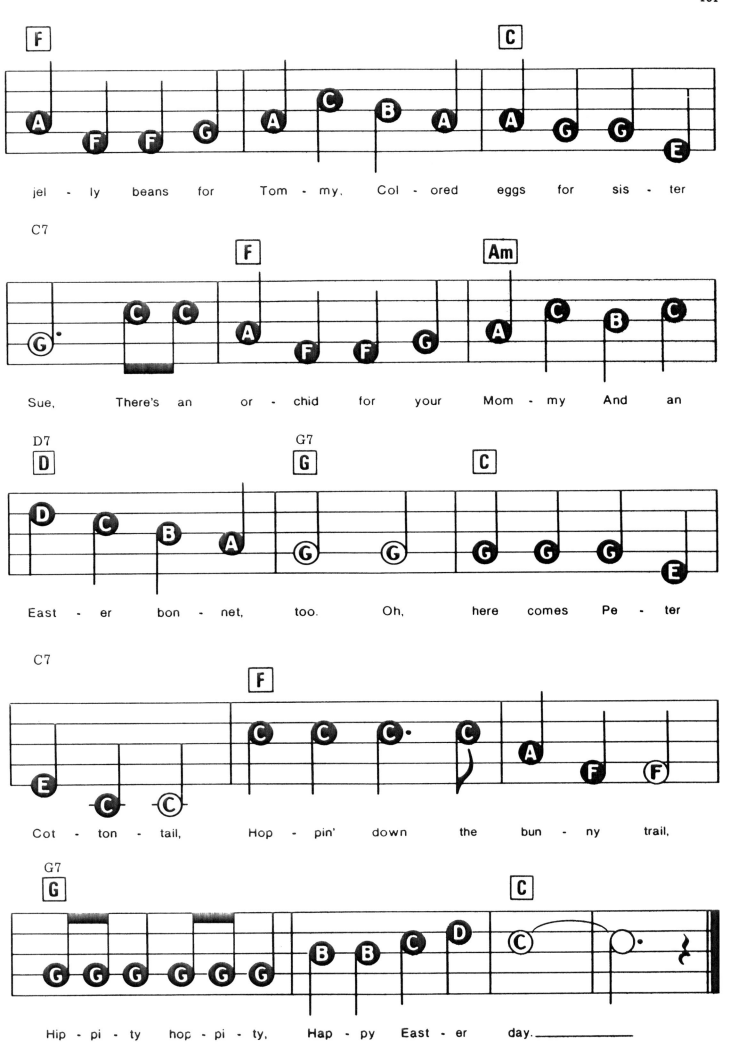

Puff The Magic Dragon

Registration 2
Rhythm: Swing

Words by Leonard Lipton
Music by Peter Yarrow

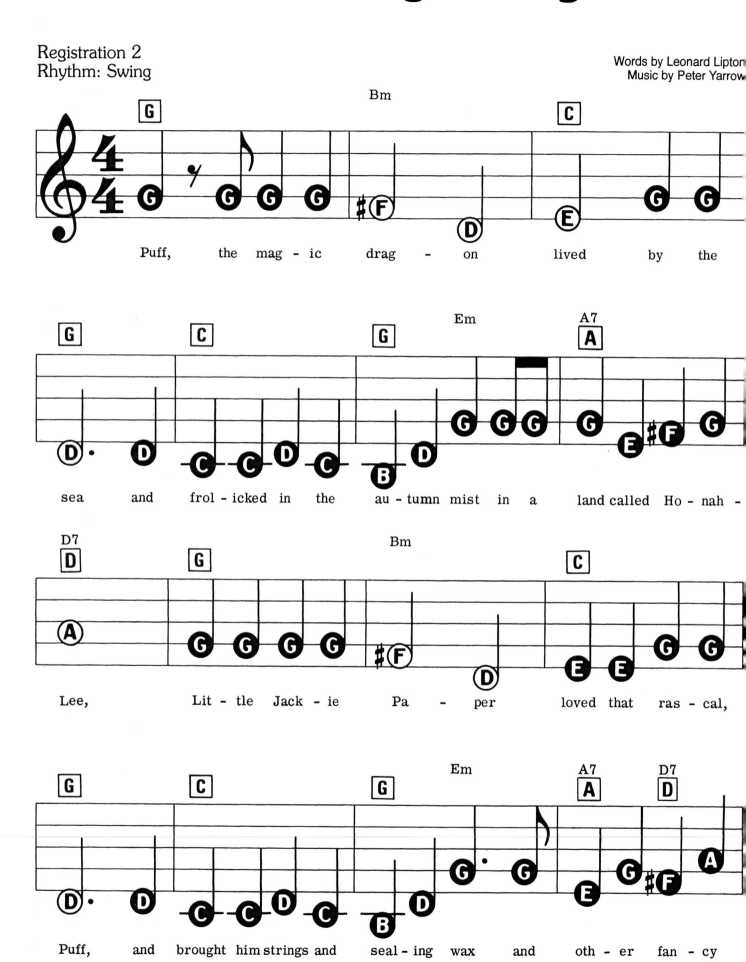

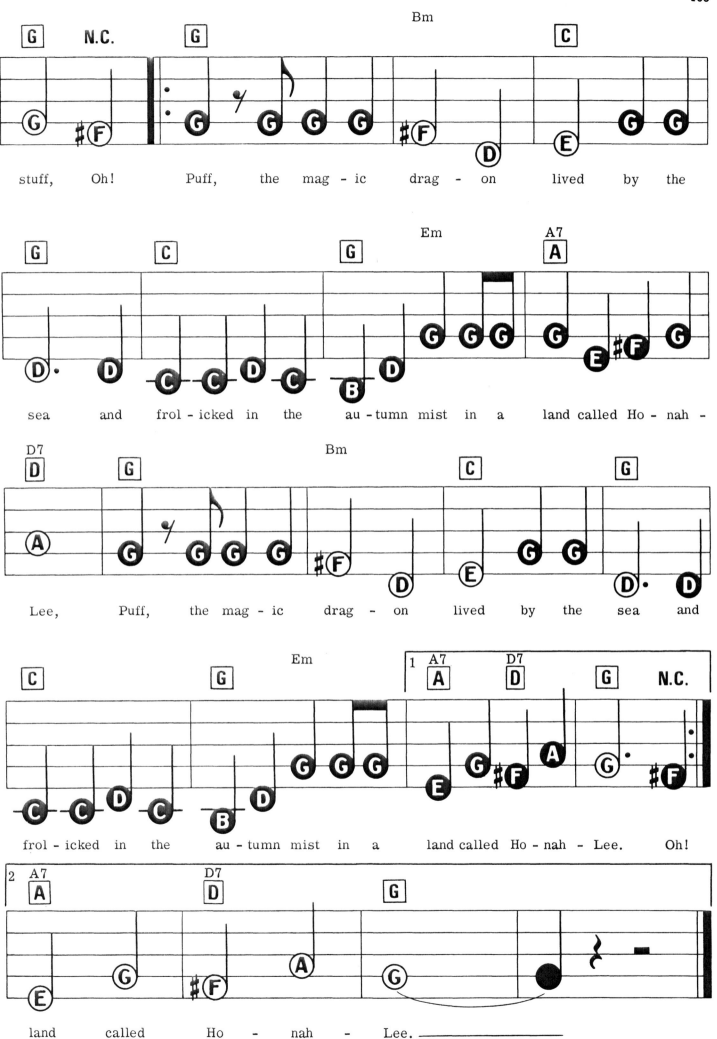

Polly Put The Kettle On

Registration 4
Rhythm: Fox Trot or Swing

Traditional

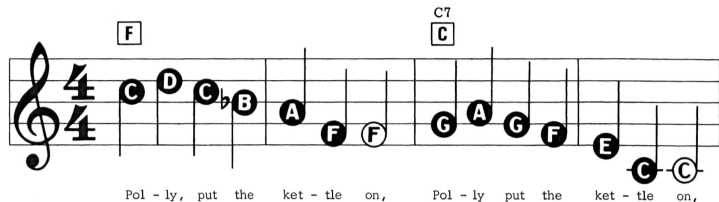

Pol - ly, put the ket - tle on, Pol - ly put the ket - tle on,

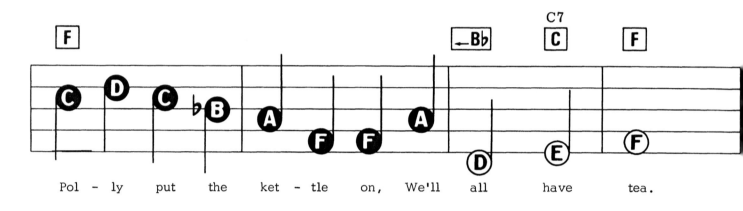

Pol - ly put the ket - tle on, We'll all have tea.

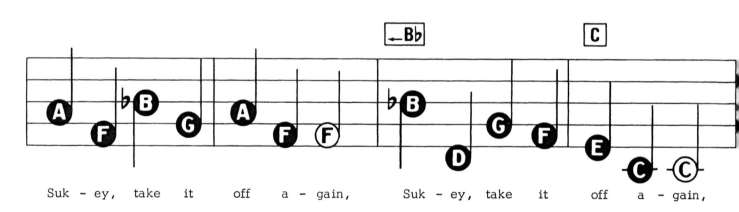

Suk - ey, take it off a - gain, Suk - ey, take it off a - gain,

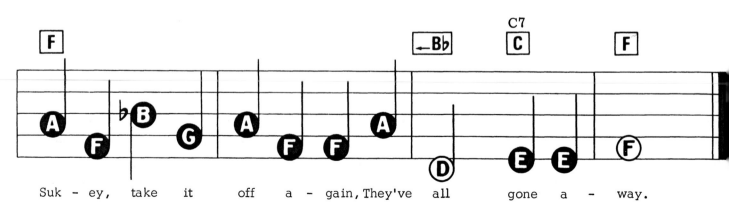

Suk - ey, take it off a - gain, They've all gone a - way.

Rubber Duckie
from the Television Series SESAME STREET

Registration 2
Rhythm: Swing

Words and Music by
Jeff Moss

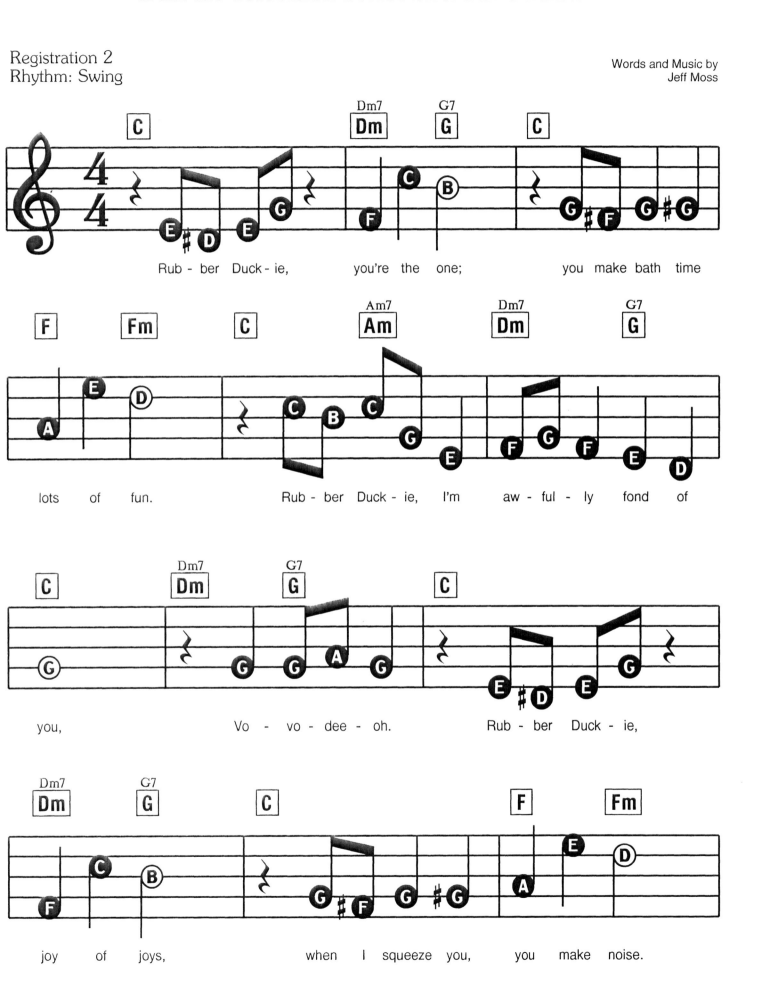

136

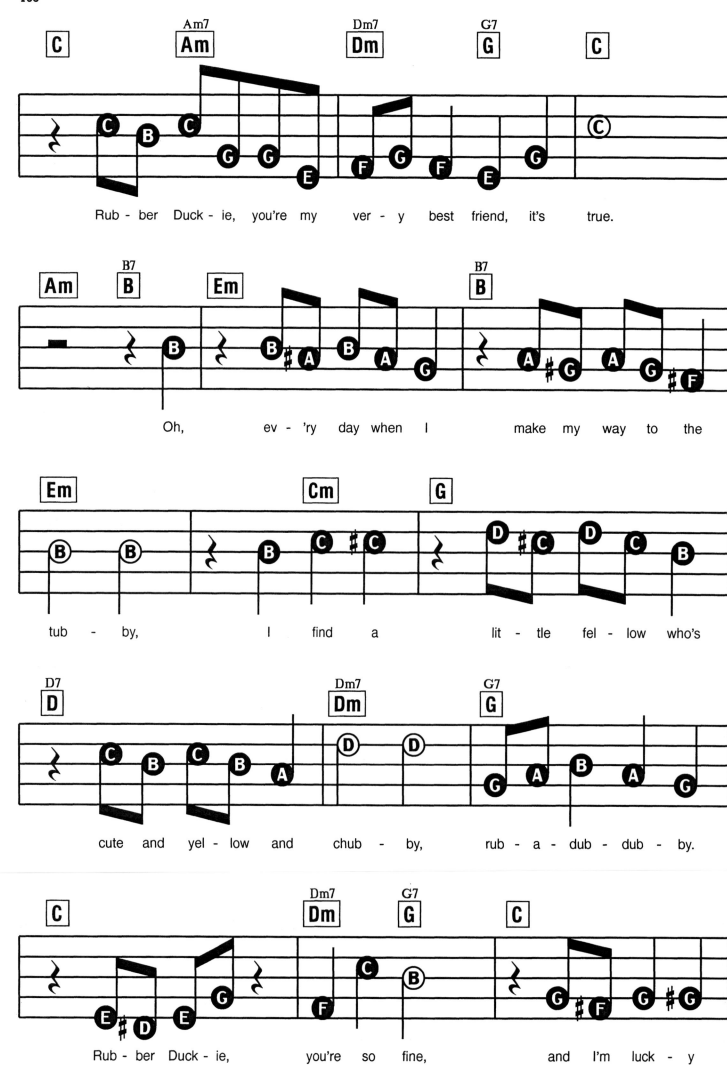

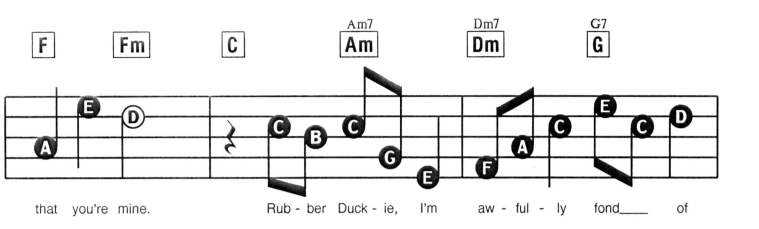

that you're mine.　Rub - ber Duck - ie, I'm　aw - ful - ly　fond＿＿ of

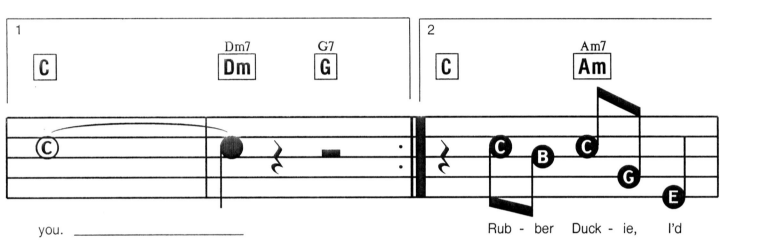

1 you. ＿＿＿＿＿＿＿＿

2 Rub - ber Duck - ie,　I'd

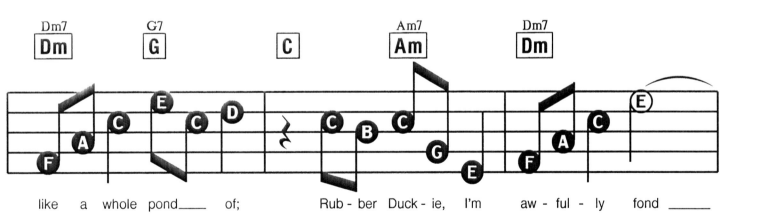

like　a　whole pond＿＿ of;　Rub - ber Duck - ie, I'm　aw - ful - ly　fond ＿＿＿＿＿

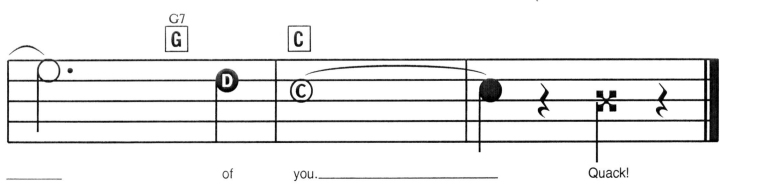

＿＿＿＿＿　of　you.＿＿＿＿＿＿＿＿＿　Quack!

Sailing, Sailing

Registration 5
Rhythm: Waltz

Words and Music by
Godfrey Marks

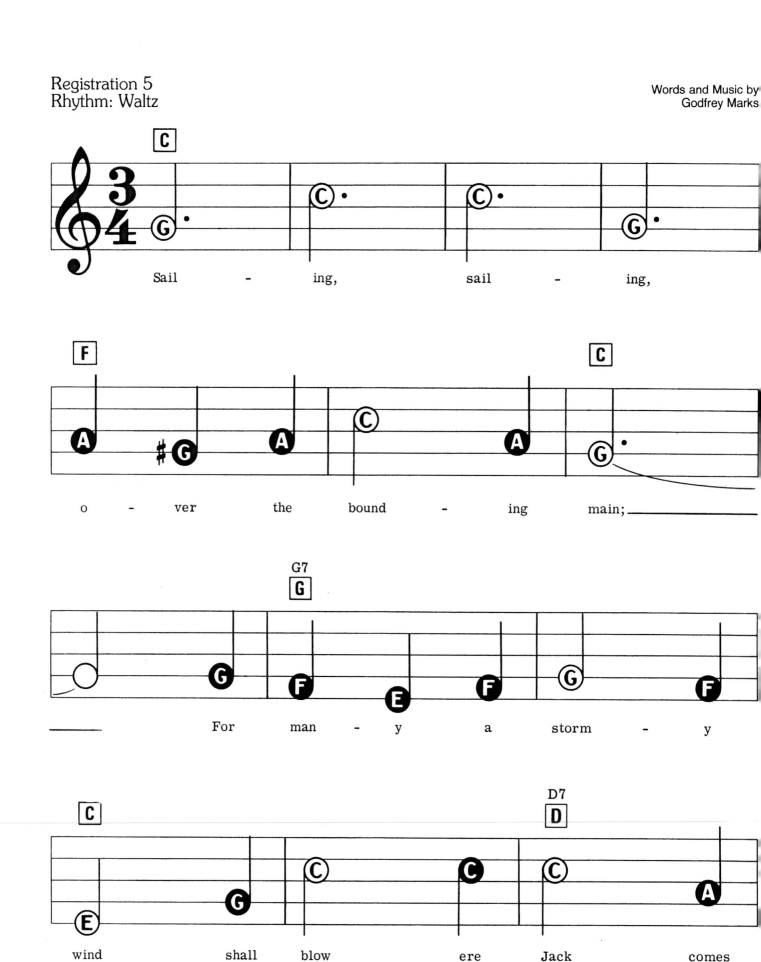

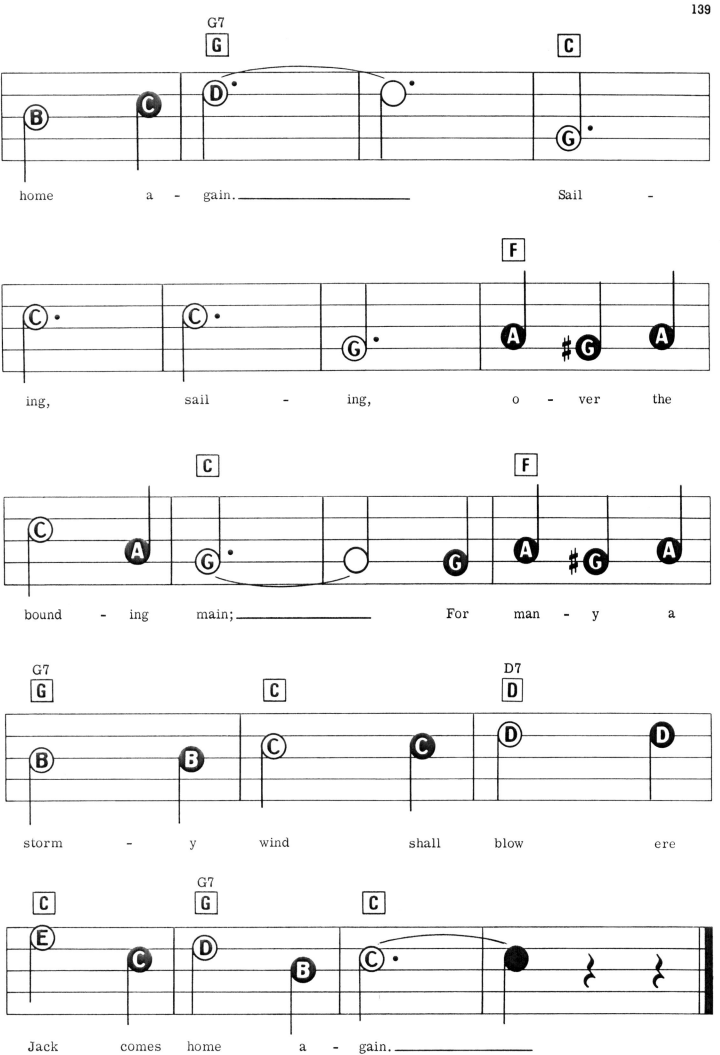

Sing
from SESAME STREET

Registration 9
Rhythm: Rock or 8 Beat

Words and Music
Joe Rap[...]

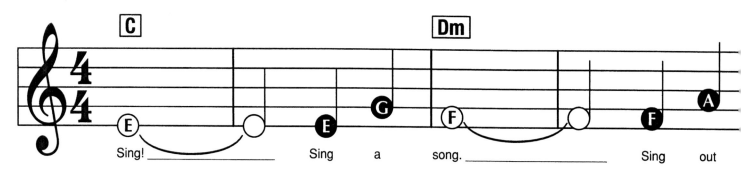

Sing! _____ Sing a song. _____ Sing out

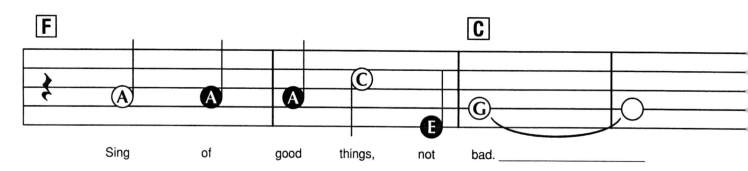

loud, _____ sing out strong. _____

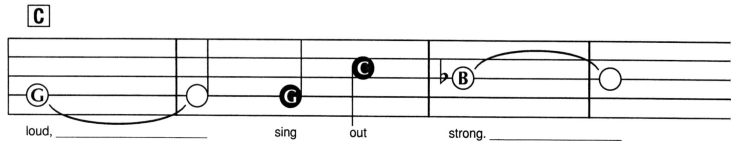

Sing of good things, not bad. _____

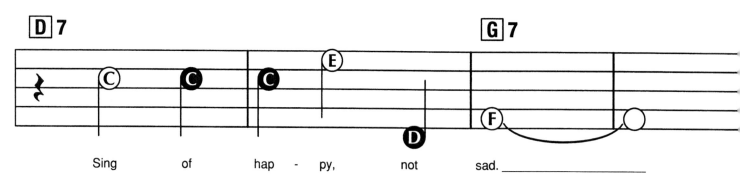

Sing of hap - py, not sad. _____

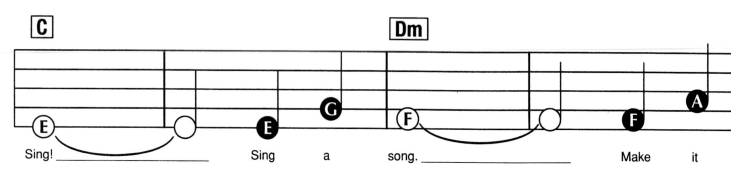

Sing! _____ Sing a song. _____ Make it

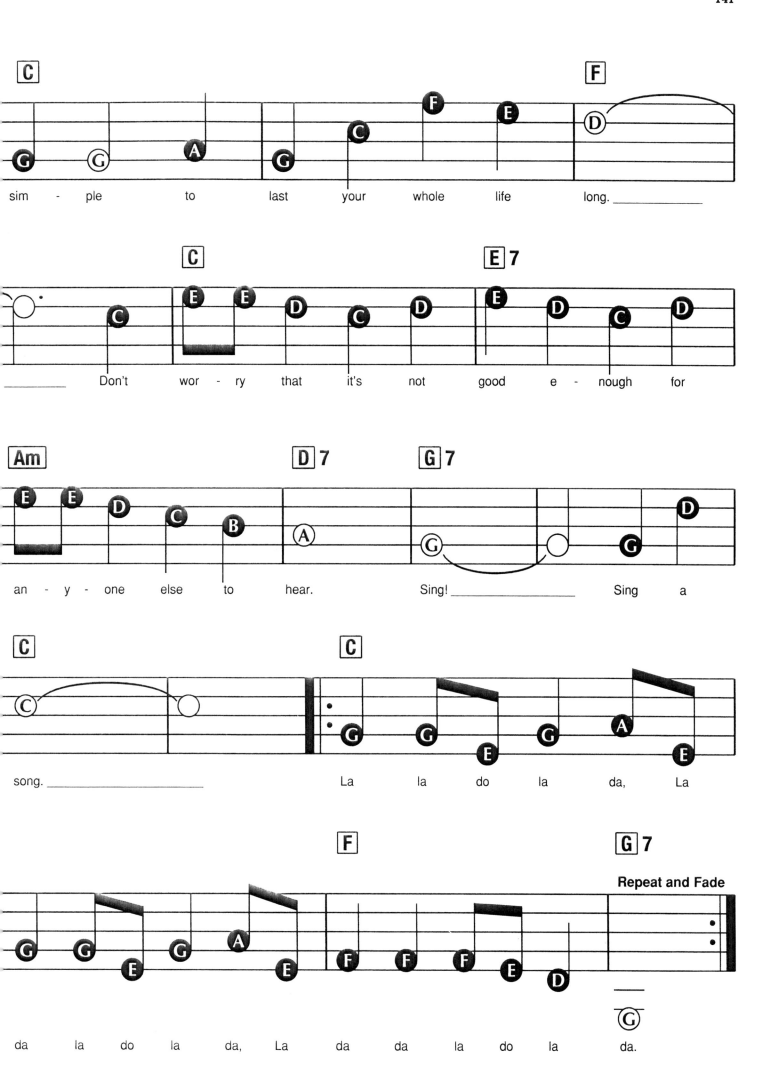

Sing A Song Of Sixpence

Registration 4
Rhythm: Fox Trot or Swing

Traditional

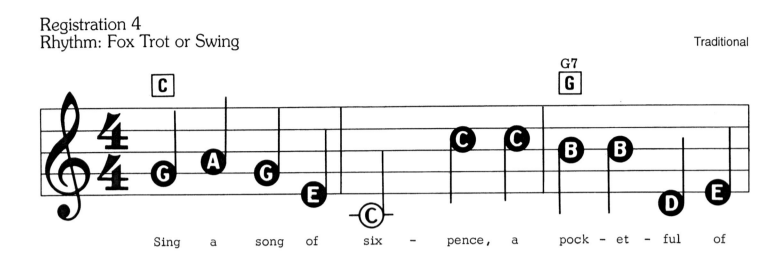

Sing a song of six - pence, a pock - et - ful of

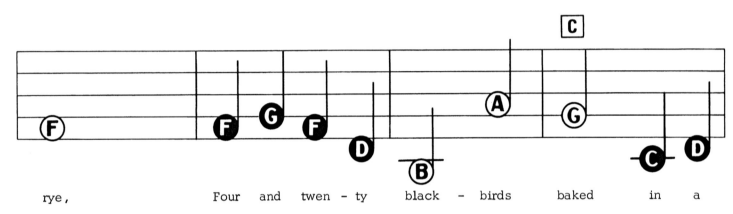

rye, Four and twen - ty black - birds baked in a

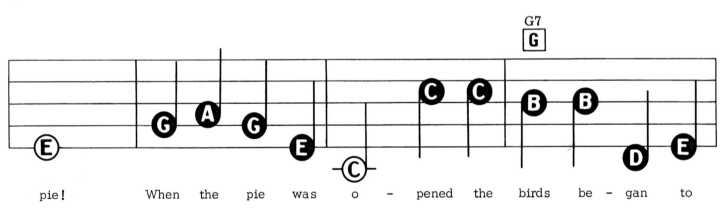

pie! When the pie was o - pened the birds be - gan to

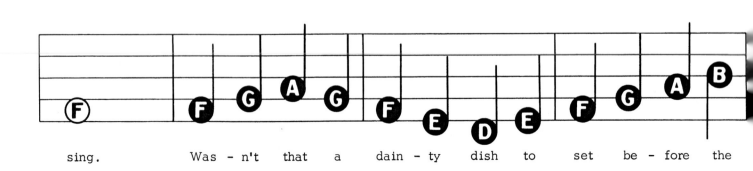

sing. Was - n't that a dain - ty dish to set be - fore the

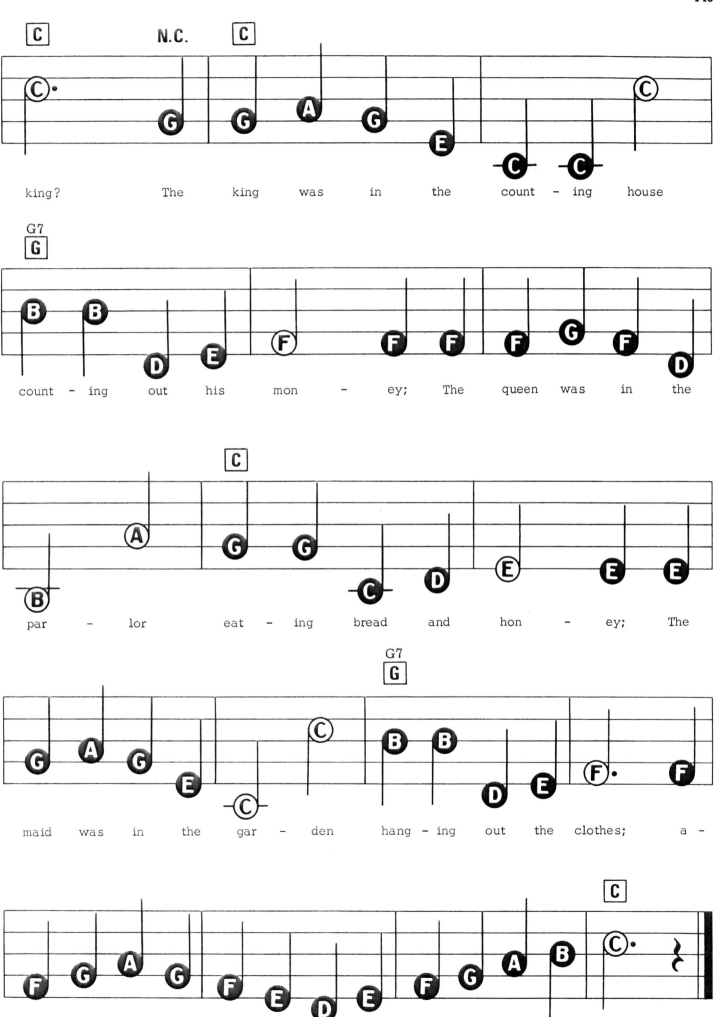

A Spoonful Of Sugar

from Walt Disney's MARY POPPINS

Registration 3
Rhythm: Fox Trot or Swing

Words and Music by Richard M. Sherman
and Robert B. Sherman

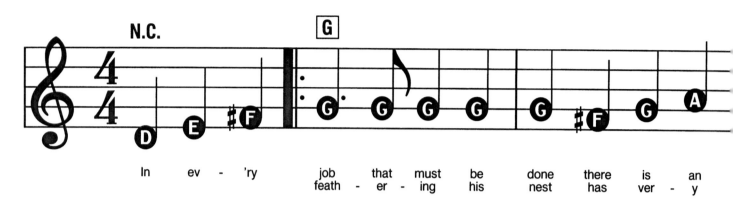

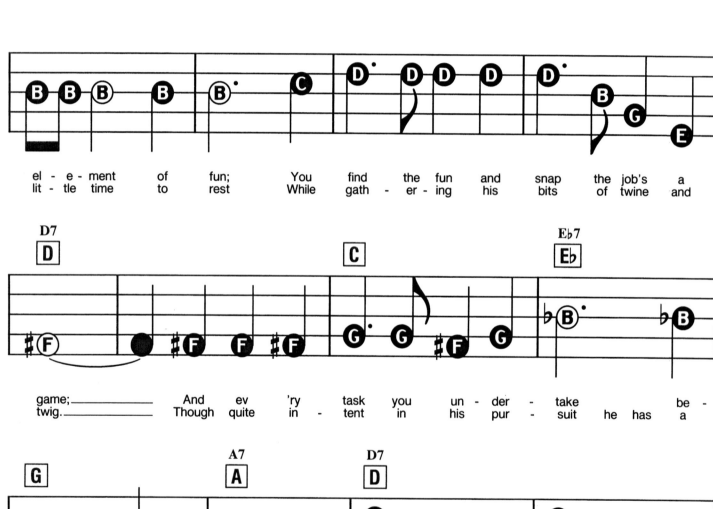

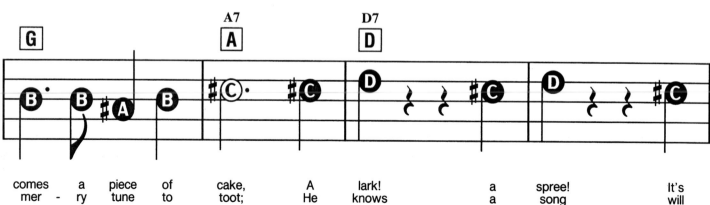

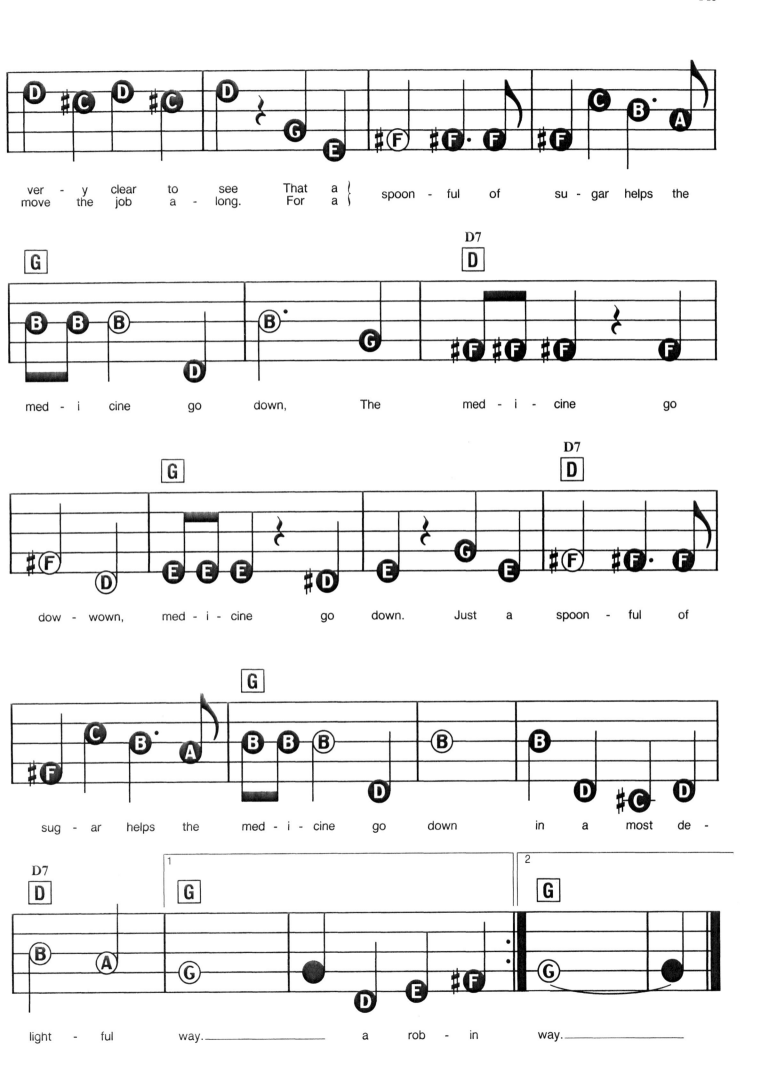

Supercalifragilisticexpialidocious

from Walt Disney's MARY POPPINS

Registration 5
Rhythm: Fox Trot or Swing

Words and Music by Richard M. Sherman
and Robert B. Sherman

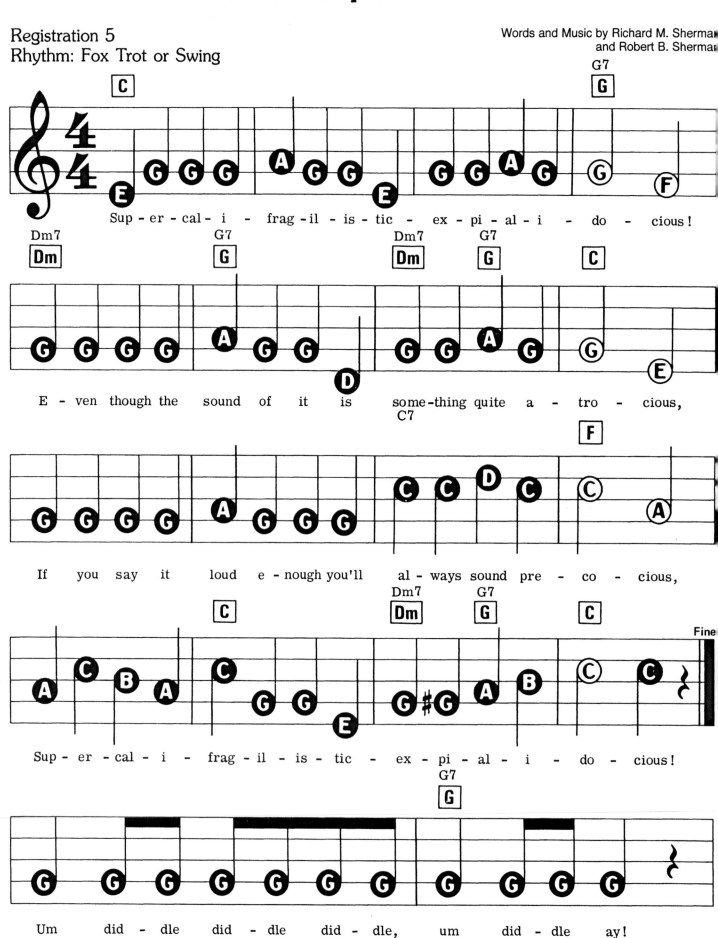

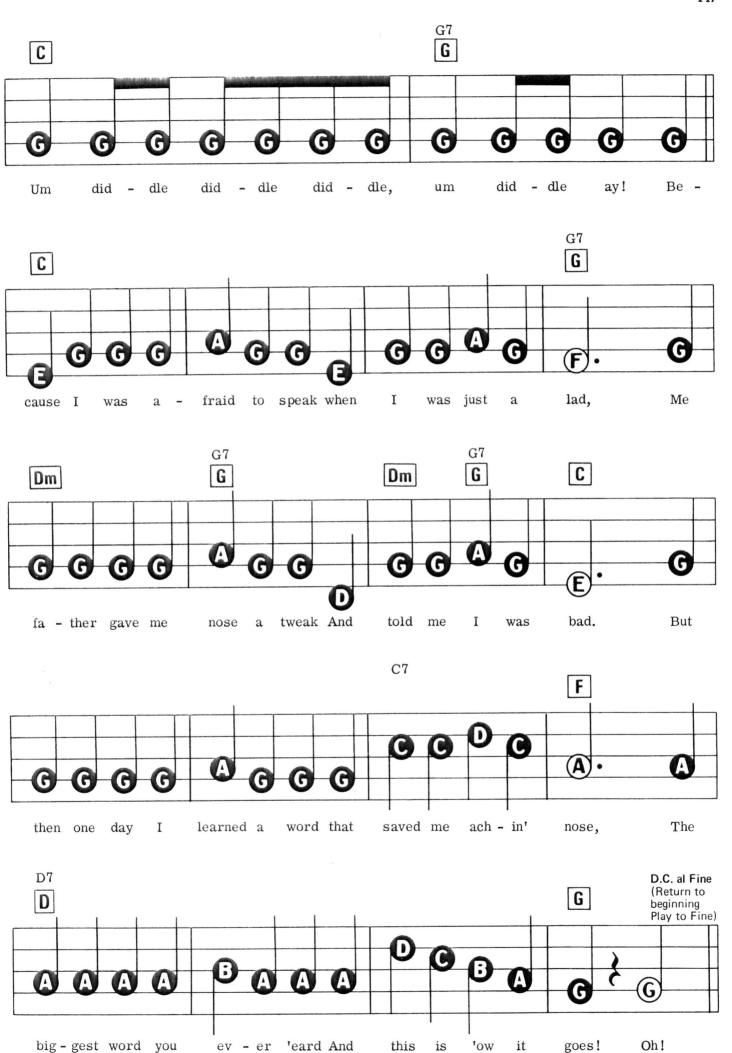

Take Me Out To The Ball Game

Registration 3
Rhythm: Waltz

Words by Jack Norworth
Music by Albert von Tilzer

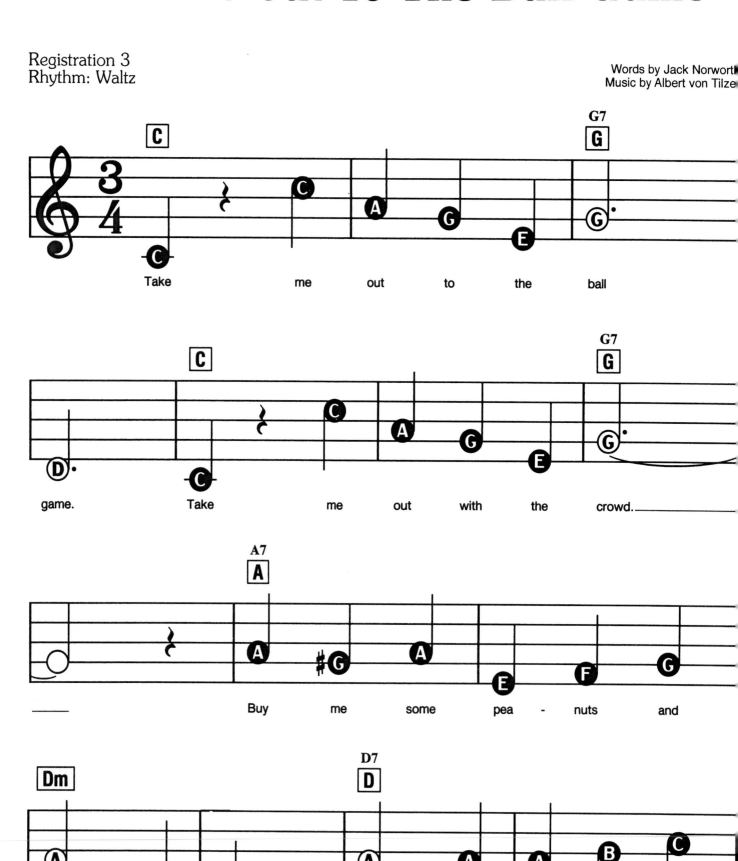

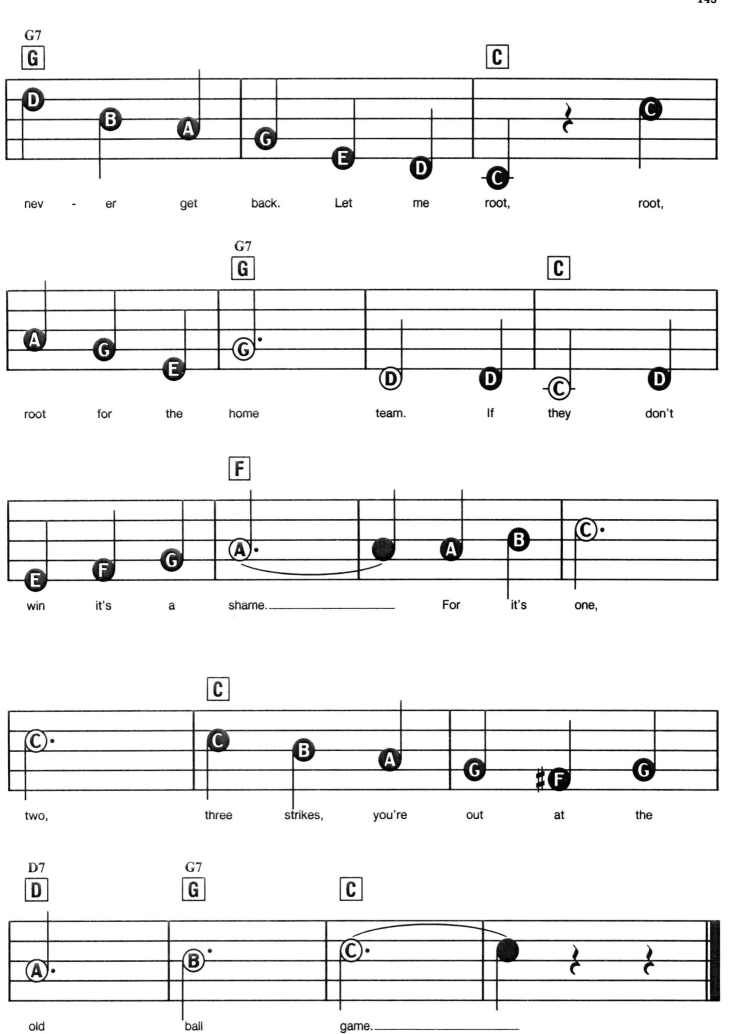

This Train

Registration 4
Rhythm: Swing

Traditional

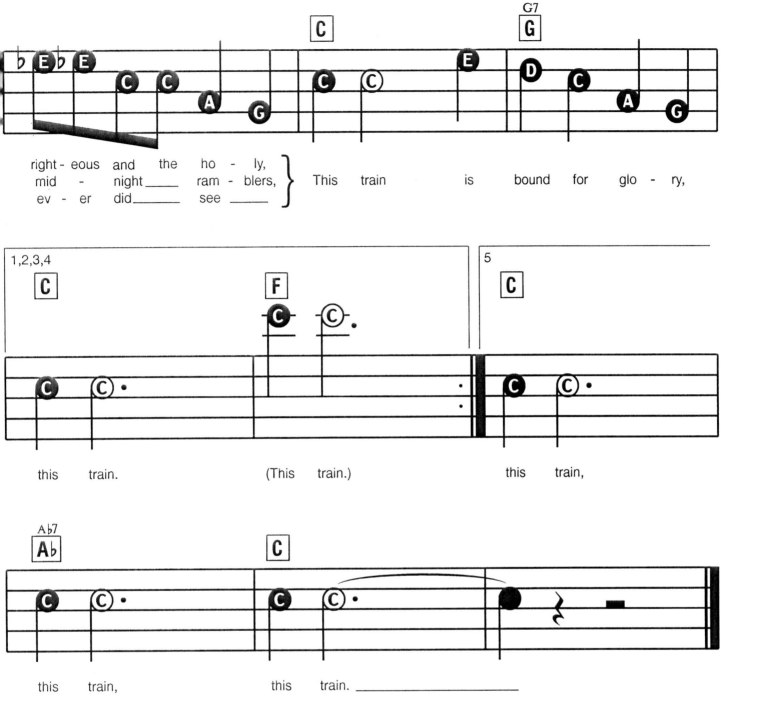

Additional Lyrics

4. This train don't carry no liars, *etc.*
No hypocrites and no high flyers.
This train is bound for glory, this train.

5. This train don't carry no rustlers, *etc.*
Side-street walkers, two-bit hustlers.
This train is bound for glory, this train...this train...this train.

There's A Hole In The Bucket

Registration 10
Rhythm: Waltz

Traditional

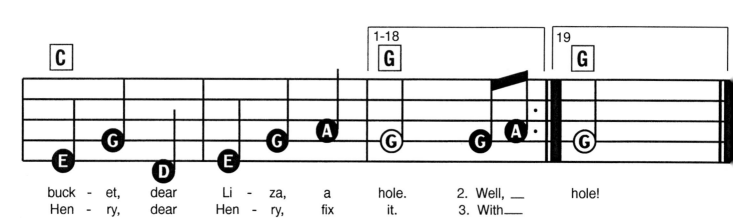

1. There's a hole in the buck - et, dear
2. fix it, dear Hen - ry, dear
3.-19. *(See additional lyrics)*

Li - za, dear Li - za. There's a hole in the
Hen - ry, dear Hen - ry. Well, ___ fix it, dear

buck - et, dear Li - za, a hole. 2. Well, ___ hole!
Hen - ry, dear Hen - ry, fix it. 3. With___

Additional Lyrics
3. With what shall I fix it, dear Liza, *etc.*
4. With a straw, dear Henry, *etc.*
5. But the straw is too long, dear Liza, *etc.*
6. Then cut it, dear Henry, *etc.*
7. With what shall I cut it, dear Liza, *etc.*
8. With a knife, dear Henry, *etc.*
9. But the knife is too dull, dear Liza, *etc.*
10. Then sharpen it, dear Henry, *etc.*
11. With what shall I sharpen it, dear Liza, *etc.*
12. With a stone, dear Henry, *etc.*
13. But the stone is too dry, dear Liza, *etc.*
14. Then wet it, dear Henry, *etc.*
15. With what shall I wet it, dear Liza, *etc.*
16. With water, dear Henry, *etc.*
17. In what shall I carry it, dear Liza, *etc.*
18. In a bucket, dear Henry, *etc.*
19. There's a hole in the bucket, dear Liza, *etc.*

A Whole New World

from Walt Disney's ALADDIN

Registration 1
Rhythm: 8-beat or Pops

Music by Alan Menken
Lyrics by Tim Rice

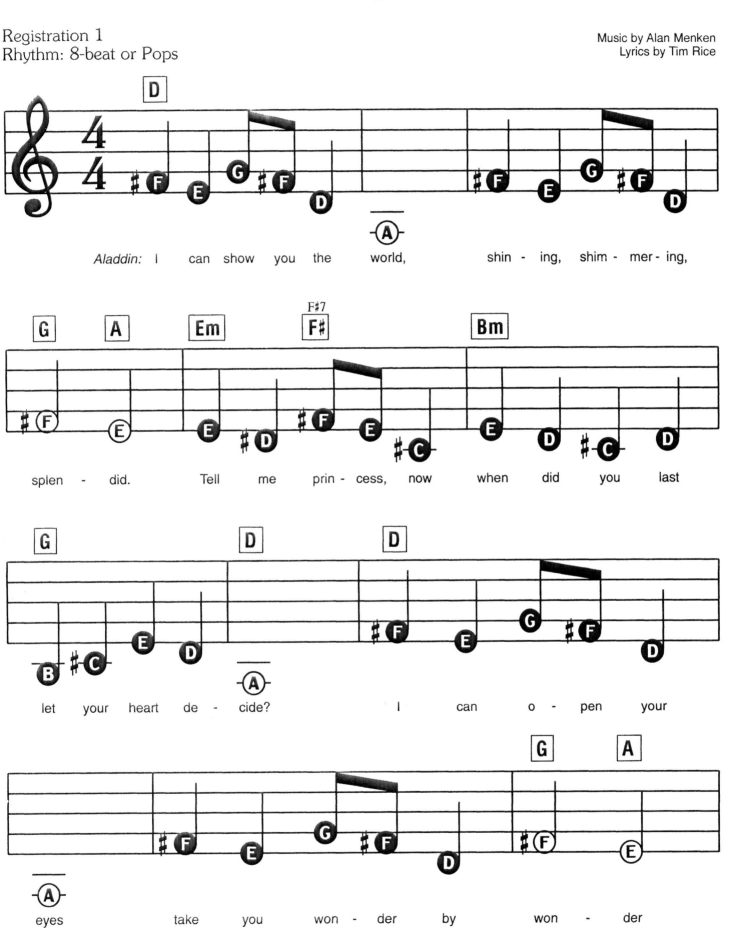

154

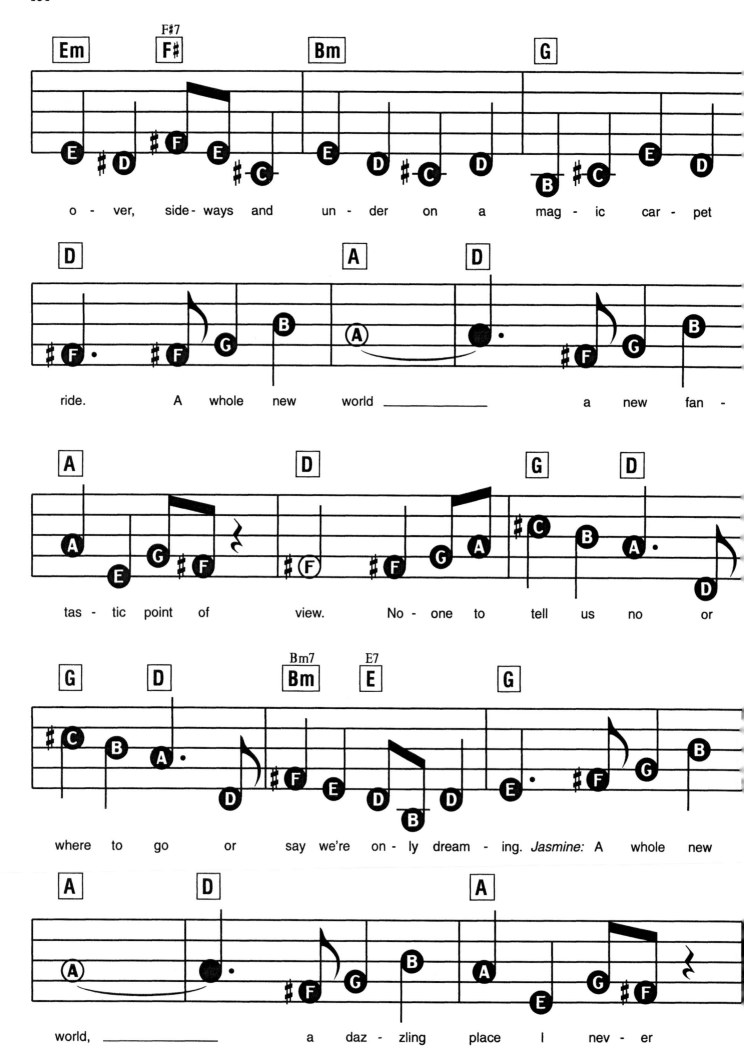

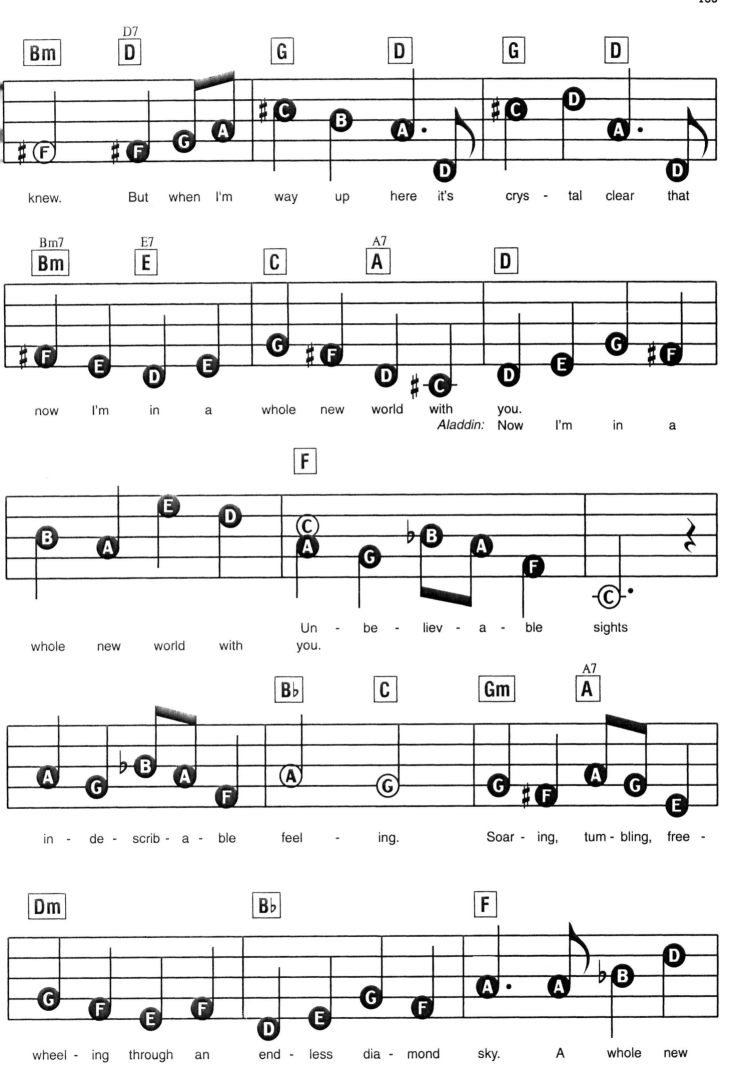

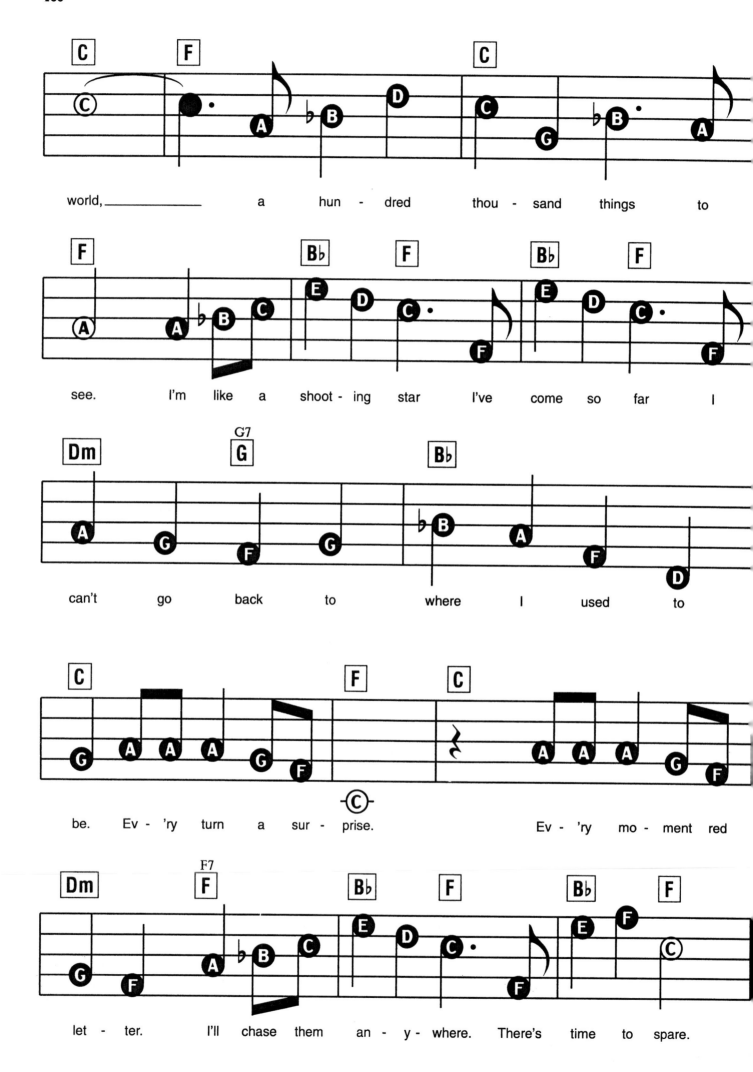

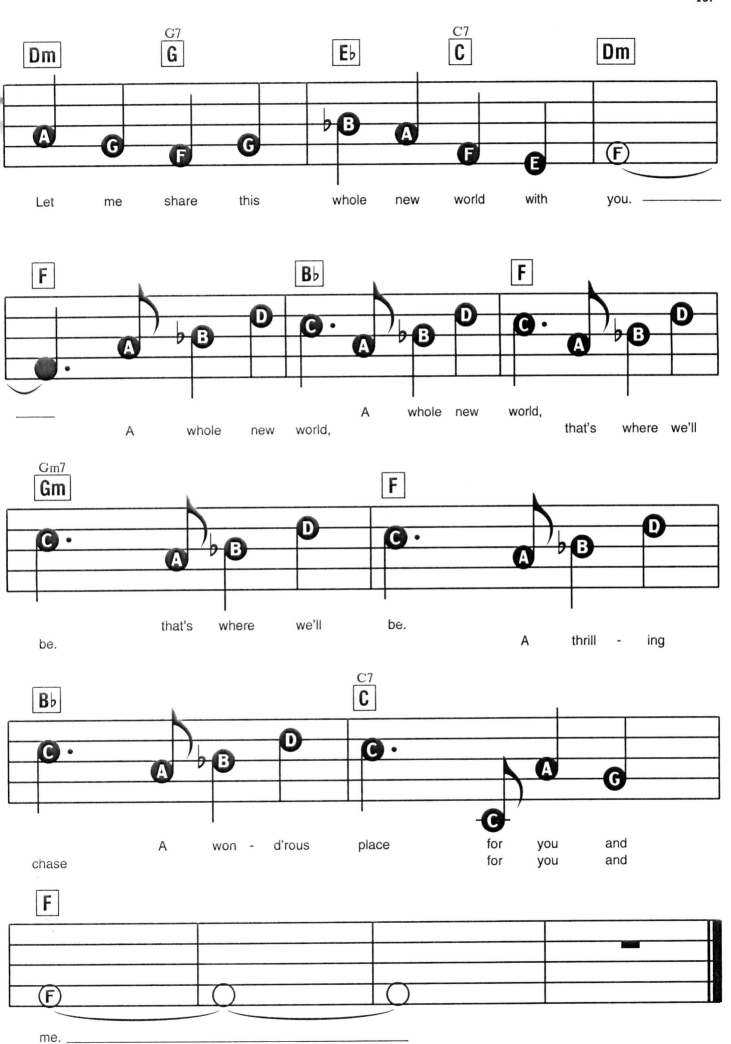

The Unbirthday Song
from Walt Disney's ALICE IN WONDERLAND

Registration 2
Rhythm: Ballad or Fox Trot

Words and Music by Mack David
Al Hoffman and Jerry Livingston

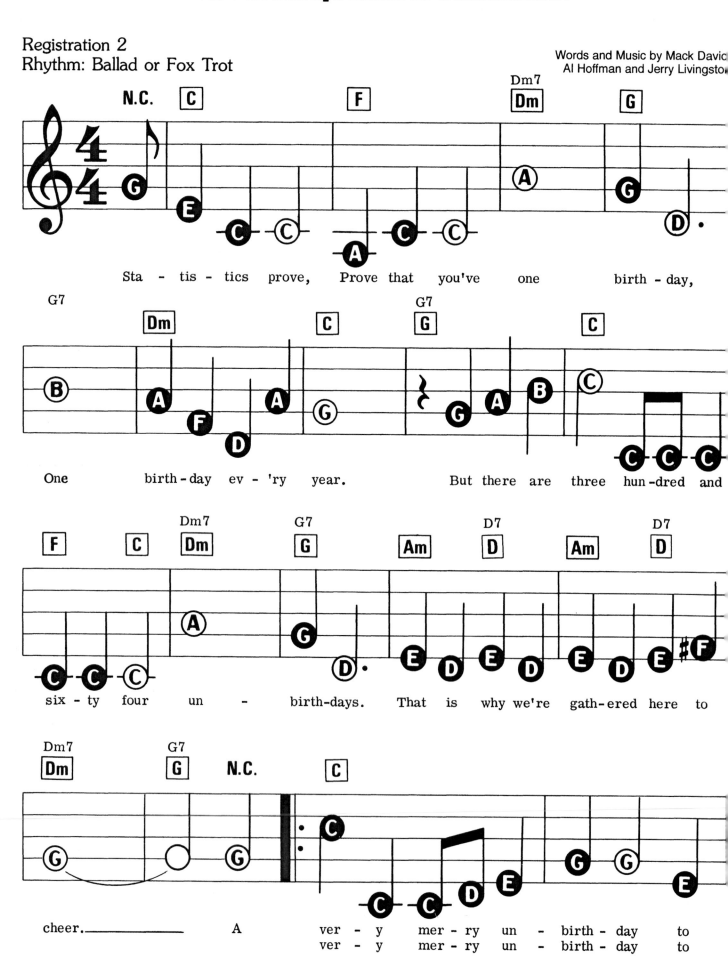

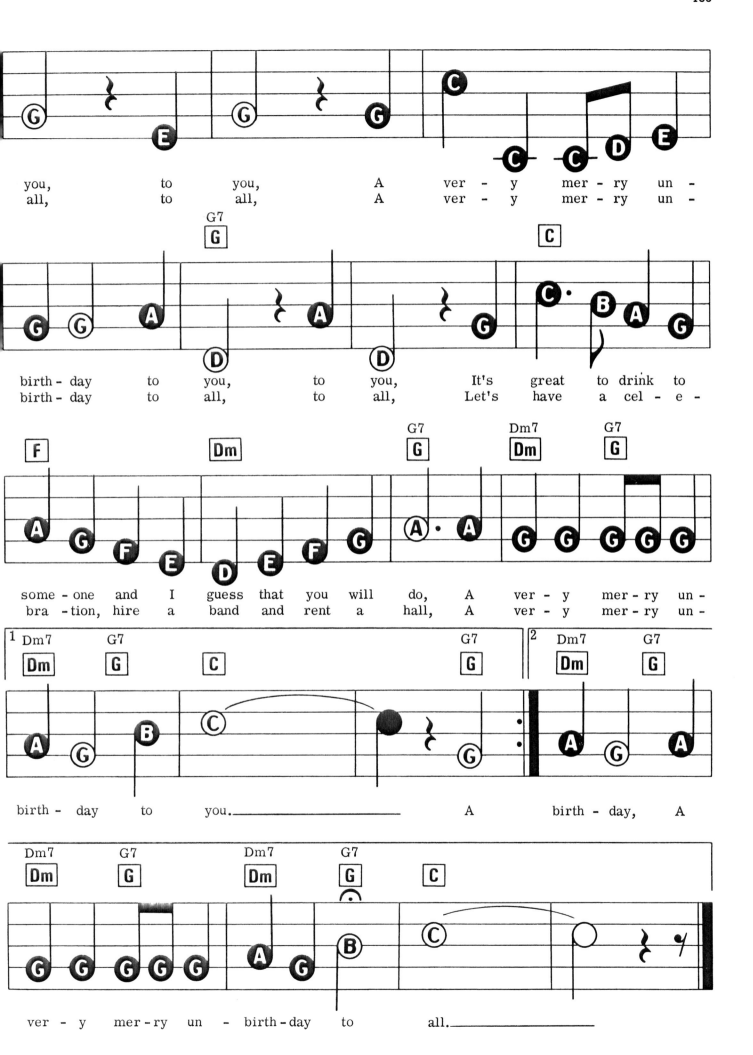

Under The Sea
from Walt Disney's THE LITTLE MERMAID

Registration 7
Rhythm: Bossa Nova or Latin

Lyrics by Howard Ashman
Music by Alan Menken

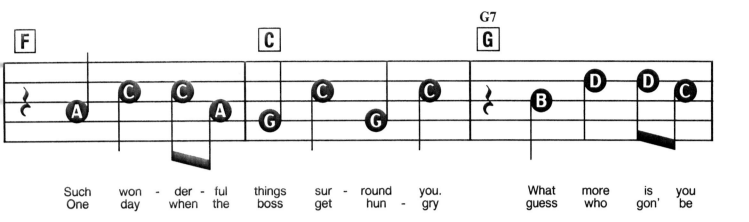

Such won - der - ful things sur - round you. What more is you
One day when the boss get hun - gry guess who gon' be

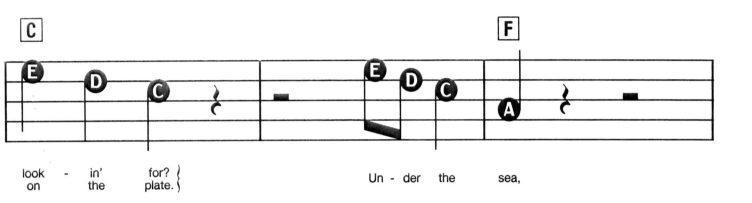

look - in' for?
on the plate.

Un - der the sea,

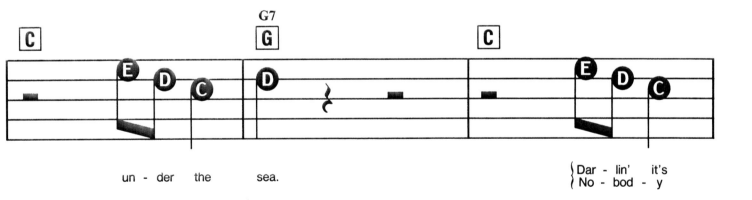

un - der the sea.

Dar - lin' it's
No - bod - y

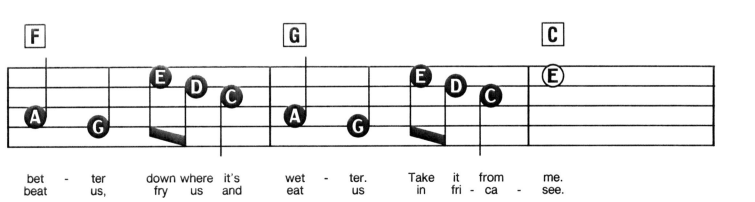

bet - ter, down where it's wet - ter. Take it from me.
beat us, fry us and eat us in fri - ca - see.

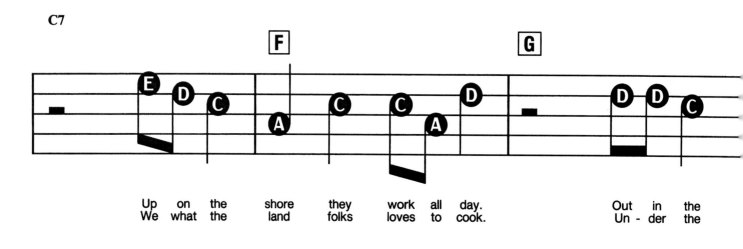

Up on the shore they work all day.
We what the land folks loves to cook.

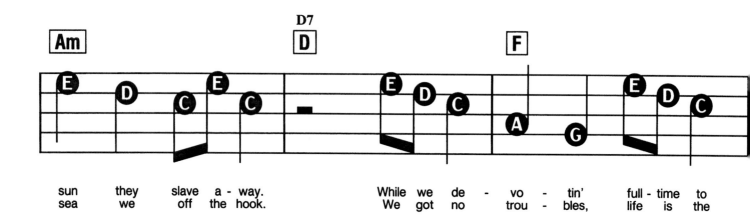

sun they slave a - way.
sea we off the hook.
While we de - vo - tin' full - time to
We got no trou - bles, life is the

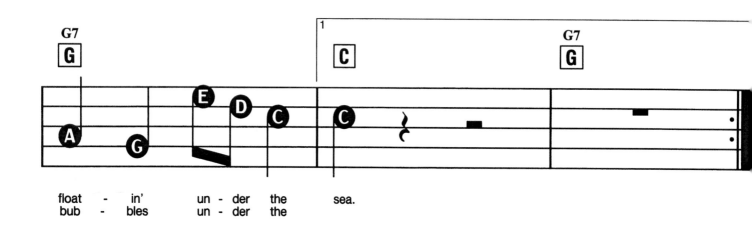

float - in' un - der the sea.
bub - bles un - der the

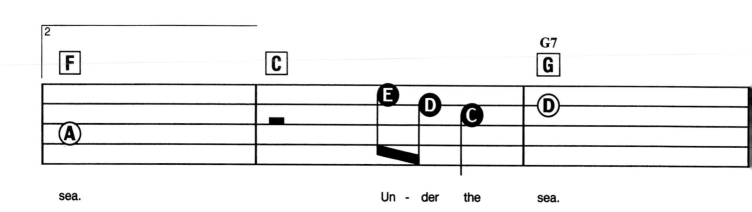

sea.
Un - der the sea.

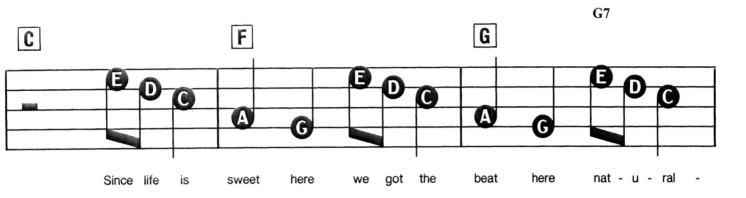

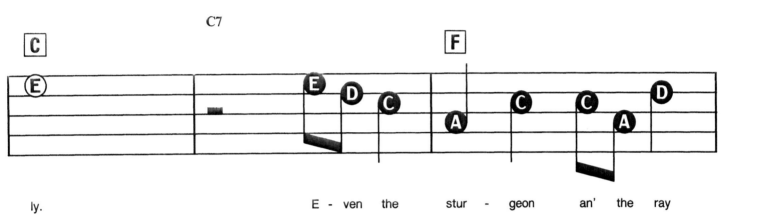

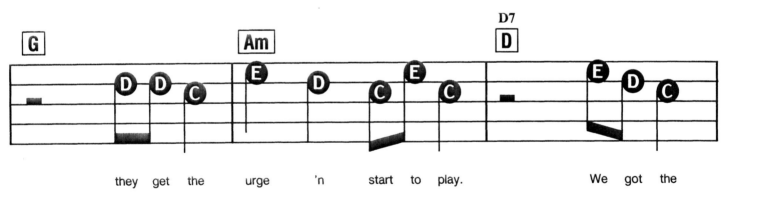

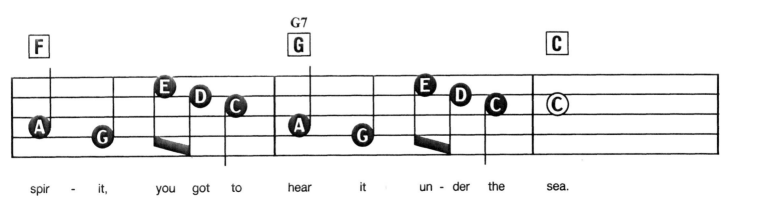

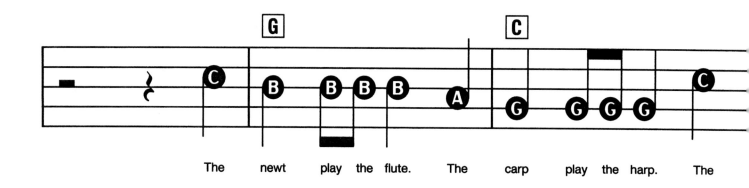

The newt play the flute. The carp play the harp. The

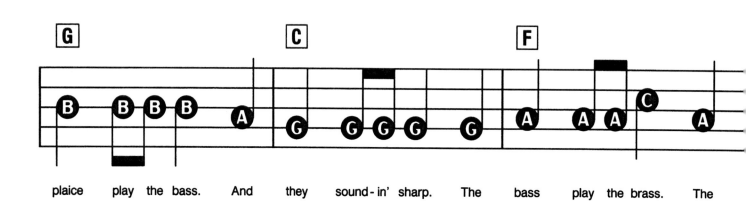

plaice play the bass. And they sound - in' sharp. The bass play the brass. The

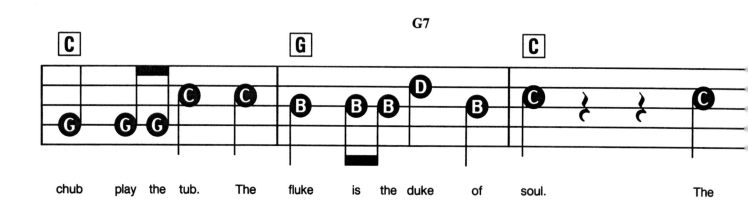

chub play the tub. The fluke is the duke of soul. The

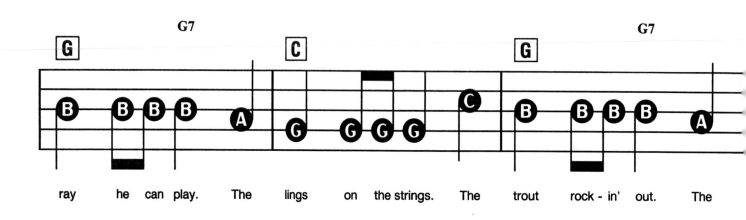

ray he can play. The lings on the strings. The trout rock - in' out. The

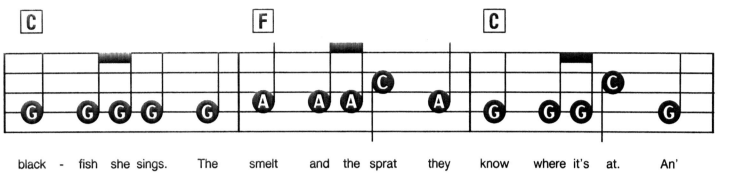

black - fish she sings. The smelt and the sprat they know where it's at. An'

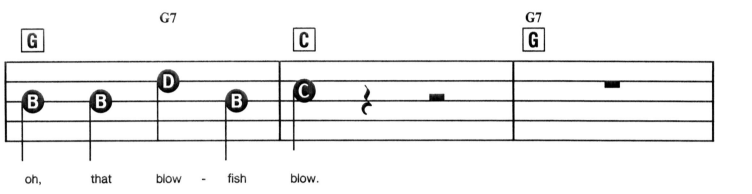

oh, that blow - fish blow.

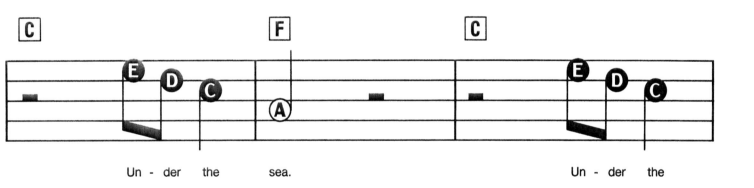

Un - der the sea. Un - der the

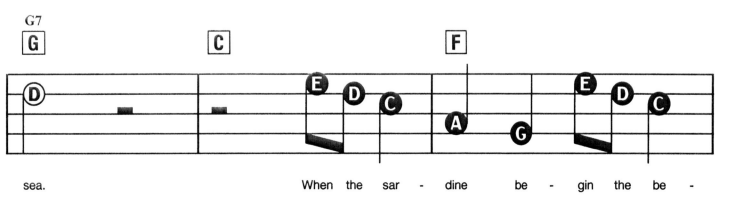

sea. When the sar - dine be - gin the be -

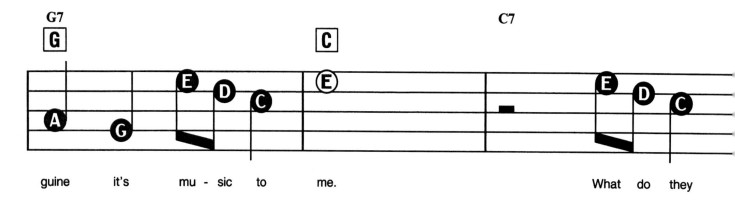

guine it's mu - sic to me. What do they

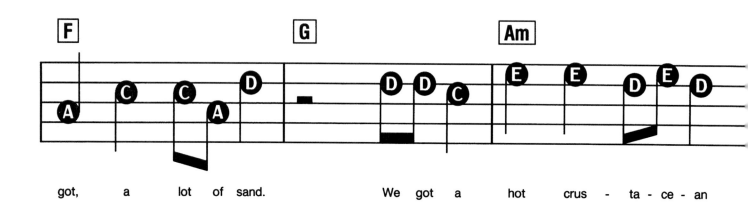

got, a lot of sand. We got a hot crus - ta - ce - an

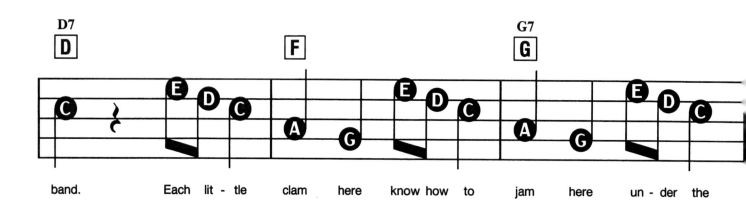

band. Each lit - tle clam here know how to jam here un - der the

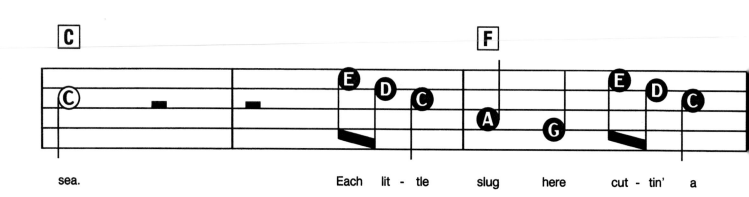

sea. Each lit - tle slug here cut - tin' a

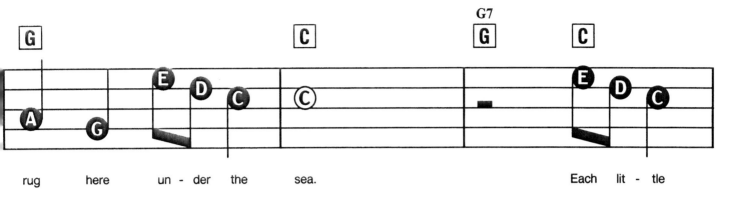

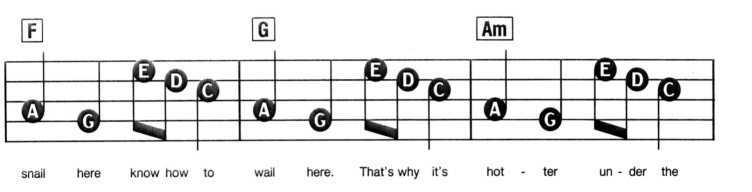

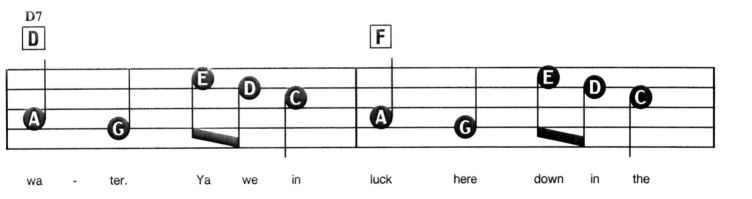

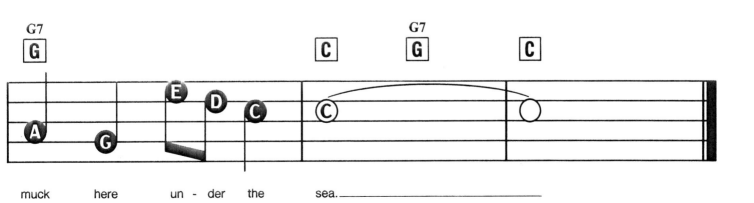

Who's Afraid Of The Big Bad Wolf?

from Walt Disney's THREE LITTLE PIGS

Registration 4
Rhythm: Fox Trot or Swing

Words and Music by Frank Churchi
Additional Lyric by Ann Rone

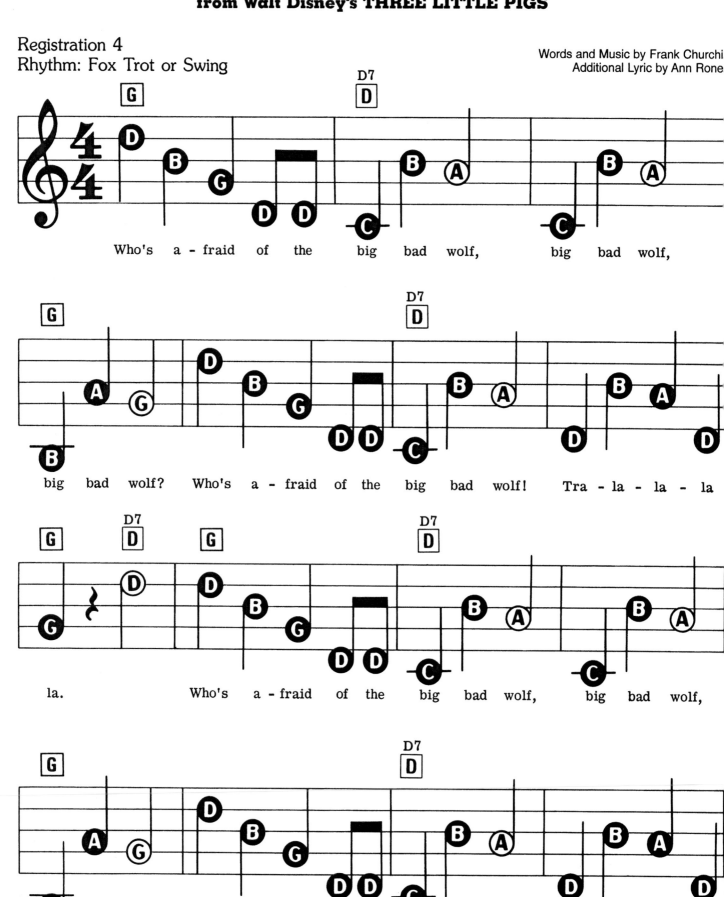

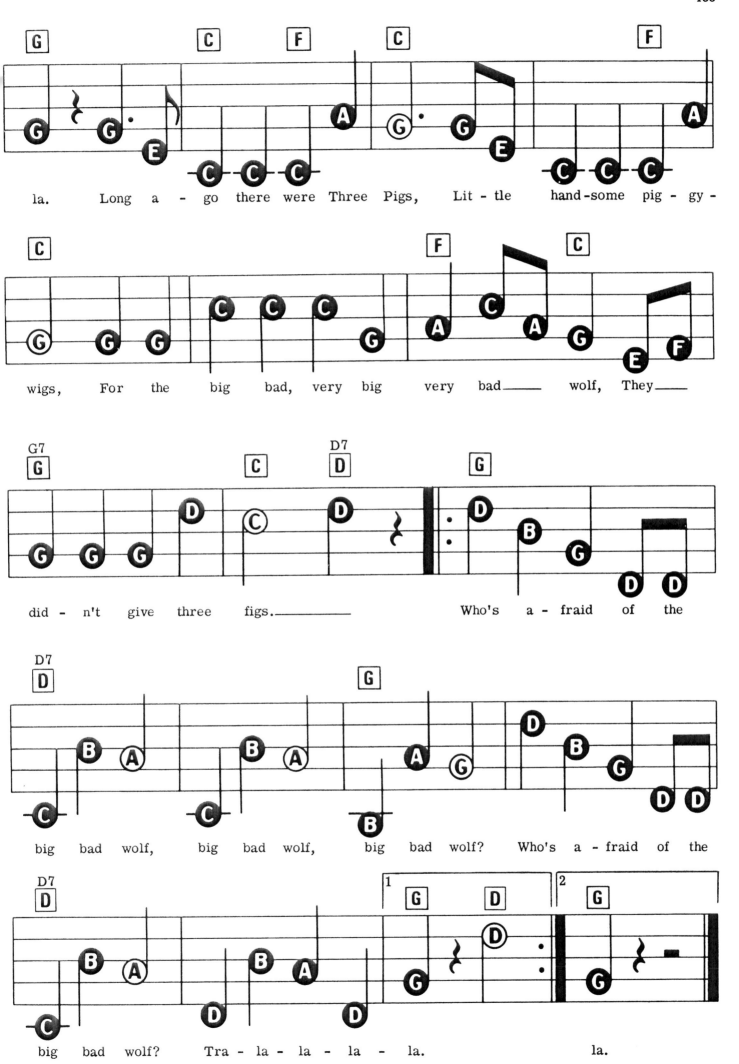

Won't You Be My Neighbor?
(a/k/a It's A Beautiful Day In This Neighborhood)
from MISTER ROGERS' NEIGHBORHOOD

Registration 8
Rhythm: Swing or Shuffle

Words and Music by
Fred Rogers

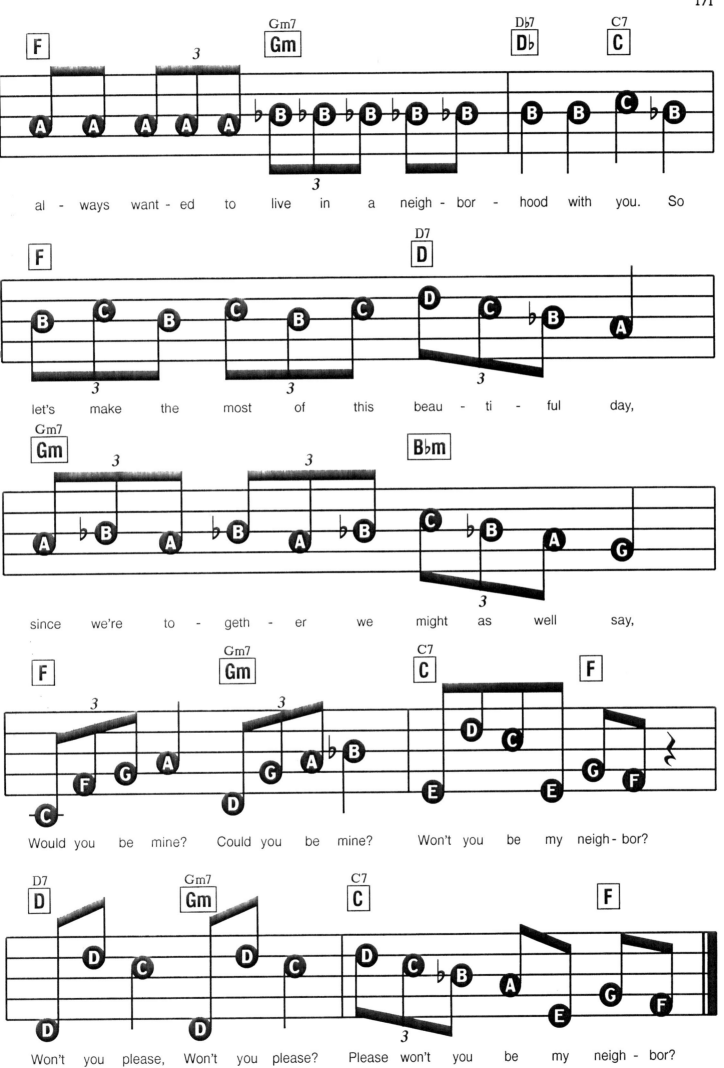

Yellow Submarine
from YELLOW SUBMARINE

Registration 2
Rhythm: 6/8 March

Words and Music by John Lennon
and Paul McCartney

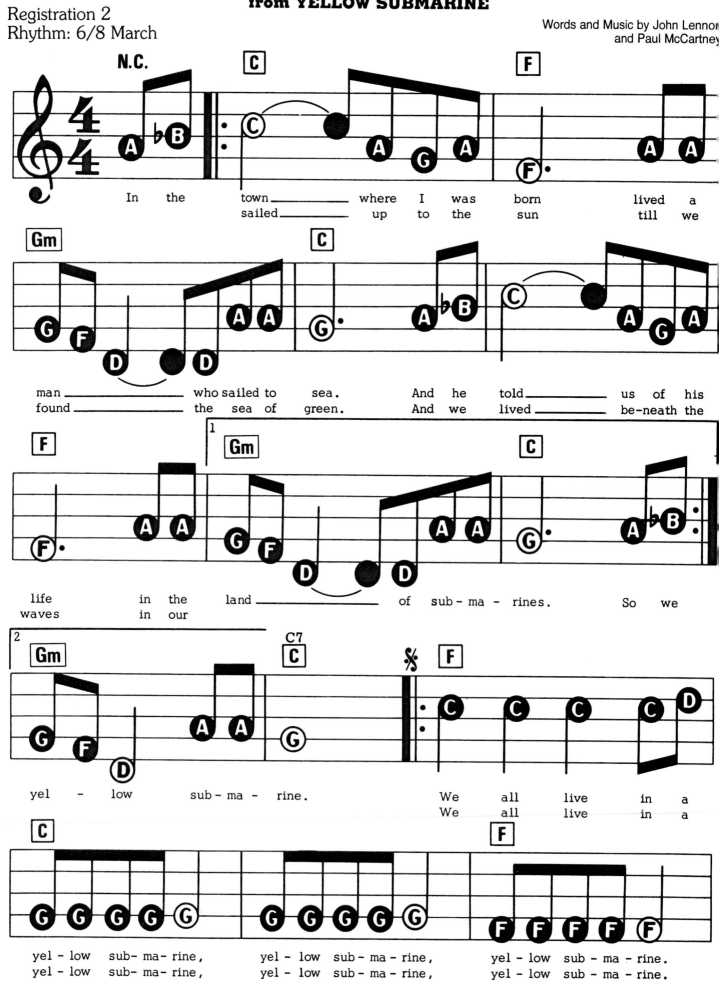

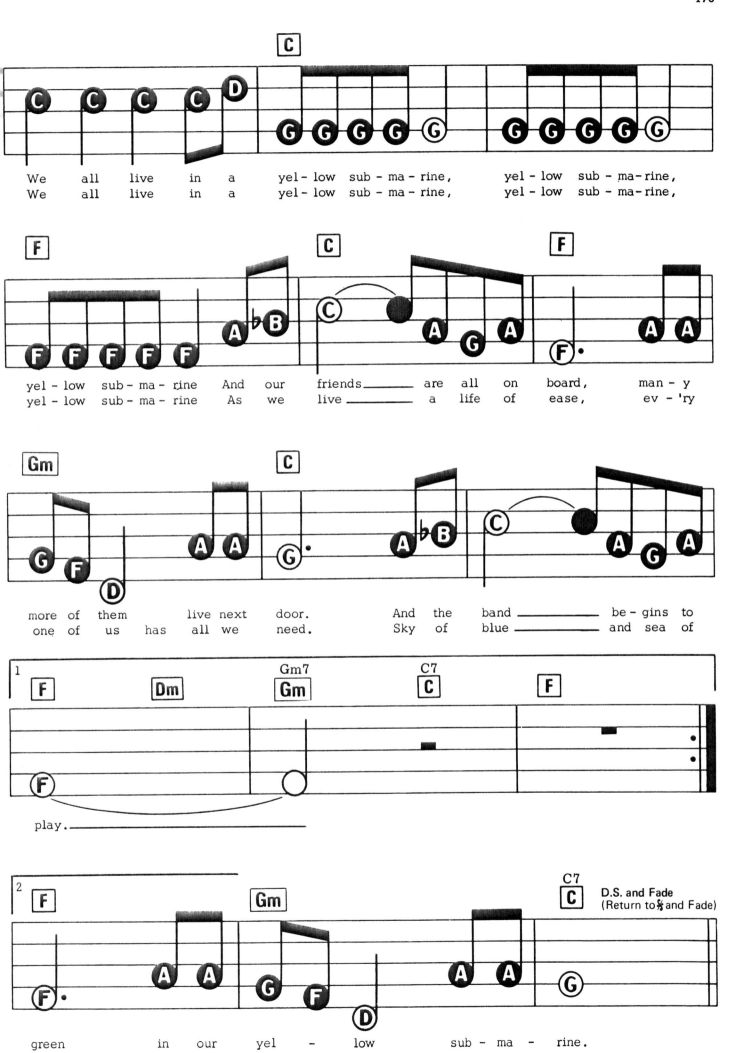

Zip-A-Dee-Doo-Dah
from Walt Disney's SONG OF THE SOUTH

Registration 8
Rhythm: Fox Trot or Swing

Words by Ray Gilbert
Music by Allie Wrubel

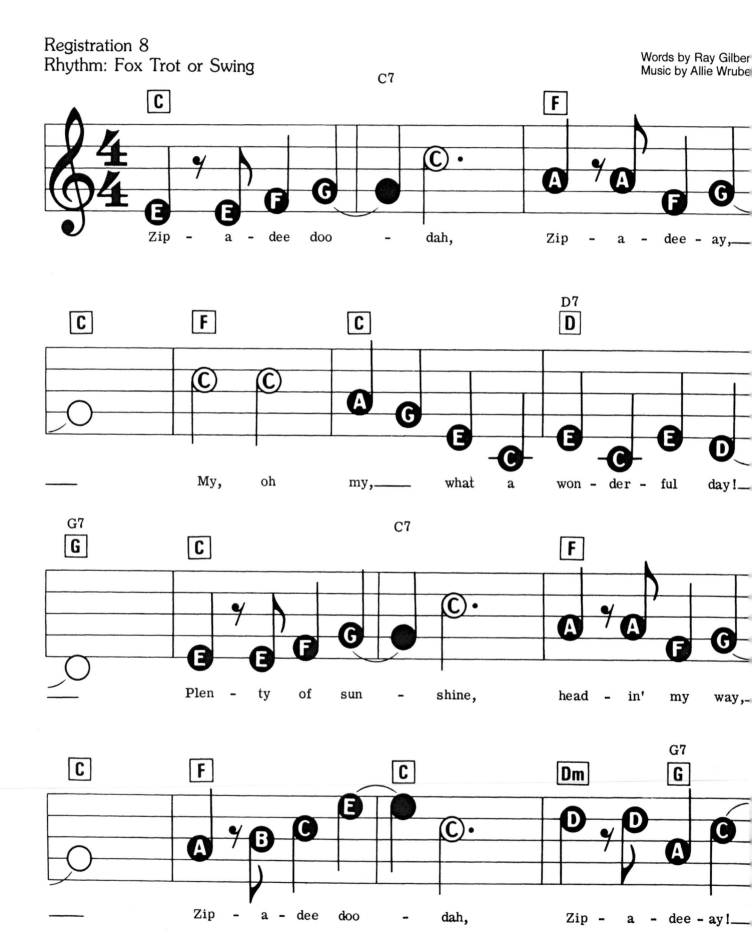

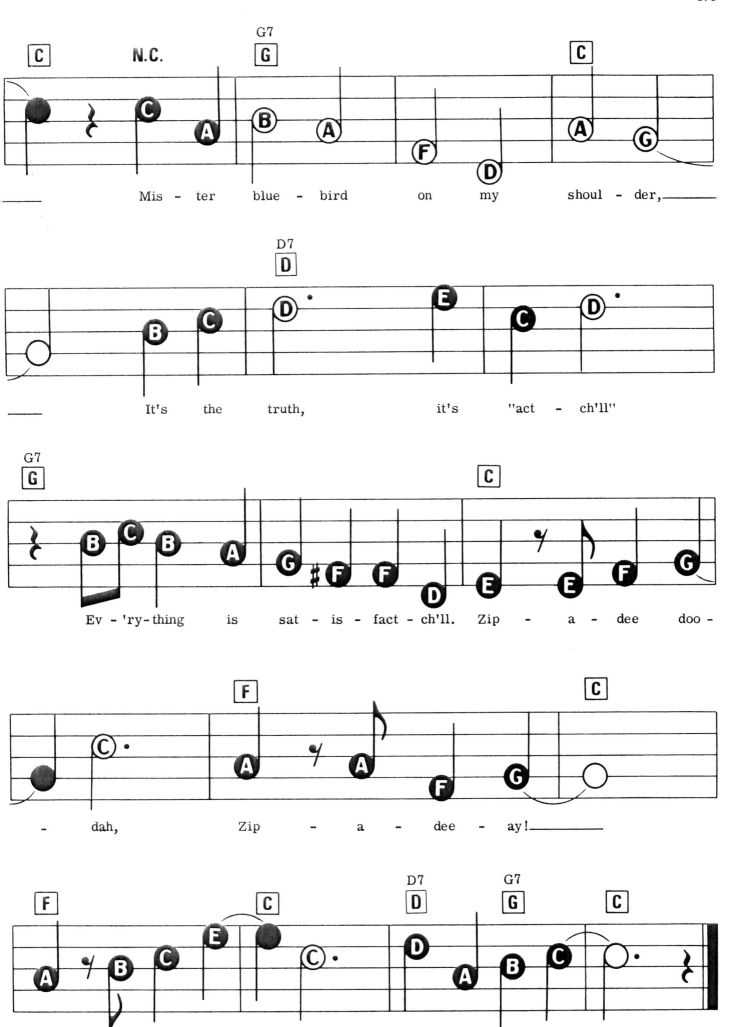

Registration Guide

- Match the Registration number on the song to the corresponding numbered category below. Select and activate an instrumental sound available on your instrument.

- Choose an automatic rhythm appropriate to the mood and style of the song. (Consult your Owner's Guide for proper operation of automatic rhythm features.)

- Adjust the tempo and volume controls to comfortable settings.

Registration

1	Flute, Pan Flute, Jazz Flute
2	Clarinet, Organ
3	Violin, Strings
4	Brass, Trumpet, Bass
5	Synth Ensemble, Accordion, Brass
6	Pipe Organ, Harpsichord
7	Jazz Organ, Vibraphone, Vibes, Electric Piano, Jazz Guitar
8	Piano, Electric Piano
9	Trumpet, Trombone, Clarinet, Saxophone, Oboe
10	Violin, Cello, Strings